PÉREZ GALDÓS

Peréz Galdós

PÉREZ GALDÓS

AND THE SPANISH NOVEL
OF THE NINETEENTH
CENTURY

BY

L. B. WALTON, M.A., B.LITT.

GORDIAN PRESS
NEW YORK
1970

Originally Published 1927

Reprinted 1970

Library of Congress Catalog Card Number - 77-114100

SBN 87752-115-8

Published by GORDIAN PRESS, INC.

TO

FERNANDO DE ARTEAGA Y PEREIRA

FOREWORD

THE contributions of permanent value which Spain has made to European literature lie in the realm of the novel and the drama. It can be claimed with some justice that Europe's greatest novel is the work of a Spaniard; and if Spain has produced no dramatist to rank with Shakespeare or Molière, her theatre has no rival for ingenuity of intrigue and richness of incident. It is the Spanish drama which has hitherto made the strongest appeal to foreign scholars and critics. The novel, while it has not been ignored, has (with the notable exception of *Don Quixote*) taken a secondary place.

This is especially true of the more recent developments in Spanish prose fiction; and the Spanish novel of the nineteenth century has been but little studied outside the Peninsula. This unmerited neglect is due in part to the popular belief that Spain has never recovered from her disastrous collapse at the close of the seventeenth century—a belief which the recent widespread interest in "la cosas de España" has as yet done comparatively little to modify. The insignificance of Spain as a political force in Europe has militated against her attaining due recognition for her achievements in other spheres; and apart from the evanescent enthusiasm for things Spanish which was manifested by some of the leading figures in the

Romantic movement of the nineteenth century, there has been comparatively little interest in the Hispanic field until our own day.

The present work is an endeavour to estimate the significance of Benito Pérez Galdós in the history of modern Spanish fiction and to show that he may justly be regarded as the creator of the modern novel in Spain. After a brief survey of the development of Spanish fiction prior to the appearance of Galdós' first novel, *La Fontana de Oro*, we have attempted, in an analysis of his principal books, to trace the evolution of his genius through the various stages of its development. Then, in a final chapter, we have called attention to those elements in his work which distinguish it from that of his predecessors; endeavouring also to estimate the influence which he has exercised upon those who succeeded him. We cannot claim to have done more than clear the ground for those who may wish to undertake more detailed studies, and although exigencies of space account for some notable lacunæ, there are several aspects of Galdós' genius which have been almost entirely ignored for the reason that, if they are to be dealt with adequately, they demand treatment apart. This applies especially to his work in the drama, and to the *Episodios Nacionales*, for the latter really constitute a separate *genre*. We have here confined our attention to those works which entitle Galdós to a place among European novelists of importance, and this study makes no claim to be exhaustive.

We should here like to acknowledge our indebtedness to the works mentioned in the bibliographical note, especially to those of El P. Blanco García, Sr. Andrés González-Blanco, "Andrenio," and Sr. Salvador de Madariaga. The latter's chapter on Galdós in his *Semblanzas Literarias Contemporáneas* has proved extremely helpful and suggestive. In order that quotations from the novels of Galdós and from the works of Spanish critics may be comprehensible to students of the nineteenth-century novel whose knowledge of Spanish is limited, we have given these extracts in an English rendering for which we are responsible. Our gratitude is due to Professor Walter Starkie, for help with the proofs and for welcome criticism and advice; also to Mr. J. A. Anderson for assistance in the compilation of an index.

L. B. WALTON.

EDINBURGH, 1927.

CONTENTS

xi

PÉREZ GALDÓS

AND THE SPANISH NOVEL OF THE NINETEENTH CENTURY

I

A BRIEF SURVEY OF NINETEENTH-CENTURY SPANISH FICTION PRIOR TO THE APPEARANCE OF "LA FONTANA DE ORO"

(a) The "Género de Costumbres"

THE eighteenth century in Spain was an age of sterility in all forms of literature, and the novel shared in the decline. Spanish fiction, however, had not ceased to be a force in Europe, for in this period, so barren of original work, the novels of the picaresque school and the masterpiece of Cervantes left their mark upon France and England in the tales of Lesage, Fielding, Smollett and Sterne.

It is not until the early years of the nineteenth century that we find signs of a coming revival in prose fiction, but already in the eighteenth we can discern the trend which that revival was to take. Such indications, however, are not to be sought in the isolated attempts at orthodox fiction which the eighteenth century is able to show. The only work of importance, Isla's *Fray Gerundio*,[1] is a satirical *tour*

[1] *Historia del famoso Predicador Fray Gerundio de Campazas, alias Zotes* (1758). Published by José Francisco de Isla under the name of his friend, Francisco Lobón de Salazar. Vide Fitzmaurice-Kelly, *History of Spanish Literature* (Spanish translation by Bonilla y San Martín, 7th ed., p. 477).

I

de force which recalls the pasquinade rather than the novel of Spanish tradition, and its undeniable merits are those of the clever pamphleteer rather than the writer of fiction.

The last years of the eighteenth and the early years of the nineteenth century were years of "Sturm und Drang"—moral, political and æsthetic. During the Napoleonic Wars men's energies were absorbed in the defence of their country against the intruder, while the bigotry and oppression of Fernando VII. rendered unfettered literary expression impossible. Those Spaniards who would have been most capable of inaugurating a literary revival at home were condemned by the despotism to exile in France—a fact which was bound to have a profound effect upon the direction which the new movement was to take when they returned. After the fall of the despotism, every amateur politician who had the "cacoëthes scribendi" hastened to express his views in print and, consequently, the early years of the literary revival are especially rich in polemical journalism. As Sebastián Miñano, one of the pioneers of the early nineteenth-century literary renascence, remarks in his *Cartas del Pobrecito Holgazán*:[1] "Now our streets are in an uproar—shouting, rioting and confusion everywhere; every day there appears a new paper with a new name—as though the old ones did not suffice."[2]

It is, then, in the realm of journalism—one of the battle-fields upon which the struggle between modern Spain and the Spain of tradition was fought—that we must seek for the modern Spanish novel in embryo, and we shall find the germ

---

[1] *Lamentos políticos de un Pobrecito Holgazán que estaba acostumbrado a vivir a costa ajena* (1820).

[2] "Ahora todo es baraúnda y confusión, y gritos, y alborotos por estas calles cada día sale un periódico nuevo con diferente título, y no parece sino que no tenían bastante con los antiguos."—*Op. cit.* lxii. vol. ii., p. 610.

of some of its most important subsequent developments in the sketches of local manners and customs which abound in the reviews and periodicals of the day. Ardent local patriotism has always been a Peninsular characteristic, and the national genius has an especial aptitude for the vivid rendering of popular scenes. The "picture of local customs" can boast of no mean ancestors, for both Cervantes and Quevedo were masters in that form of art,[1] while, late in the seventeenth century, Juan de Zabaleta, a literary Velázquez, cultivated it in his admirable *El día de fiesta por la mañana y por la tarde*, a book which had to wait for due appreciation until long after it was first published in 1654.[2] The *genre* had the prestige of tradition; it was one for which the Spanish genius has an especial aptitude, and it could serve easily as a vehicle for social satire and polemic.

It was not, however, to national masterpieces that the early nineteenth-century writers turned in their search for inspiration. During their exile in France, Spanish men of letters had become imbued with the spirit of trans-Pyrenean romanticism, and their admiration for the protagonists of the French Romantic movement led them only too frequently into an uncritical and undiscerning imitation of everything French. In their revival of a thoroughly national type of literature they sought their models not in Cervantes, Quevedo or Zabaleta, but in M. Jouy,[3] a now forgotten writer who won

---

[1] Cf. El P. Blanco García, *La Literatura Española en el Siglo XIX* (3rd ed., 1909), part i., cap. xvii., pp. 328–9.

[2] El P. Blanco García (op. cit., p. 329) gives, erroneously, 1666.

[3] Victor Joseph Etienne de Jouy, author of various books upon Parisian customs. His *L'Hermite de la Chaussée d'Antin ou Observations sur les Mœurs et les Usages français au commencement du XIXᵉ Siècle* was especially popular in Spain (6th ed., Paris, 1815). Vide Cánovas del Castillo, *El Solitario y su Tiempo* (1883) (Colección de Escritores Castellanos), vol. i. cap. iv., pp. 139–40.

fleeting fame during the First Empire and the Restoration. A large proportion of early nineteenth-century "costumbrista" literature is mere plagiarism, and it would scarcely be an exaggeration to say that the same criticism could with some justice be made of the pioneer work in other literary forms. These early years of the new era are, in fact, an age of translation and imitation—both of an inferior character. The political subjugation of Spain by France, begun in the eighteenth century with the establishment of the Bourbon dynasty and culminating in the accession to the throne of Joseph Bonaparte in 1808, was accompanied by a similar process in thought and letters. It is difficult throughout this period to point to a single Spanish work of real originality; and, indeed, France has continued to exercise a considerable influence upon Spanish literature to this day. There are, however, some among the pioneers of the nineteenth-century revival whose names deserve to be remembered as worthy inaugurators of the modern Spanish novel of customs; some whose work, while not unaffected by their reading of French authors, has the authentic Spanish ring. Of these Serafín Estébanez de Calderón, "*El Solitario*"[1] is, according to his latest biographer, Antonio Cánovas del Castillo, the first and the most original.[2] Pulpete and Balbeja, the two "paladines de capa y baldeo"[3] of the *Escenas Andaluzas*, are drawn in the best style of the "gusto picaresco." The story of their duel for the hand of the vivacious Doña

---

[1] Calderón resided in Madrid from 1830 to 1834, occupying during his career there many important public positions. His *Escenas Andaluzas* appeared in 1847. He attempted the historical novel in *Cristianos y Moriscos* (1838).

[2] Vide A. Cánovas del Castillo, *El Solitario y su Tiempo* (1883) (Colección de Escritores Castellanos), vol. i. cap. iv., pp. 138–9, where the author establishes "El Solitario's" priority.

[3] *Escenas Andaluzas* (1847 ed.), pp. 1–7.

Gorja, who finally snubs them both for their pains, might almost rank as a *conte* if the sketch were more amply filled in; while as to Manolito Gázquez, a Spanish Tartarin de Tarascon —"there was no talent with which he was not endowed to an eminent degree, no adventure, however extraordinary, which had not come his way, nor any striking event at which he had not been present."[1] He is an indication of what "El Solitario" might have done had he chosen to carry the short story beyond the stage of the rough sketch. One certainly cannot accuse the author of the gallicism which mars the work of so many of his contemporaries. Always a sturdy opponent of alien influences which tended to undermine Spanish national characteristics, he is true to the intention which he expresses in the Introduction to the "Andalusian Scenes," to confine himself to the portrayal of districts "where Spain lives and reigns, free from any mixture or blending with alien heresies."[2] It is perhaps unfortunate that his zeal for realistic accuracy led him into the constant use of words and expressions in local *argot* which are quite unintelligible to the average Spaniard unpossessed of a dialect dictionary.[3] He erred, however, in the right direction, and his vigorous prose, for all its obscurity, is preferable to the emasculated language,

[1] "No había habilidad en que no descollase, aventura extraordinaria por la que no hubiera parado, ni ocasión estupenda en que no se hubiese encontrado"—*Escenas Andaluzas* (1847 ed.), pp. 51–61.

[2] "Donde vive y reina España, sin mezcla ni encruzamiento de herejía alguna extranjera." Vide "Dedicatoria a Quien Quisiere" (*Escenas Andaluzas*, 1847 ed.). See also "Toros y ejercicios de la Gineta" (op. cit., p. 183), where he explains the object of his works: "My chief purpose is to reveal and describe the manners and customs of Spain in a way which shall be as peculiar to our soil as possible."

["Mi principal propósito se cifra en revelar y relatar los usos y costumbres españolas por el modo más peculiar de nuestro suelo que posible sea."]

[3] Cf. El P. Blanco García, op. cit. vol. i., p. 333.

B

overladen with neologisms, which characterises the work of the gallophiles.

Ramón de Mesonero Romanos,[1] founder of the *Semanario Pintoresco Español*, enjoyed an even wider vogue than "El Solitario." Under the pseudonym of "El Curioso Parlante," he published several editions of his famous *Escenas Matritenses*,[2] the second series of which appeared in *El Semanario*. In these brilliant sketches of the life of the capital we can follow, step by step, the gradual transformation which Spain underwent after her eclipse as a great European Power; and although they are read nowadays rather by the student of social history than by the lover of literature, they mark an important stage in the development of the nineteenth-century novel of customs. Mesonero was well versed in the master-pieces of Spanish literature and, if the *Escenas Matritenses* are obviously inspired by the inevitable Jouy, some of them have the true Castilian flavour which constitutes the chief merit of "El Solitario's" work. In technique Mesonero is superior to his predecessor. The description of isolated incidents advances a step further towards the short story, but there is still a tendency, noticeable in all these sketches of local customs, to confine character-drawing to the delineation of isolated types. In "El Barbero de Madrid," [3] a scene in the first volume of the *Escenas Matritenses*, we have the makings of a picaresque novel in miniature, but the second part is devoted mainly to the description of individual characters: "El Religioso," "El Periodista," "El Poeta Bucólico," "El Contratista," and so on.

[1] Mesonero Romanos edited *El Semanario Pintoresco Español* from 1836 to 1842. He also published many articles in *La Ilustración Española y Americana*.
[2] 1842.
[3] Vide *Artículos Escogidos de las Escenas Matritenses* (Biblioteca Universal), 1879, vol. i., p. 84–92.

The nearest approach to the short story proper is to be found in *Una Noche de Vela*,[1] which did more than any other of the "Madrid Scenes" to establish the author's reputation as a writer. The story is, briefly, as follows. The Count of Tremedal, a gifted and wealthy aristocrat, falls ill upon his return from a ball. As he lies mortally sick, he reflects upon the futility, in his present position, of all his social advantages. All these gifts "were useless to him in his present situation—a prisoner in his bandages and ligatures, powerless, 'done for,' of no more importance than the most insignificant inmate of the public hospital."[2] His wife, an old friend, a sister, who hoped to inherit his fortune, together with various other rapacious relatives, surround his bed. The conversation which ensues between these human vultures is reported with delicious irony. Certain of his demise, they talk of nothing but the probable disposition of his wealth in the event of his dying intestate. The climax is reached with the death of the count and the appearance of a notary who announces, to the dismay of the company, that one of the count's natural sons will inherit, according to the terms of a secret will.

Mesonero's *Memorias de un Setentón*[3] form a valuable supplement to the *Escenas Matritenses*. The author was a personal witness of many of the events which he describes, and the work is a vivid and intimate record of Spanish social and political history from 1808 to 1850. As a prolegomenon to the *Episodios Nacionales* of Galdós the *Memorias* are of the

[1] Vide op. cit., vol. ii., pp. 61–82.
[2] ". . . para el paso actual no le servían de nada, preso entre vendas y ligaduras, inútil y agobiado, ni más ni menos que el último parroquiano del hospital" (op cit., p. 63).
[3] First published in *La Ilustración Española y Americana*, and later in a separate volume (Madrid, 1881).

greatest interest, for the *Episodios* are history recorded in a similar intimate manner, with a leavening of fiction to stimulate the reader. If Mesonero lacked the technical skill and the powers of imagination essential to the novelist, his observation is not merely journalistic and superficial. Nor was he blinded by party prejudice. He divined that human nature could not be altered by political legerdemain, and that reform affects the name of the institution which is changed rather than the institution itself. Prior to Galdós, no other Spanish writer succeeded in expressing the life of Madrid, in all its varied aspects, with more clarity and vigour.

It is not, however, until the advent of Mariano José de Larra that we meet with an author who, if he had possessed greater powers of application, might have been a figure of European importance in the history of nineteenth-century Spanish fiction. We shall have occasion to treat of Larra in tracing briefly the early development of the romantic novel. It is sufficient here to call attention to his work as a satirist, by which he will be remembered rather than by his attempt at an historical romance. Some critics refuse to recognise Larra as an "escritor de costumbres," and see in him only the writer of embittered polemics (in striking contrast with Mesonero's genial irony) against the corruption of his age. But *El Duende Satírico del Día*,[1] *El Pobrecito Hablador*,[2] and his contributions to various periodicals, are more than acrimonious pasquinades. They are mordant descriptive and character sketches worthy of the pen of Quevedo—with whom, indeed, Larra has a certain temperamental affinity.

[1] 1828. These articles he excluded from his collected works.
[2] Vide *Colección de artículos dramáticos, literarios, políticos y de costumbres, publicados en los años* 1832, 1833, 1834 (1835 y 1836) *en "El Pobrecito Hablador," "La Revista Española," "El Observador," La Revista Mensajero," y "El Español," por D. Mariano José de Larra* (1835-7, 4 vols.).

Among writers of minor importance in this form of literature were D. José Somoza [1] who, in his *Recuerdos e Impresiones*, gives a brilliant picture of the manners and customs of eighteenth-century Spain, and Antonio Flores [2] who deserves special mention because it is possible that Galdós was influenced by *Ayer Hoy y Mañana* in his *Episodios Nacionales*. Flores also attempted the novel proper in *Fé, Esperanza y Caridad*,[3] a literary monstrosity which is interesting only as the work of a pioneer. In *Ayer, Hoy y Mañana*, Flores covers the period of Spanish history already treated by Mesonero in his *Escenas Matritenses*, continuing, however, his survey beyond the point at which Mesonero left off. The world of Goya, the younger Moratín, and Ramón de la Cruz; the "age of confusion" which links the eighteenth century to the modern world, is admirably portrayed in the various scenes of *Ayer*, where all social types, from the aristocrat to the beggar, are represented. Flores exaggerates at times and abuses (as does Galdós) the device of allegorical personification, but in spite of all defects the sketches of *Ayer* can still afford pleasure to modern readers who have some knowledge of modern Spanish history and a taste for the "things of Spain." The crude realism of certain descriptive passages is an indication of the influence, obvious in *Fé, Esperanza y Caridad*, which the works of Eugène Sue exercised upon the Spanish writer. Unfortunately Flores succeeds in reproducing only the faults and absurdities of *Les Mystères de Paris* in his attempt to supply a

---

[1] The most convenient edition of Somoza's works was published in 1913, with a critical introduction by José R. Lomba y Pedraja.

[2] Flores's most important works were: *La Historia del Matrimonio, gran colección de cuadros vivos matrimoniales* (1852), and *Ayer, Hoy y Mañana, o la Fé, el Vapor y la Electricidad. Cuadros sociales de 1800, 1850 y 1899 dibujados a la pluma* (1853).

[3] 3rd ed., 1851.

Spanish equivalent, and in this he resembles the vast majority of imitators who endeavoured to establish the didactico-romantic novel in Spain. *Fé, Esperanza y Caridad* is one of the earliest Spanish efforts in the *genre*, and it is on this account only that it has any interest for us. It is a cumbersome farrago of impossibilities occupying some twelve hundred pages. Flores raises our hopes by calling it a "novel of customs"—and we are tempted to believe that here at last we have the "cuadro," with its undeniable merits, amplified into a really original Spanish novel. The "customs," however, are not those of the "Madrid Scenes," but rather those of a Suesque Paris indifferently disguised as Madrid. We quickly recognise in Visco the infamous Prince Rudolph; Crispín, el Zapatero, recalls the M. Pipelet of Sue's tale, and there are also general resemblances which afford ample evidence of the French origin of this wearisome novel.

By 1843, when *Los españoles pintados por sí mismos*, a "sketch of local customs" in which many distinguished Spanish writers collaborated, was published, the vogue of this literary form had reached its height. This work marks the close of the "journalistic" period of what was eventually to develop into the novel of customs proper.

(b) The Romantic Novel and the "Roman à Thèse."

THE development of the nineteenth-century romantic novel opens, as did that of the novel of customs, with an era of translation and imitation.

So far as the romantic novel is concerned, Sr. González-Blanco has hit the mark when he describes the Spanish romantic movement as "a French plant with British graftings." [1] If the eyes of Spanish novelists were turned most frequently towards France, they found time for an occasional glance at Richardson, whose *Clarissa Harlowe* enjoyed a considerable vogue when, in 1829, it appeared in Spanish dress. *Clarissa* proved a formidable rival to *La Nouvelle Héloïse*; while *Atala, René* and *Le dernier Abencérage* vied with them both in public favour. These works, together with those of Bernardin de Saint-Pierre and Ann Radcliffe, ran into many editions but did not inspire any original Spanish works of importance. The public appeared to be satisfied with the wretched translations which were published in the various "Bibliotecas" and anthologies of the time,[2] and this state of affairs lasted throughout the first three decades of the century.

With the appearance of Madame Cottin's *Mathilde* in a Spanish translation,[3] the attention of Spanish authors was directed to the historical novel, a literary form in which one would have expected them to excel. No country possesses a history richer in dramatic episodes and situations than does Spain, and the gift for picturesque and stirring narrative which is exhibited in many mediæval Spanish chronicles would seem to augur well for the future of the historical novel in that country. The sterility of the *genre* in modern Spanish literature is a curious and unexpected phenomenon. There is, indeed, no lack of such novels in Spanish, but it is difficult to name

[1] "Un vegetal francés con injertos británicos." Vide A. González Blanco, *Historia de la Novela en España desde el Romanticismo a nuestros días* (1909), cap. i., p. 81.

[2] The most important of these were Cabrerizo's *Colección de novelas*, which began publication in 1818; the *Colección de novelas históricas originales españolas* of Repullés (1833-4); and Jordán's *Nueva Colección de novelas*, the first series of which appeared in 1831.

[3] *Matilde, o memorias sacadas de la historia de las Cruzadas*. Traducidas en castellano por D. M. B. García Suelto (Madrid, 1821).

a single one which rises above the mediocre.[1] This is especially true of the historical novel in its early period, when Scott and Dumas reigned in undisputed sway over the imaginations of Spanish writers. A glance at the numerous "collections" of the period will convince one of the enthusiasm with which Scott was devoured by Spanish readers, and it is significant that Jordán[2] changed the title of his collection, from the fifth volume onwards, to *Nueva Colección de novelas de Sir W. Scott, etc.* There are nineteen volumes in the series, and among the translations they contain are versions of *Woodstock*, *The Pirate*, *The Heart of Midlothian*, *Ivanhoe* and *The Antiquary.*

Nearly all these translations of Scott are extremely poor, especially those which were made from French renderings of the original. The same, unfortunately, must be said of the "original" Spanish works which they inspired. Whether the model be Scott, Dumas or Madame Cottin, the copy is generally a distortion which exaggerates all the defects in the original and destroys most of its merits. Cabrerizo's collection contains samples of the worst that Spanish romantic novelists can do. That of Repullés[3] is by far the most interesting and important, for it contains Larra's *El Doncel de Don Enrique el Doliente* (1834), one of the least incompetent historical novels which nineteenth-century Spain produced. In this work the influence of Scott is unmistakable. The "machinery" of the novel; the long descriptive passages; the chapter-headings, and the introductory note dealing with the period of the setting—all recall the work of the master.

---

[1] Larreta's *La Gloria de Don Ramiro* (1908) is a notable exception, but Larreta is a South American.

[2] The first volumes of Jordán's *Nueva Colección de Novelas de diversos autores traducidas al castellano por una sociedad de literatos*, appeared in 1831.

[3] Vide supra.

With these superficialities, however, and certain similarities of detail such as the incident of the "juicio de Dios," (cf. *Ivanhoe*) and the broken drawbridge (cf. *Kenilworth*), the resemblance ceases.[1] The theme of the novel—the unhappy love of Macías, El Enamorado, for the wife of Enrique de Villena—is entirely national and traditional, and it has been treated by many Spanish writers, including Lope de Vega.[2]

El Doncel de Don Enrique el Doliente, while it is unquestionably the most interesting of these early attempts at the historical novel, lacks a solid basis of erudition and the treatment is far too subjective to produce the illusion of reality. The hero, Macías, is in the Rousseaucsque tradition—a modern "désillusionné" rather than a fifteenth-century troubadour, while Larra's treatment of Enrique de Villena is quite untrue to history. *El Doncel* is "Larra's" novel, and in the hero he gives us a picture of himself dressed according to period. He owes nothing to Lope in his conception of Macías, and in so far as he follows anyone he imitates Dumas rather than Scott. Fernán Pérez de Vadillo and Elvira recall at times the Duchess of Guise and St. Méguin of *Henri III. et Sa Cour*.

Espronceda, who was closely akin in temperament to Larra, attempted the historical novel in his *Sancho Saldaña*,[3] one of his few writings in prose. Neither Espronceda nor Larra was at home in a *genre* which sets so stern a limit to subjective expression; but Larra's tale is vastly superior to that of the great Spanish lyric poet. José García Villalta's *El Golpe en Vago*[4] marks a further advance in the development of the

[1] Cf. Enrique Piñeyro, *El Romanticismo en España* (cap. i., p. 16).
[2] In *Porfiar hasta morir* (1638).
[3] *Sancho Saldaña o el castellano de Cuellar, novela histórica original del siglo XIII* (Madrid, 1834).
[4] *El Golpe en Vago, cuento de la décimaoctava centuria* (1835).

historical romance, being a step towards the type of historical fiction to which Galdós was especially attracted—a fusion of the historical novel proper with the novel of tendency. The action of *El Golpe en Vago* takes place in eighteenth-century Spain, but the work is, in reality, a thinly disguised attack upon the Jesuits, and in this it foreshadows the anti-clericalism of the Galdosian politico-historical *genre*.

It would be profitless to discuss further the numerous attempts at the historical romance of the orthodox type which flooded Spain at one period of the romantic revival. Apart from Larra, Espronceda, Villalta, Martínez de la Rosa,[1] and, possibly, Enrique Gil who, in his *El Señor de Bembibre*,[2] produced a fairly creditable imitation of *The Bride of Lammermoor*, no Spanish writer succeeded in producing work of any value or interest in a form of literature from which much might reasonably have been expected.[3] Its vogue, however, easily eclipsed that of all other types of novel, and from *El Doncel* and *El Señor de Bembibre* down to the fantastic productions of the indefatigable Manuel Fernández y González,[4] the printing presses flooded Spain with volume after volume of romantic extravagance which is without significance for the student of rational fiction.

For the failure of the historical romance the early developments of the "thesis novel" offer some compensation. The use of the novel as a vehicle for the expression of social unrest has become in modern times so normal that we are nowadays

---

[1] The defects of Martínez de la Rosa's *Doña Isabel de Solís, Reina de Granada* (1839) are redeemed by beauty of style.

[2] 1844.

[3] Cf. A. González-Blanco, op. cit., cap. i., p. 131.

[4] Manuel Fernández y González, a typical writer of feuilletons, enjoyed an enormous popularity in his own time. Among the least preposterous of his works are *El Cocinero de su Majestad* (1857) and *Men Rodriguez de Sanabria* (1853).

a little astonished when we meet with a book which is totally devoid of any "tendencious" element. Very many novelists, including Galdós, have frankly regarded the *genre* as a means for the propagation of humanitarian ideas, a means which its admitted popular ascendancy over other forms of literature renders peculiarly effective. In France, Eugène Sue had employed it in the cause of "socialism," and Octave Feuillet, in his *Histoire de Sybile*, found it a convenient medium for Liberal-Catholic propaganda, to which George Sand replied with her *Mlle. de la Quintinie*.[1] It was only to be expected that Spain, ever since *El Conde Lucanor* especially rich in didactic literature, would follow in this respect the example of the rest of Europe. She found her first modern "thesis" novelist in a Cuban lady, Gertrudis Gómez de Avellaneda. "La Avellaneda" consciously endeavours to imitate the daring unconventionality of Sand in her mode of dealing with social problems, professing, as she does, intense sympathy with the rebel and the "under-dog" in whatever walk of life he, or *she*, may follow. Those who have been long accustomed to regard Spain as a "backward" country in which the free expression of revolutionary ideas in politics and morals has always been practically impossible, will be amazed by the advanced feminism of this Spanish Sand. The comparison, however, is too great a compliment to "la Avellaneda," who possessed too inadequate a knowledge of life and too superficial an insight into the workings of the human mind ever to have produced great fiction.

Sab, Guatimozín and *Espatolino* are of small intrinsic literary merit. The first was written when "la Avellaneda"

[1] Vide Preface to *Mlle. de la Quintinie* (1863 ed.) where George Sand embarks upon a spirited defence of the *roman à thèse*.

was a mere child, and of it and of *Guatimozín* she seems to have been a little ashamed, for neither are included in the authorised edition of her collected works.[1] In *Sab*, inspired probably by *Uncle Tom's Cabin*, she boldly tackles the problem of slavery, demanding for the negro not merely adequate wages but also full rights of citizenship. The story which forms the background of the thesis is, however, scarcely convincing. Sab, the slave, is in love with his mistress, who is engaged to be married to a man whom Sab knows to be worthless; and with unaccountable quixotism he does all he can to further the union, eventually sacrificing his life in order to bring it about. In *Guatimozín* she advocates the theory of purification by love which Octave Feuillet espouses in his *Rédemption*; while in the person of Espatolino, the Italian bandit, she embodies the revolt of the individual against the conventions of society. In *Dos Mujeres*, she depicts the alleged "slavery" of marriage from the woman's point of view, while in *Dolores* she aims a blow at Spanish tradition by attacking the mediæval conception of honour. Her shorter novels and *contes* are in a less controversial vein, many of them being based upon national legends and folk-lore. In these she gives free rein to the lyrical and mystical side of her temperament.

In spite of the immaturity and extravagance which mar her work, "la Avellaneda" played an important part in the development of the Spanish novel of manners. Her books will, at any rate, still bear reading—which is more than can be said for the majority of Spanish attempts at historical fiction. In her we find for the first time a nineteenth-century Spanish *novelist* who possesses some sense of situation and some power of gripping a reader.

[1] Vide *Obras Literarias* (1869–71).

The lachrymose tradition of *Werther* and *Obermann* is not well represented in the Spanish novel of this period, but the lyric poet Nicomedes Pastor Díaz attempted, in *De Villahermosa a China*,[1] to supply the want. The hero, Javier, a notorious Don Juan who had already seduced one victim, Irene, inspires a violent passion in Sofia, who breaks off her engagement to Enrique, a virtuous but uninteresting youth. Meanwhile Javier meets once again his old love, who has entered a convent. Her passion for him is revived, but she succeeds in resisting temptation and, finally, in converting her dissolute lover. Together they endeavour to convince Sofia of the futility of her passion, and Javier, who has become a priest, eventually marries her to Enrique. He then goes out to China as a missionary, solving the problem of existence by a life of self-sacrifice—a conclusion more to the taste of a Catholic novelist than the orthodox Wertherian suicide. It is easily divined that the novel is the work of a poet, and its chief merits lie in the lyrical beauty of isolated passages. As the only example of its kind, it has a certain interest for students of the Spanish novel, but it will scarcely be remembered on account of its intrinsic worth. It is, indeed, difficult, throughout the period we have very briefly reviewed, to point to a single novel of permanent literary value. Spain had not yet succeeded in breaking free from the subservience of the previous century, and these early attempts are of interest not so much for what they are in themselves as for their pioneer

---

[1] *De Villahermosa a China. Coloquios de la vida íntima* (1858). The novel is in four parts, the first of which was published in *La Patria* in 1848 (vide the Foreword to the 1858 edition). Pastor Díaz apologises for the book, which he refuses to describe as a novel. "I do not know whether the public will call it a novel: I have not dared to do as much." ["No sé si el público le llamará novela; yo no he atrevido a tanto." *Advertencia*, p. ix.].

work in the creation of a public for the novel, in providing an audience for the great Spanish writers of the latter half of the century. The "modern novel" which aims at portraying society in all its varied aspects, the novel which is at once a criticism and a reflection of the ideals of the age, was as yet unborn in the Peninsula.[1]

(c) From Romanticism to Realism. Fernán Caballero and Pedro Antonio de Alarcón.

THE changes in the social and political life of Spain which were effected towards the middle of the nineteenth century find a parallel in the literary history of the period. During the premiership of Brabo Murillo (1851–2) a step was taken towards reconciliation with the Holy See—a move foreshadowing the reaction in favour of moderation which followed the revolutionary upheaval of 1854 and the period of social unrest which culminated in the break between Espartero and O'Donnell in 1856. From 1856 until the dethronement of Isabel II. the moderate and radical parties alternated in power. The

---

[1] Cf. Revilla's *Bocetos Literarios* (*Revista Contemporánea*, 15 March, 1878, vol. xiv., pp. 117–8). "The modern novel, that which portrays the society of our own day and embodies the ideals and passions which animate our age, that which unites the dramatic interest of events and the psychological interest arising from the skilful portrayal of character with the social interest engendered by the problems which are dealt with in the work; that which has replaced and improved upon the ancient epic, and which paints with startling veracity and in brilliant colours the complex life and troubled conscience of contemporary society, remained uncultivated in Spain." ["La novela moderna, la que retrata la sociedad actual y encarna los ideales y sentimientos que a nuestro siglo animan; la que al interés dramático de los sucesos une el interés psicológico producido por la acabada pintura de los caracteres y el interés social engendrado por los problemas que en ella se plantean; la que sustituye con ventaja a la antigua epopeya y representa con pasmosa verdad y brillantes colores la vida compleja y la conciencia agitada de la sociedad presente, no tenía cultivadores en España."]

revival of Catholic orthodoxy had considerable influence upon the development of contemporary literature, which mirrored the growing prestige of moderate and anti-revolutionary views. In the early romantic period it was usual for poets of rebellion to express their dislike for established authority by a studied neglect of formal perfection. Their verse is frequently as insubordinate as their temperament. In the later period, however, there was far greater respect for authority both in life and in literature, a respect which, in letters, took the form of an effort to combine the lyric spontaneity of romanticism with the balance and formal beauty of classicism; while in life men sought for a rule to follow, bowing either to the authority of the Church or the sovereignty of reason.

The novel of the early romantic period suffered from the extravagance and exaggeration which is apparent in other literary forms. It was frequently cultivated as a "side-line" by men whose interests lay in the direction of politics and journalism rather than serious fiction, and the majority of the novels of the period bear obvious signs of having been written in haste. Spain produced innumerable novels, but no "novelist" in the orthodox sense of the word. The *genre* was not taken seriously until the fury of the romantic storm had given place to the lull which heralded the advent of Spanish realism after the decline of the historical romance. Two types of fiction now predominate: the novel of tendency crudely initiated by "la Avellaneda," and the novel of customs, of which we can discern the beginnings in the work of the early "costumbrista" writers. It remained to weld these two varieties of fiction into an harmonious whole—the modern "realistic" novel of manners—and to Cecilia Böhl de Faber, a Spanish lady of German extraction who wrote under the pseudonym

of Fernán Caballero, fell the task of initiating the process
which culminated in the novels of Benito Pérez Galdós. Until
1850 the Spanish novel had merely reflected the dominant
tendencies of foreign literatures; but now, in Fernán Caballero,
we at last find a writer of independence and originality, an
author who is not content with mere imitation. Avoiding
the alluring net spread by Scott and Dumas, she attempts
to create original works based upon personal observation of
the life she knew so well: the varied, colourful existence of
Andalusia. Temperamentally she was well equipped for her
task, for she had, in addition to the fertile imagination of the
Spaniard, the Teuton's love of accuracy and detail. Passionately attached to her adopted country, she saw great
possibilities in the sketch of national and local customs. She
determined to develop it beyond the stage of the *ébauche* at
which it was left by "El Solitario," Mesonero, and the rest.
Although it is not altogether free from the defects of the
"romantic" tradition which had dominated Spain for half
a century, *La Gaviota*,[1] the first-fruits of her labours, is a
creditable piece of work. The story is extremely simple;
indeed its author admits in her Preface [2] that it can scarcely
be termed a "novel" in the accepted sense of the word. It is
divided into two parts. The scene of the first is laid in the
neighbourhood of the imaginary town of Villamar, and the
action centres upon the relations of a young German doctor,

[1] *La Gaviota. Novela original de costumbres españolas.* 2 vols. (1848).
[2] Vide op. cit. 1921 edition. Prólogo, p. v.: "And, indeed, it was not
our purpose to write a novel, but rather to give an exact, true and
genuine idea of Spain, and especially of the present state of its society,
of the modes of thought peculiar to its inhabitants, of their idiosyn-
crasies, tastes and customs." ["Y en verdad, no nos hemos propuesto
componer una novela, sino dar una idea exacta, verdadera y genuina de
España, y especialmente del estado actual de su sociedad, del modo de
opinar de sus habitantes, de su índole, aficiones y costumbres."]

Friedrich Stein, with the inhabitants of the district—among whom the Catalán fisherman, Pedro Santaló, and his daughter Marisalada ("La Gaviota") play the most important part. Marisalada is the centre of interest throughout the story, and in her portrayal of this strange, wild creature, Fernán Caballero shows herself to be a psychologist of no mean order. Marisalada is a bizarre compound of the "noble savage" dear to Rousseau, and the modern "emancipated" woman of the Sandian tradition. A creature of instinct and passion, she is the complete antithesis of her lover who, we may imagine, is an expression of the Teutonic element in the author's character, as Marisalada is that of the Spanish. The minor figures in the first part—la tía María, Dolores, Manuel, Don Modesto Guerrero, "Rosa Mística," "Turris Davídica," Momo and Gabriel—are admirably drawn. In her portrayal of the two old "devotas" Fernán Caballero anticipates the delicious irony of Galdós, who delighted in rendering such types. The first part of the novel might aptly be likened to a portrait gallery, a series of *genre* studies to which we are introduced one by one. Stein, as one would expect, falls in love with the alluring "Gaviota" and determines to marry her and give her the opportunity of cultivating her remarkable voice, for this creature of the wilds has in her the makings of a prima donna.

He is assisted in this project by the Duque de Almansa, who, badly injured while hunting, is cured by Stein. In the second part of the novel the scene is transferred to Seville, where we are introduced to various types representative of Andalusian society—General Santa María, the ardent patriot; Eloisa, the cosmopolitan; the Condesa de Algar; the Marquesa de Guadalcanal; Pepe Vera, the "torero"; and the incredible

c

Englishman Sir John Burnwood. The erratic temperament of Marisalada remains, however, unchanged in this atmosphere of distinction, and, finding in Pepe Vera a lover more to her primitive taste, she is unfaithful to Stein who, broken-hearted, emigrates to Havana and there dies of yellow fever. This second part is, on the whole, unconvincing. It brings out clearly a cardinal defect in the literary equipment of the author, a defect which she is able to conceal when she deals with more primitive types. Fernán Caballero had no adequate experience of life. Her aristocrats, especially, smack of the novelette, and her Englishmen are fantastic. She moved in a restricted circle and lacked the gift, peculiar to great genius, of making a little experience go a very long way. It is, indeed, impossible to join unreservedly in the pæan of unqualified praise with which La Gaviota was greeted by certain Spanish critics.[1] Apart from the superficiality of its author's observation, revealed by many of the characters in it, La Gaviota is a badly constructed book. It is far too long. There is a notable insufficiency of plot and action to justify two volumes, the first of two hundred and three, the second of two hundred and thirty-six, pages.[2] The author has not succeeded in emancipating herself completely from the evil traditions of the neo-chivalresque school, and deliberate imitations of the style and mannerisms of Scott appear in La

---

[1] Vide Eugenio de Ochoa's *Juicio Crítico* (p. **xxxi**.), which prefaces the 1921 edition of *La Gaviota*: "It is certain that *La Gaviota* will be in our literature what *Waverley* is in English literature—the early dawn of a glorious day, the first flower in the glorious crown of poetry which will encircle the temples of a Spanish Walter Scott." ["Ciertamente *La Gaviota* será en nuestra literatura lo que es *Waverley* en la literatura inglesa, el primer alba de un hermoso día, el primer florón de la gloriosa corona poética que ceñirá las sienes de un Walter Scott español."]
[2] 1921 edition.

Gaviota, and strike one as being utterly out of place. She indulges frequently in sentimental rhetoric and long, wearisome digressions; her description of Seville might have been taken straight from the pages of Baedeker; she allows herself to be led into a tiresome didacticism—these are but a few of the charges one might bring against this well-meaning pioneer of realism in the Spanish novel. Fernán Caballero lacked, in fine, the resources of heart and mind which are inseparable from genius. She had, however, none of that arrogance which so often characterises the mediocre artist. Her pretensions are modest; and she herself, in a letter to one of her admirers, M. Germond de Lavigne, has well defined the scope of her own talent: "Je n'ai cherché," she says, "à mettre dans mes récits ni étude du cœur et du monde, ni invention, ni art, ni inspiration; c'est la peinture exacte de notre société actuelle, des mœurs, des sentiments, du langage poétique, spirituel, moqueur avec gaieté et sans fiel de notre peuple. Ce sont des types espagnols vrais en tout genre, des descriptions exactes en toute matière."

Her claims to "españolismo" are amply justified, for her work, in spite of certain affectations due to borrowing from Scott, has the authentic flavour of the soil, and in it we can discern the love of truth, the power of observation and the effort to express the hidden beauty and significance of ordinary life which is characteristic of the realistic novel at its best. When Fernán Caballero entered the literary arena, the Spanish public was weary of the dull and interminable pseudo-historical romance. It yearned for a truer presentation of life; and found what it required in *La Gaviota, Clemencia, Lágrimas* and *La Familia de Alvareda*. These works by Fernán Caballero renewed European interest in Spanish

literature, an interest which had been steadily on the wane
since its momentary [1] revival by the Schlegels in the early
years of the century.

The intimate relationship between politics and literature
which existed throughout the nineteenth century is especially
remarkable after the revolution of 1868. With greater liberty
of the press and freedom of speech, there came into being
numerous reviews and political clubs,[2] which reflected the
democratic spirit of the age. The majority of contemporary
writers entered the arena either as champions of the new order
or defenders of the old, and did not hesitate to use whatever
literary medium they possessed as a means of party propaganda. In *Los Gritos de Combate* [3] the lyric poet, Nùñez de
Arce, expresses his bitter disillusionment at the failure of
liberal ideals to alter human nature; while in the drama
Tamayo y Baus[4] is the prophet of "neo-Catholicism" and
enlightened social reform.

[1] Signor Benedetto Croce, in an article to which Professor Starkie has
kindly called our attention (*Scritti di Storia Letteraria e Politica. XVII*.
Seconda edizione riveduta, Bari, 1921, pp. 207–25) writes in glowing
terms of Fernán Caballero, even placing her above George Sand in
the hierarchy of women lyricists: "Migliore vena di poesia," he says
"e anche di poesia idillica che non nella celebratissima Sand a me par
di trovare nella modesta scrittrice spagnuola, che si celava sotto il
nome di Fernán Caballero. . . . vedo in lei una solidità di mente, una
semplicità di cuore e una vivezza di fantasia, che l'altra con tanto
maggiore facondia e virtuosità, non possedeva" [op. cit., p. 207].
He regards her as a worthy sucessor of the great Spanish novelists
of the Golden Age: "Ma Fernán Caballero, tutta spontaneita com era,
vivendo intensamente le figure che creava, sapeva a tratti narrare con
forza e sobrietà e mostrarsi degna erede della progenie dei narratori
spagnoli, da colui che scrisse il *Lazarillo*, al gran Cervantes e agli
autori di romanzi picareschi. *La Gaviota* è piena di cose bellissime. . . ."
(op. cit., p. 219). May we venture to suggest, with all deference to
Signor Croce, that this praise is, possibly, a little extravagant?
[2] One of the most famous of these, "La Fontana de Oro," supplied
the title of Galdós' first novel.
[3] 1875.
[4] 1829–98.

The novel, however, naturally became the favourite medium of propaganda, for it lends itself more easily to digression and appeals to a wider public than either poetry or drama. The novel in the last decades of the nineteenth century is a faithful mirror of the ideals, religious, social, and political, of that turbulent and complex age, and it was during these stormy years that the Spanish novel, the "modern" novel which endeavours to be at once a representation and a criticism of life, grew to maturity. If Fernán Caballero was its initiator, and Galdós, in the fullest sense of the word, its "creator," Pedro Antonio de Alarcón did much to indicate the direction it was to take. Contemporary with Fernán Caballero and Galdós, he enjoyed a greater vogue among the intellectuals than the former and for some years vied with the latter in popularity. He is remarkable for his power of invention, his ability to create character and, above all, for his originality, his "españolismo neto," for if, to some extent, he acquired his technique from Scott, Dumas, Balzac and George Sand, his individuality was never dominated by that of any foreign genius. We divine in his work a constant struggle between two opposing sides of his temperament, the side which made him, in his early years, an advanced liberal and that which eventually brought him to espouse the cause of neo-Catholicism. He stands towards the latter in much the same position as does Galdós towards radicalism. Alarcón published only one novel prior to the appearance of Galdós' *Fontana de Oro* in 1870: *El Final de Norma* (1855). It is a youthful work which has most of the defects of immaturity. Serafín, the hero, falls madly in love with an opera singer, Brunilda, "the daughter of heaven." He loses sight of her for a long time, and when they meet again she tells him that she is pledged to a certain individual who claims to have saved her father's life—and whom her father has commanded her to marry. It eventually transpires, however, that this gentleman was in reality the betrayer and not the saviour of her parent. This discovery leads to the conventional "happy ending" of what is in many respects a typical feuilleton. The story is commonplace in conception and execution, and it is difficult to understand the reason for the enormous vogue it once enjoyed not only in Spain but also in France and America. It does, however, in some respects, mark an advance upon *La Gaviota*; for it has a well-defined plot and plenty of incident, and if the character-drawing is not subtle it is at least convincing. It is, also, definitely Spanish in tone, and this "españolismo" is, perhaps, the most striking characteristic of Alarcón's work. It is nowhere more apparent than in *El Sombrero de Tres Picos*,[1] "a picture as truly Spanish as the grace of Sevillan girls or the colour of the wines of Jerez," [2] and in this revival of the *gusto picaresco* he leads the Spanish novel back into the highway of national tradition. *El Sombrero* was, however, only an interlude, and Alarcón returned to the platform in 1875 with *El Escándalo*. In this novel he deals with the notorious problem as to whether, in any conceivable circumstances, the end may justify the means. General Fernández de Lara, father of Fabián Conde, the hero of the book, dies the victim of an unjust accusation of treachery to his country. Can Fabián vindicate his father's honour by utilising documents which, if genuine, would have proved the charges

---

[1] Published for the first time in the *Revista Europea*. *El sombrero de Tres Picos, historia verdadera de un sucedido que anda en romances, escrito ahora tal y como pasó* (Madrid, 1874).

[2] "Un cuadro bien genuinamento español como la gentileza de las sevillanas o el color de los vinos de Jerez" (vide Luís Alfonso's Prologue to 7th ed.).

untrue? Father Manrique, the Jesuit priest, decides that he would not be justified in so using them—thus giving the lie to one of the most widely spread charges against the morality of his order. *El Escándalo* brought down upon its author the wholesale condemnation of the radicals, who accused him of being a Jesuit spy, and in order to prove that he was not so reactionary as they imagined, he wrote his next novel, *El Niño de la Bola* (1880), in a less orthodox vein; while in its successor, *La Pródiga*, he returns to the novel of customs. From 1881, the year in which he published, in addition to *La Pródiga*, his last novel, *El Capitán Veneno*, Alarcón lived a retired life, concentrating upon his *Historia de mis libros* (1884), in which he reviewed and defended his own works. He died in 1891.

An erratic genius, it is difficult to assign him to any particular school, for he was easily influenced by the changing literary fashions of the day. It is as a connecting-link between Fernán Caballero and Galdós, as the inaugurator of the last stage in the development of the nineteenth-century novel, that Alarcón most interests us here. To Galdós belongs the honour of "creating" the modern Spanish novel in the full sense of the word, for when his *Fontana de Oro* was published in 1870, no prose fiction of European significance had yet appeared in Spain, with the exception of Pereda's *Escenas Montañesas*,[1] which is a collection of "cuadros de costumbres" rather than a novel. Galdós was the first writer of indisputable genius to embark seriously upon the task of reviving modern fiction in Spain.

[1] 1864.

II

CONCERNING the life of the man who, by the vast scope of his work and the amazing fecundity of his genius, is certainly entitled to rank as the greatest Spanish novelist of the nineteenth century, we know surprisingly little. The reticence, born of an engaging modesty not usually found in eminent novelists, which Galdós invariably manifested with regard to his personal affairs, has become a byword among Spanish critics.[1] From the few data we possess we gather that Galdós spent the greater part of his life in scholarly retirement, and the adventures which contributed to the formation of his genius had as their sphere the mental and spiritual rather than the material stage.

Benito Pérez Galdós was born at Las Palmas, Grand Canary Island, on 10 May, 1843.[2] His parents were moderately well-

---

[1] Vide Clarín's *Galdós* (Madrid, 1912), p. 5: "One of the most significant biographical details which I have been able to worm out of Pérez Galdós is the fact . . . that he, who is so fond of telling stories, does not want to tell his own." ["Uno de los datos biográficos de más sustancia que he podido sonsacarle a Pérez Galdós es . . . que él, tan amigo de contar historias, no quiere contar la suya."] Also Luís Antón del Olmet and Antonio García Carraffa's *Galdós* (Madrid, 1912), *passim*. The latter (a record of various interviews) is the most complete biography we possess, and upon it this section is largely based.

[2] A stone now marks the house in the Calle de Elcano, where he was born. It bears the following inscription: "Here was born Pérez Galdós, the greatest, most genuine and most universal glory of the Canary Islands." ["Aquí nació Pérez Galdós, la gloria más grande y más legítima y más universal de las Islas Canarias."]

28

to-do, and Galdós, who throughout his life enjoyed the advantages which an independent income alone can give, was not one of literature's many wrestlers with poverty. It is interesting to note that he received his early education at an English school in Las Palmas, a fact which played its part in the moulding of his literary tastes and, some would have it, of his temperament.[1]

At the age of thirteen he proceeded to the Colegio de San Agustín, where he studied, with considerable success, for his "bachillerato." From this period date his first efforts at journalism—in the local papers *El País* and *El Eco*.

In 1864 he was sent by his family to Madrid for the purpose of studying law, a subject which he cordially disliked. It cannot be said that he proved an assiduous student at the University; but in a long life of practically unremitting labour these few Bohemian years may be regarded in the light of a holiday before the event! In the rough-and-tumble existence of boarding-houses [2] and cafés he certainly acquired that grounding in knowledge of human nature which is more essential than book-learning to the would-be novelist; and of this period of Galdós' life a vivid picture may be found in *El Doctor Centeno*. Academic activities would seem to have played a very small part in his existence as an undergraduate, and apart from a testimony of respect and affection for Camús, who then occupied the Chair of Latin, and Fernando Castro, Professor of History, Galdós has left little on record concerning

[1] Vide Clarín, op. cit., p. 34: "Galdós, like various characters in his last novels, tends to be a Spaniard 'a la inglesa.'" ["Galdós tiende a ser, como varios personajes de sus últimas novelas, un español a la inglesa."]

[2] He first lodged at a boarding-house in the Calle de las Fuentes, 3, and it was here he met León y Castillo, another Canary Islander, and a great friend of his at this period. Galdós soon moved to the Calle del Olivo (now Calle de Mesonero Romanos), where he lived for over six years. (Vide Olmet y Carraffa, op. cit. cap. iv., pp. 27, et seq.)

his university career. One can find ample evidence in his novels, however, of his dislike for academic prodigies,[1] and one gathers that he was more at his ease intellectually among the brilliant dilettanti who frequented the Café Universal, than in the lecture-room. Among his café acquaintances of this period were a future liberal minister, Amós Salvador; a future general, Ochando; and Ricardo Molina, who was eventually to become a judge of the Supreme Court, but who, at this time, was as obscure as Galdós himself. To Molina Galdós owed his introduction to La Nación, then owned by Pascual Madó and Santín de Quevedo; and in La Nación appeared his first attempts, in the metropolis, at literary and dramatic criticism.

Criticism, however, was not his goal. Although the early years in Madrid had been barren of original work so far as any external manifestations were concerned, his mind, he tells us was throughout this period in a ferment of activity. Ideas for novels and plays, especially plays, crowded through his brain, bearing fruit only in the shape of innumerable jottings destined, no doubt, to serve him in good stead when faced with the task of formal composition.

His ambitions at this period of his career were, he tells us, concentrated upon the theatre.[2] He wrote a romantic drama in the style of Echegaray entitled La Expulsion de los Moriscos, which he sent to Manuel Catalina, then manager of the Teatro del Príncipe. Catalina professed to be delighted with it, was "on the point" of producing it, but, fortunately, perhaps, for Galdós' reputation as a dramatist, it was never staged. One gathers that this was only one of many similar youthful disillusionments.

[1] e.g. The satirical portrait of Jacintito in Doña Perfecta.
[2] "My dreams were of the theatre." ["En el teatro tenía puesta mi ilusión."]—Op. cit. cap. iv., p. 29.

Two events which occurred at about this period exercised, Galdós tells us, a profound influence upon his mind: the massacre of the *Noche de San Daniel* (10 April, 1865), and the revolt of the sergeants of San Gil barracks—of both of which incidents he was a witness.[1]

In May 1867, Galdós visited Paris for the first time, and was in the French capital on the occasion of the visits of the Sultan of Turkey and Wilhelm of Prussia. He saw the first Exposition Universelle; and gained, within a very brief period, an amazingly thorough knowledge of the city, which he tramped, map in hand. Paris moved and fascinated him profoundly; but the dominating influence of this period is to be sought in the novels of Balzac—all of which he bought and read from cover to cover.

Upon the literary relationship between Balzac and Galdós we shall say more elsewhere: it is sufficient to note here that the novel was in future to be the *genre* of his predilection. He had been wavering for some time between the novel and the theatre, and his early failures in the drama doubtless first impelled him towards prose fiction. His study of Balzac, however, proved to be the determining factor in his ultimate decision, of which *La Fontana de Oro*, an historical-cum-thesis novel, begun in 1868, was the first fruit.

In that year, after a brief visit to Madrid, he returned to Paris with his family. *La Fontana de Oro* was concluded at Bagnères de Bigorre, whence he proceeded, after a brief period of residence, to Marseilles. From Marseilles he went to Perpignan, and from Perpignan across the Pyrenees by

---

[1] "These events left vivid memories in my soul and they have exercised a considerable influence upon my literary temperament." ["Estos sucesos dejaron en mi alma vivísimos recuerdos y han influído considerablemente en mi temperamento literario."]—Op. cit. cap. iv., p. 30.

coach to Gerona, and thence by train to Barcelona, where he witnessed the revolutionary disturbances of September 1868. In Barcelona he met Nuñez de Arce, the famous lyric poet. From Barcelona he went by boat, with his family—who were returning to Las Palmas—as far as Alicante. He was in Madrid on the occasion of the entry of Prim and Serrano into the capital. "That of Prim, especially," he said, "will never be erased from my memory. It was one of the most magnificent spectacles I have ever witnessed in my life. I say again that I shall never be able to forget that extraordinary event."[1] The period of Galdós' most intense journalistic activity opens in the year 1869, the year in which he definitely concluded his legal studies. Hitherto he had regarded his newspaper articles as mere frivolities; but now he had to work at them in earnest. Anibal Alvarez Osorio had just founded *Las Cortes*, and Galdós became a member of its brilliant editorial staff. To him was given the task of reporting the sessions of Congress, and he was present at all the meetings of the "Constituent Cortes," hearing all the most famous speeches of Castelar, Echegaray, Figueras, Pi y Margall, Cristina Martos, Nocedal, Salmerón, etc. Galdós, always an indefatigable worker, excelled himself at this period of his career. Rarely, he tells us, did he leave his office before two A.M. He was living then in the Salamanca quarter of Madrid, Calle de Serrano, No. 8. The house was owned at that time by Sr. García Torres, Director de Rentas, who occupied the "principal," while Galdós had the "piso tercero." Galdós' connection with *La Revista de España* dates from

---

[1] "La de Prim especialmente no se borrará nunca de mi memoria. Fué uno de los espectáculos más grandiosos que he contemplado en mi vida. Repito que nunca podré olvidar aquel extraordinario suceso." Vide op. cit., cap. v., p. 33.

1870, in which year he was introduced to that journal's founder, Alvareda, by a mutual friend, Ferreras. Alvareda, with the aid of Prim, founded later *El Debate*, of which Galdós was for some time editor. Its columns, he tells us, are crowded with his articles.[1] Many celebrated journalists were his colleagues, including López Guijarro, Nuñez de Arce, Ramón Correa and Ferreras. After Pavia's *coup d'état*, Alvareda became the editor-in-chief of *El Debate*, which passed later into the hands of Nuñez de Arce.

La Sombra—a "cuento largo"—and *El Audaz*, his second novel proper, appeared as serials in the *Revista de España* for the year 1871.

The year 1873 saw a radical change in the mode of life which Galdós had hitherto pursued. Although of a reserved and retiring disposition, he had always taken part in the distractions of the journalistic and political circles in which he moved. He was a familiar figure at the "tertulias" of the principal cafés of Madrid; he had many friends and acquaintances; was fond of social life and visits to concerts and theatres.

Then, with startling suddenness, he cut himself aloof from ordinary life and became, for a considerable period, almost a recluse. In 1873 he wrote and published four of his *Episodios Nacionales*, a series of novels in which he aimed at giving in the form of fiction a faithful picture of Spanish political and social history during the nineteenth century.[2] In 1874 there appeared four more, and so on, one *Episodio* every three months until 1876—the year in which he wrote *Doña Perfecta*,

---

[1] "Their columns are full of my work. I wrote innumerable articles on politics, literature, art, criticism." ["Sus columnas están llenas de trabajos míos. Hice innumerables artículos de política, de literatura, de arte, de crítica."]—Op. cit. cap. vi., p. 37.

[2] Vide Section III., also Bibliography.

the first of the *Novelas Contemporáneas*. From 1876 onwards the latter alternated in appearance with the "Episodes," and Galdós grew rapidly in popular esteem. The first public expression of this general admiration took the form of a banquet in his honour, organised by Leopoldo Alas ("Clarín") in March 1883. At this banquet laudatory speeches were delivered by such eminent Spaniards of the day as Cánovas del Castillo, Castelar and Echegaray.

In 1883 Galdós visited England, spending most of his time in London, a city for which he conceived a far greater affection than for Paris. His ambition was to know London as well as he knew Madrid, and he would spend hours tramping the streets with a Baedeker in his hand. He especially delighted in visiting the haunts immortalised by Dickens, whose works he devoured as eagerly as he had done those of Balzac. Galdós returned again and again to England, staying sometimes with his friend José Alcalá Galiano (grandson of the famous orator Antonio Alcalá Galiano) who was Spanish consul at Newcastle. With José Alcalá Galiano, Galdós undertook many long tours of Europe, visiting Holland, Germany, Denmark, Sweden, Italy. On his third visit to England Galdós visited Stratford-on-Avon, which became the theme of an essay entitled *La Casa de Shakespeare*.

After this period of travel abroad, Galdós made many journeys through Spain, riding third class in order to obtain a first-hand acquaintance with popular customs.[1] No part

[1] Vide op. cit. cap. xi., p. 60, where Galdós' account of one of these excursions is given as follows: "You cannot imagine what picturesque scenes I witnessed and what delightful 'argot' I heard in third-class carriages and at the inns where I lodged. I remember how much I enjoyed a trip I took from Bribiesca to Burgos. I travelled by a goods train which had only one third-class coach, a train which they call 'the donkey.' The convoy stopped for a long time at all the stations. Owing to this

of the country was neglected. His life in Madrid was un-eventful, most of his time being spent either in his study or in the library of the old "Ateneo." [1] To this institution he was deeply attached, and he there made the acquaintance of many celebrated contemporaries, including Manuel de la Revilla, the critic; Villanova, the geologist; Menéndez Rayón, the antiquarian; Julio Burell, the poet; and various professors of the Universidad Central. The even tenor of his quiet, scholarly existence was enlivened only by his theatrical successes, with which we are not here immediately concerned, and an occasional excursion into politics.[2] In 1897 he was admitted to the Spanish Academy: he was a liberal deputy for Porto Rico from 1886 to 1890, and in 1907 he was elected deputy from Madrid by the Republican party. His sight, which had for long been failing him, grew steadily worse until, in 1912, he became totally blind. He died on 4 January, 1920, mourned throughout two continents.

circumstance, and to its lack of speed, it was many hours late. Nevertheless I found the journey an extremely pleasant one, with its constant ebb and flow of villagers in and out of my coach, the conversations which were started and the picturesque customs which I discovered." ["No se pueden Vds imaginar qué escenas más pintorescas presencié y qué lenguajes más bonitos oí, en los vagones de tercera y en los mesones en que me hospedaba. Recuerdo que gocé mucho en un viaje que hice de Bribiesca a Burgos. Realicé la jornada en un tren de mercancías que llevaba sólo un coche de tercera y que llaman la *burra*. En todas las estaciones se detenía el convoy largos ratos y debido a esto y a su escasa velocidad, tardó en hacer el recorrido muchas horas. Pero a mí la excursión me resultó amenísima con el constante entrar y salir en el vagón de aquellas gentes aldeanas, con los diálogos que entablaron y con las costumbres pintorescas que me iba descubriendo."]

[1] Vide op. cit. cap. xii., pp. 63–7.
[2] For an interesting account of Galdós' political views vide op. cit. caps. xx. and xxi., pp. 113–33.

III

THE EARLY POLITICO-HISTORICAL NOVELS AND THE "EPISODIOS NACIONALES"

(a) The Early Novels: "La Fontana de Oro" and "El Audaz"

THE didactic element in Spanish fiction, from *El Conde Lucanor* down to the present time, has always been conspicuous. The crude realism of the first "picaresque" tales was soon leavened, if only for reasons of policy, with a dash of sermonising; and the misdoing of the hero-rogue was followed by his repentance and apotheosis. Prior to the birth of the "género picaresco" in novel form, Juan Ruiz had announced, probably with his tongue in his cheek, that his records of dissolute conduct were set down in order that his readers might beware of falling into sin themselves.[1] Such intrusions of "the moral" were, undoubtedly, in many cases, examples of the tribute which vice pays to virtue; but the desire to point a moral, if only as a cloak for cynicism, was there. It is present, to a lesser degree, in the Spanish drama of the "Golden Age," which abounds in religious themes: and it repeatedly tends, in Spanish literature of the last century, to oust the main business of telling the story or constructing the play. We have remarked upon it in the novels of "la Avellaneda," Fernán Caballero and Alarcón: and it is equally noticeable in the plays of Tamayo y Baus. It is, then, only to be expected that the father of modern Spanish realism,

[1] Vide Prologue to *El Libro de Buen Amor*.

36

Benito Pérez Galdós, should have had little sympathy with the Flaubertian theory of "l'art pour l'art." [1] Moving, as he did, in the political and literary circles of the "Ateneo" of his day, and ill-fitted, by his retiring disposition, to hold his own in verbal polemic, it was only natural that he should turn to the newspaper article and the novel as the most convenient means of expressing his views upon, and suggesting his remedy for, what he conceived to be the abuses of his time. It is interesting in this connection to note that he was not immediately attracted by the novel as an art-form, his ambitions being directed, as we have already indicated, rather towards the drama.[2] Only after many early disillusions [3] as a playwright did he definitely make up his mind to concentrate his energies upon the novel, and even when he took this resolution he had hopes of future greatness as a dramatist, hopes which were, as it proved eventually, to be amply justified. His first two novels belong to the journalistic period of his career, and it was not until after they were written that he began to formulate the more ambitious project of that

[1] Vide op. cit. cap. xvi., p. 93. In reply to the questions of his interlocutors as to whether he approves of "el arte por el arte," Galdós replies, "No, never. I believe that literature should instruct and set an example." ["No; jamás. Creo que la literatura debe ser enseñanza, ejemplo."]

[2] Vide op. cit. cap. iv., p. 29: "Nevertheless the literary *genre* which fascinated me most, the one for which I felt the keenest enthusiasm, and the one which I first cultivated, was the drama. My dreams were of the theatre." ["Sin embargo, el género literario que más me seducía, por el que sentía mayores entusiasmos y el que cultivé primero . . . era el género dramático. En el teatro tenía puesta mi ilusión."]

[3] Vide op. cit. cap. iv., p. 30, where, speaking of his verse drama, *La Expulsión de los Moriscos*, Galdós is reported as saying: ". . . It was on the point of being played, but . . . it was not played. Why? Because the work of beginners is never played. 'Come to-morrow, come again the day after.' Always the same eternal reply." [". . . Estuvo a punto de representarse, pero . . . no se representó. ¿Por qué? Por lo que no se representan siempre las obras de los que empiezan. 'Que venga Vd. mañana, que vuelva Vd. pasado.' Lo de siempre, lo eterno."]

D

Spanish "Human Comedy" which grew out of the "historia novelada" of the *Episodios Nacionales*.

He confesses, in his introductory note to *La Fontana de Oro* (1870), a book which he began in 1867, that he was led to write it on account of "the connection which one might discover between many of the events here set forth and some of those which are happening here and now"[1]—by which he means the political upheavals of 1868–70; and in the condition of Spain after the expulsion of Isabel II. in 1868 we do certainly find a remarkable parallel to the state of affairs which existed during the period of Spanish history of which *La Fontana de Oro* treats—the absolutist régime of Fernando VII. and its final overthrow.

In 1868, as then, reaction fought for supremacy with revolution, and the voice of moderation was drowned by the clamour of excess. The story of Spanish social and political disturbances in the nineteenth century does not make pleasant reading for democrats—for never did a people show themselves more unfitted for the task of governing themselves than did the Spaniards of that unhappy time. Galdós, with his hatred of extremes, felt that it was an opportune moment for the publication of a novel which should have as its chief object the portrayal of disasters consequent upon violent measures; and the circumstances of its publication are the best indication of the light in which it can well be considered as a work of fiction. In it Galdós attacks not only Fernando VII. and the extreme reactionaries who surrounded that monarch—men of the type of the Marquis de Loja in Galdós' own day—but also the "exalted" liberals who, in 1824 as in 1868,

---

[1] "La relación que pudiera encontrarse entre muchos sucesos aquí referidos y algo *de lo que aquí pasa*" (vide 1906 ed., p. 5).

did much to provoke measures of repression. True, he attributes many of the revolutionary disturbances of 1820–4 to the nefarious activities of "agents provocateurs" employed by Fernando, but at the same time he does not attempt to disguise his lack of sympathy with the anarchical elements in Spanish politics and his contempt for the rhetorical vapourings of the political clubs, among which "The Friends of Order," under the leadership of Alcalá Galiano, occupied an important place.[1] This novel, indeed, degenerates at times into a mere frame-work of events upon which the author hangs a series of personal opinions, expressed sometimes directly, sometimes through the mouths of his characters. The book is, in consequence, of greater interest as a social "document" than as a work of fiction; for it is diffuse, prolix and lacking in coherence. It opens with a description of the public manifestations of the democratic spirit which turned the streets of Madrid into a bear-garden from 1820 to 1823: "The mob . . . stirred the whole city into motion, turning its streets into a vast theatre of immense rejoicing or crazy uproar."[2] There follows a description of the Madrid of that age, a description in which Galdós reveals that intimate acquaintance with the history and topography of the capital which characterises all his "metropolitan" works. He mentions the chief political clubs of the period—"La Fontana de Oro," "El Grande Oriente," "Lorencini," "La Cruz de Malta," etc.; and introduces us to

---

[1] The "Friends of Order" met at a café which went by the name of "La Fontana de Oro." The "Fontana's" most important rival was "The Patriotic Society of the Friends of Liberty," which met at a café in the Puerta del Sol under the presidency of Gorostiza. Vide Martin Hume, *Modern Spain* (1899), pp. 209–10.

[2] "El pueblo . . . ponía en movimiento a la villa entera; hacía de sus calles un gran teatro de inmenso regocijo o ruidosa locura" (*La Fontana de Oro* (1906 ed.), cap. i., p. 7).

the Carrera de San Jerónimo as it was then, with its countless shops and taverns frequented by ardent politicians of all creeds. Among the best known of the demagogues is the barber, Gaspar Calleja, a hero of the revolution of 1808 and "one of Fernando's greatest enemies in '14."[1] After presenting us to Don Anatolio Mas, the perfumer and haberdasher, and to Doña Ambrosia, the vendor of silks, Galdós goes on to discuss the genesis of the political clubs, and in one of those arresting portraits for which his books are remarkable, to introduce us to one of the chief characters in the novel, Gil Carrascosa, a Spanish Vicar of Bray,[2] who decided, after serving the monarchy in an ecclesiastical capacity, to adopt radical journalism as a career. Upon the return of Fernando he again favoured absolutism; but deserted the king after the latter had accepted the Constitution of 1820. Carrascosa then joined the "Comuneros"—the famous anarchist society of which the poet Espronceda was once a member—and became an avowed "exaltado." An argument between Carrascosa and Calleja puts us at once *au fait* with the merits and demerits of the rival leaders of the time.[3]

We are then admitted to a closer acquaintance with "La Fontana de Oro."[4] A detailed description of the premises is

[1] Op. cit. cap. i., p. 10.
[2] Cap. i., p. 15. "He was undersized, and his head was set almost directly upon his trunk with only just enough neck to prevent him from being a complete hunchback. His abdomen was fairly bulky, and he had a trick of folding his hands upon it and stroking it, as though he were affectionately protecting it." ["Su estatura era pequeña y tenía la cabeza casi inmediatamente adherida al tronco, *sin más cuello que el necesario para no ser enteramente jorobado.* El abdomen le abultaba bastante, y generalmente cruzaba las manos sobre él *con movimiento de cariñosa conservación.*"]
[3] Cap. i., pp. 15–18.
[4] Cap. ii.

given,[1] and we listen to a speech by Alcalá Galiano.[2] After the meeting is over, we are introduced to another of the principal characters in the story, the villain of the piece, the ultra-reactionary Elías,[3] who engages in a political dispute with the barman. Chapter iii. initiates the main action of the novel. Elías is attacked while on his way home by a band of intoxicated radicals, led by Calleja, and is saved from death at their hands by a mysterious captain, whose name and antecedents are not disclosed until much later in the story. More than a page [4] is devoted to a rhetorical declamation from the captain upon the inevitable failings of democracy in its early stages. Galdós seems to be a little conscience-stricken about this rather wearisome digression, and frankly admits that he does not profess to give the captain's exact words.[5] The inappropriateness of these remarks, addressed as they are to an unfortunate individual who has narrowly escaped being thrashed to death by a gang of bullies, is almost ludicrous. Passages of this description are, unfortunately, only too frequent throughout the book. Galdós rarely misses an opportunity of mounting the rostrum in order to deliver an address upon liberty, equality, et cetera; and this tendency to sermonise is a fault which, even in his best books, he never entirely succeeds in correcting.

At the home of Elías, or "Coletilla," as he is nicknamed by the liberals, we meet Clara—a young girl whose position in the house is ambiguous, and with whom the susceptible captain immediately falls in love. As a man of the world, he is fascinated by her immaturity and innocence. He determines

---

[1] Cap. ii., pp. 20–2.   [2] Ibid., p. 24.
[3] Ibid., p. 25.   [4] Cap. iii., pp. 33–5.
[5] Ibid., p. 34. "Es probable que el militar no empleara estos mismos términos; pero es seguro que las ideas eran las mismas."

to pursue the matter further—after a vain attempt to elicit information from the girl as to her relations with Elías. We are then given a detailed account of the life and personality of Elías [1]; and this method of "polishing off," his characters in isolated chapters is characteristic of Galdós' methods as a novelist. While it has undeniable advantages, it is upon the whole a clumsy procedure, especially when the information as to the *status quo* of the most important characters is introduced into the story long after we have made their acquaintance.

Several chapters elapse before we are given the history of the mysterious Clara,[2] who turns out to be the daughter of a Segovian colonel killed at Sagahún while leading a revolt against Napoleon in December 1808. She has been adopted by Elías, who sends her to a convent school. The account of her education there, under the terrible Madre Angustias, gives Galdós an opportunity to attack ecclesiastical methods of instruction, which included, by way of punishment, the imprisonment of young girls in a damp and insanitary cell infested by rats.[3] Elías eventually removes her from this unsatisfactory establishment. Chapter vi. introduces us to the hero of the novel—Lázaro, son of Elías' sister Marta, with whom Clara is now living at Ateca. This fact gives rise to the "love interest" of the story, for Lázaro quickly falls a victim to Clara's charms. He is a would-be Demosthenes whose chief ambition is to establish himself in the capital, where, he imagines, his talents as an orator will meet with the appreciation they deserve. He is deeply affected upon the removal of his immediate interest, Clara, to Madrid—where she is to keep house for her adoptive father, and he soon finds a

[1] Cap. iv., pp. 44-9.   [2] Cap. v., pp. 50-8.   [3] Cap. v., p. 56.

pretext for a journey to the capital, armed with a letter to his uncle, Elías.[1] Meanwhile, we return to the adventures of Clara,[2] whose feminine love of personal adornment is sternly repressed by her adoptive father—for whom she conceives an intense dislike. Shortly after her arrival in Madrid the meeting with the captain—recorded in an earlier chapter [3]—takes place, and we are given to understand by Pascuala, the servant, that the stranger is desirous of renewing an acquaintance which has obviously given him considerable pleasure. Elías, however, treats Clara as a prisoner and issues strict injunctions that no one is to be admitted to the house without his knowledge and consent.

We then hear of Lázaro's arrival in Madrid and of his meeting with an old friend, Javier, whom he had known in Ateca. The two youths go together to the "Fontana de Oro" (Lázaro is unaware of his uncle's reactionary opinions) and the unfortunate youth receives a severe rebuff when he attempts to impress the sophisticated "madrileños" with his oratory—which eventually proves to be his downfall, for he is soon arrested and imprisoned as the result of his activities at a revolutionary demonstration. In the meantime Clara is anxiously awaiting Lázaro's arrival.[4] In place of her lover, however, the captain appears upon the scene. He has effected his entry in the traditional way of the "cloak and sword" comedy, by suborning the servant. Elías surprises the captain with Clara, venting his wrath upon the latter, whom he persists in regarding as a wanton. He announces his intention of confiding her to the care of "tres señoras devotas"—the "señoritas de Porreño." Elías had rendered some service to

[1] Cap. vii., pp. 65-9.   [2] Cap. viii., pp. 69-76.
[3] Cap. iii.   [4] Cap. xiii.

the impoverished house of Porreño, and these three old maids
have often expressed a desire to install Clara in their household. María de la Paz Jesús, Salomé, and Paulita Porreños are
types such as Galdós delights to ridicule, and the three
"beatas" are an early indication of what was to be his
favourite theme—the evil results of a perverted religiosity.
We are soon formally introduced to "the three wrecks," as he
contemptuously styles them. Of the three, Doña Paulita—
who is destined to play an important part in the story—is,
psychologically, the most interesting. She is an "abnormal"
type such as Galdós frequently depicts, especially in his later
works, and such as would delight the followers of Freud or
Jung—a neurotic spinster whose suppressed sexuality is
concealed by a thin disguise of piety. The scene in which
Clara meets these three harpies for the first time is remarkable for a skill in dialogue and character-drawing worthy
of the author's later and more mature works. In it Galdós
aims at contrasting the natural and innocent instincts of
Clara with regard to love and marriage with the perverted
religiosity of the three old maids, who see in love nothing but
the foulness of uncontrolled bestiality. Especially remarkable
are the passages in which Clara replies to the inquisitorial
catechism of her guardians.[1] Her passionate "I want to live"
is reflected in the lives of many Galdosian heroines.

Meanwhile Lázaro is visited, in his prison cell, by his uncle,
who delivers a tirade against liberalism, to which Lázaro
makes a spirited reply.[2] Subsequently, Elías and the ex-priest
Carrascosa pay a visit to "the three wrecks."[3] Carrascosa (who
is in league with the captain) wishes to obtain the consent of
the old women to Clara's taking part in a religious procession.

[1] Cap. xvi., p. 133.   [2] Caps. xvii. and xviii.   [3] Cap. xix.

They are horrified by his ill-disguised worldliness, for he confesses that, in his choice of virgins for the ceremony, he is guided by physical as well as by moral comeliness! This incident gives rise to an amusing misunderstanding which allows full play to Galdós' powers as a humorist. The old women imagine at first that he is asking one of them to take part in the procession. They of course indignantly refuse their permission for Clara to attend the ceremony. We are then initiated into the secret of the mysterious captain's antecedents.[1] His name is Claudio Bozmediano y Coello, and, indeed, as the author somewhat naïvely remarks, "It was already time to tell you his name."[2] We are given details of his plot to arrange further meetings with Clara, with whom he is now quite genuinely in love, and we hear of his efforts to obtain Lázaro's release from prison; for he hopes, by effecting this release, to ingratiate himself with Clara. Then we find ourselves once again present at a meeting of "La Fontana de Oro."[3] References are made to the "agents provocateurs" and their inflammatory speeches. Lázaro, by reason of his connection with Coletilla, is—together with other Aragonese members—suspected, and this leads to a "split" in the club. Meanwhile changes are materialising for the Porreños household,[4] and Elías informs the three sisters that he wishes Lázaro to live with them. Upon his arrival Paulita is strongly attracted to Lázaro, and her cry of rebellion—"I must live!"—is misunderstood by Clara. Paulita finds it increasingly difficult to conceal her passion for Lázaro, but he has as yet no suspicion of the truth.

The "exalted" liberals now invite Lázaro to join their

[1] Cap. xx.
[2] Cap. xxii.
[3] Cap. xx., p. 155.
[4] Caps. xxiii. and xxiv.

party,[1] and Elías, seeing in their activities a possible weapon for the cause of reaction, encourages his nephew in the latter's advanced views.[2] Returning to the Porreños household, we there learn that arrangements have been made to view the procession from a neighbour's window. Lázaro joins the party and, while they are watching the procession, Salomé's reticule falls into the street.[3] Lázaro goes in search of it, finds it, and, instead of rejoining the party immediately, rushes back to see Clara. Bozmediano, however, has already taken the opportunity, afforded by the absence of the "three wrecks," of finding Clara alone.[4] She rejects his advances and declares her love for Lázaro. At this juncture Lázaro himself bursts in, and Clara endeavours to explain the situation. He is, however, unsatisfied and determines to seek out Bozmediano, who has contrived to effect his escape from an awkward interview. Meanwhile the three harpies have decided to turn Clara out into the street on account of what they regard as her intrigue with the captain. Lázaro is informed of the expulsion, and reasserts his determination to unearth Bozmediano, who, when he is eventually discovered, explains his "honourable intentions" and joins Lázaro in his search for the now homeless Clara. We then follow the fortunes of the heroine, who, after wandering aimlessly about the streets of Madrid, finally decides to seek refuge with Elías' old servant, Pascuala—now married and living in the Calle del Humilladero—in whose house Bozmediano and Lázaro finally discover her.[5] We are then acquainted with the dire results of the activities of the "agents provocateurs."[6] Lázaro makes a speech in favour of moderation, but his efforts are

[1] Cap. xxvi.   [2] Cap. xxvii.   [3] Cap. xxviii.
[4] Cap. xxix.   [5] Cap. xxxix.   [6] Cap. xl.

futile. There is a riot, and the mob is fired upon by the soldiers. Fernando VII., however, (of whom we are given a vivid portrait in chapter xli.), is not pleased with Elías' work, and Galdós brings out the mean cowardice and treachery of the king in the graphic scene where the wretched " Coletilla " is dismissed with contumely.[1]

We then return to the Porreños ménage and to Paulita, who tries to persuade Lázaro to elope with her. Upon his horrified refusal, she indulges in a rhetorical tirade in defence of "the weakness of human nature," and the story winds up with Lázaro's departure from Madrid with Clara. He decides to renounce his political career. Paulita retires to the inevitable convent, where she quickly comes to be regarded as a saint, for, as Galdós ironically remarks, "eight theologians proved it by means of eighty syllogisms." [2]

The conclusion of the novel is unsatisfactory: one feels that Galdós has grown rather tired of the story, and that he wishes to finish it off as quickly as possible. *La Fontana de Oro* has, indeed, many grave defects—of which, it is clear, Galdós himself was not unconscious. The characters tend to become mere mouthpieces through which the author voices his own opinions; and there are, throughout the book, clear indications of party bias. In *La Fontana de Oro* and *El Audaz* Galdós is at the parting of the ways. The journalist and the politician are at war in these pages with the creative artist. The latter must have hesitated to make of Elías so inhuman a villain, and it is demanding too much of our credulity when we are asked to suppose that any loyalist, however perfervid, would have tolerated such base ingratitude as that exhibited here by Fernando VII. Galdós believed that much of the extreme

---

[1] Cap. xli., p. 313.   [2] Cap. xliii., p. 331.

radical propaganda, not only in 1823 but also in his own day, was due to the activity of "agents provocateurs"; and he thought that *La Fontana de Oro* would do much to popularise this view among the liberals of 1868. That the "agent provocateur" was a common figure at the meetings of the political clubs cannot be doubted; but one feels that in his enthusiasm for the cause of democracy Galdós is a little too willing to seize upon any plausible justification of revolutionary excesses. The result of this somewhat too evident bias is that the historical part of the book fails to ring true. Vague, sentimental humanitarianism of the Rousseauesque type has ceased to convince; and yet much of what appears nowadays to be empty rhetoric would, at the time of the publication of *La Fontana de Oro*, create a very different impression. *La Fontana* is, in consequence, the book of an age, and to foreign readers unacquainted with the intricate details of political intrigue in nineteenth-century Spain it makes no great appeal. To the serious student of Galdós, however, both it and *El Audaz* are deserving of careful study, for in them we can discern the germ of greater things. In his portrayal of the neurotic spinster, Paulita, Galdós reveals a keen psychological insight which penetrates beneath the surface of the conscious mind down into the realm of the subconscious motives of human action. The terrible disillusion which arises out of a sudden realisation of prolonged self-deception is admirably brought home to the reader. The scenes in which the spinster attempts to seduce Lázaro are, however, rendered unconvincing by the latter's almost fatuous simplicity. Perhaps we are not intended to take this simplicity *au pied de la lettre*—but in view of other taxes which the author makes upon one's credulity one inclines to think that it is meant seriously. Nearly all that concerns the "three wrecks" is, however, excellent. Galdós is always at his best in dealing with feminine human nature which has been in some way warped—usually, in his novels, either by an excess of piety or by an inordinate passion for luxury. Upon these two themes he rings the changes throughout his later works; and if Clara is but a feeble anticipation of the typical Galdosian heroine immortalised in Rosario and Gloria, in "the three wrecks" we find the germ of a Doña Perfecta.

As a prolegomenon to the later works *La Fontana de Oro* is, in many respects, significant. We find here the vivid and detailed descriptions of Madrid and the life of its common people—descriptions based upon intimate personal knowledge and observation—together with many examples of the author's wonderful facility in portraiture. We find also the chief faults which mar his best work—only here the defects are more glaring. The book is badly constructed. It is far too long, and too much time is allowed to elapse before one is introduced to the main characters of the story.[1] It abounds in the long, wearisome digressions and improbable situations of the Spanish romantic tradition, and reads in some parts more like a political pamphlet than a novel.

Upon it *El Audaz*, also a novel of tendency, as its sub-title, *Historia de un Radical de Antaño* indicates, marks a distinct advance. By way of introduction to this book Galdós quotes an extract from a letter written by Eugenio de Ochoa to the editor of *La Ilustración de Madrid*.[2] In this letter Ochoa brings out very clearly the purpose of the novel, which, like *La Fontana de Oro*, presents the events of one period as a criticism of those of another. With the same *arrière pensée*

[1] The chapter devoted to Bozmediano is a striking example of this fault (cap. xx.).
[2] The letter appeared in No. 42 of this publication.

which prompted *La Fontana*, Galdós gives us in *El Audaz* a vivid picture of the condition of Spain at the close of the eighteenth and the opening of the nineteenth century, a picture (in the words of Ochoa) of "that society which said the rosary every night and trailed about the anterooms of the Príncipe de la Paz every morning; that society which filled the towns with monasteries and the roads with highwaymen; which embraced all the vices and scandals of our own age together with others against which, in our day, the very stones would rise." [1]

We are introduced in the first chapter of the book to the protagonist, Martín Martínez Muriel, who is engaged upon an argument with a certain Padre Jerónimo Matamala. Galdós has evidently learned something about the construction of a novel since he wrote *La Fontana*, for he remarks with reference to Martín that "it is fitting that he should be introduced before we report in detail . . . the animated dialogue which took place between these two persons in the garden of the monastery." [2] Martín has come to Madrid in order to seek restitution for a wrong done to his family by the noble house of Cerezuelo, which allowed his father to die in prison, the victim of a false accusation. Martín also believes that the Count of Cerezuelo owes his father a large sum of money, and this sum he hopes to regain by way of compensation for the injustice which his father has suffered. El Padre Jerónimo de Matamala, to whom Martín bears a letter of introduction and with whom he

[1] "Aquella sociedad que rezaba el rosario todas las noches y se arrastraba por las mañanas en las antesalas del Príncipe de la Paz; que tenía los pueblos llenos de conventos y los caminos infestados de salteadores, que abrigaba todos los vicios y todos los escándalos de la nuestra, con otros más, ante los cuales se sublevarían hoy hasta las piedras" (vide Introduction to *El Audaz* (1907 ed.), p. 5).

[2] "Conviene darle a conocer antes que refiramos textualmente . . . el acalorado diálogo que ambos personajes sostuvieron en la huerta del convento" (op. cit. cap. i., p. 8).

discusses, in the first chapter, the political condition of Spain, recommends the youth to his friend Buenaventura Rotondo. Martín, an ardent liberal, discovers in the latter a kindred spirit—but receives little encouragement from him as to the possibility of obtaining redress from the Cerezuelos. Don Buenaventura Rotondo is admirably drawn,[1] and *El Audaz*, like *La Fontana de Oro*, abounds in vivid character-sketches. We are also introduced to Martín's friend Leonardo, a penniless "second son" who shares Martín's radical views.[2] He has fallen in love with a fascinating widow, Doña Engracia, who lives with her shrewish mother, Doña Bernarda. Don Lino Paniagua, a chaste ecclesiastical "go-between," is endeavouring to arrange a meeting between Leonardo and the widow.

The "chorus" of the tale is a demented dotard, José de la Zarza, who imagines himself to be living in France at the time of the Revolution, and we hear through him of a plot which is on foot to overthrow Godoy.[3] A brilliant description of a picnic-party [4] gives Galdós an opportunity to satirise various social types of the period—Don Narciso Pluma, "one of the best-mannered youths of his age," [5] Pepita Sanahuja, "a poetess . . . who was crazy about pastoral literature," [6] and Antonia de Gibraleón, the political blue-stocking, who models herself upon the deceased Princesse des Ursins.[7] This chapter is one of the best things in *El Audaz*, and for penetrating irony it can scarcely be surpassed by anything in the later novels.[8] The party is enlivened by the appearance of Martín and Leonardo, who are introduced by Don Lino Paniagua as strangers to Madrid. Martín, with doubtful taste, delivers a fiery attack

---

[1] Vide op. cit. (1907 ed.), cap. ii., pp. 29–30.
[2] Cap. ii.   [3] Cap. iii.   [4] Cap. iv.
[5] Cap. iv., p. 59.   [6] Ibid., p. 62.   [7] Ibid., p. 64.
[8] Note especially the satire on pastoral poetry, ibid., pp. 73–7.

upon the society of the age, especially the clergy. He is introduced to Susana Cerezuelo, daughter of his enemy the count, and tells her, somewhat impolitely, of his reasons for visiting Madrid.

We are then transported to the mansion of the Count of Cerezuelo, and hear of the arrival of Martín's young brother, Pablo, who has been committed to the count's charge by the dying Muriel.[1] Pablo is made a page in the count's household, but, finding the situation little to his taste, soon runs away, and Martín, upon a visit to Alcalá, hears of his brother's escape.[2] Meanwhile, Doña Bernarda discovers the intrigue between her daughter Engracia and Leonardo,[3] who, in Martín's absence, has been summoned to appear before the tribunal of the Inquisition.[4] His home has been searched and his books have been confiscated. Lino Paniagua advises Martín to seek the aid of Susana Cerezuelo on behalf of Leonardo, and after a fierce moral struggle he submits to this humiliation, Susana eventually agreeing to intervene.

Then, in a long digression, we hear a discussion between various highly-placed Government officials upon the political and social condition of Spain, and are introduced to Don Tomás de Albarado y Gibraleón, the Grand Inquisitor.[5] After this interlude we begin to perceive the conflict of wills upon which the psychological interest of the novel hangs. Susana loves Martín, but wishes him to forsake his radicalism and elevate himself to her rank in society, while he wishes her to throw in her lot with him and become a "filia plebis." In this chapter, also, we are introduced to the brutal demagogue Sotillo, in the portrayal of whom Galdós attacks extreme

[1] Cap. v.   [2] Cap. vi.   [3] Cap. vii.
[4] Cap. viii.   [5] Cap. x

radical views.[1] We then learn how Don Felix, Marquis of Fregenal, who loves Susana, reveals Martín's visit to Tomás de Albarado, and are treated to another long digression— one of those vivid pictures of low life in Madrid for which the novels of Galdós are especially famous.[2] In *El Audaz* we have an early indication of his ability to delineate social types as widely apart as the "maja," "La Pintosilla," and the "précieuse" Pepita Sanahuja. Galdós is at home with all classes of society, but, as we shall have occasion to remark later, he excels especially in his portrayal of the Madrid bourgeoisie, which, however, does not figure to any great extent in this novel.

We then hear of the kidnapping of Susana by the radicals [3] so that she may be held as a hostage until the release of Leonardo is secured. She is confined in the same room with the lunatic José de la Zarza, who imagines her to be the Princesse de Lamballe. Meanwhile, El Padre Jerónimo Matamala reproaches Martín for his indiscretion in speaking openly against the Church,[4] and we hear of Susana's treatment at the hands of the revolutionaries.[5] Martín visits her and attempts to justify the violent measures adopted to secure Leonardo's release and further the radical cause: "In the heart of all great crimes there lies a mysterious and inexorable logic which connects them with other crimes perhaps greater and more unpardonable,"[6] he says, in reply to her bitter

---

[1] Vide cap. xi., p. 153: ". . . his doctrine . . . consisted in setting fire to every city and sending to the gallows all the nobles, friars, and royal personages in the Peninsula." [". . . su doctrina . . . consistía en pegar fuego a todas las ciudades y llevar al cadalso a cuantos nobles, frailes y gente real se hallaran en la Península."]

[2] Caps. xiii. and xiv.   [3] Cap. xv.   [4] Cap. xvi.   [5] Caps. xvi.–xxii.

[6] "En el fondo de todos los grandes delitos existe una lógica misteriosa y tremenda que los enlaza a otros crímenes, quizá mayores y más imperdonables." Cap. xxi., p 245.

E

reproach. In much the same way, no doubt, would Galdós justify, to some extent, the revolutionary excesses which he, in his soul, abhorred.

Then follows a peaceful interlude which takes us to the house of the Sanahuja family at Aranjuez.[1] Pepita, who has been affected by her reading of pastoral poetry in much the same way as was Don Quixote by the romances of chivalry, is looking for a "shepherd" to accompany her upon sentimental excursions. She finds the desired "pastor" in Pablo Manuel, who since his escape from the Cerezuelo mansion has been leading the life of a vagabond. Meanwhile, the final development of the radical plot is revealed.[2] Martín, in an impassioned speech, denounces the Bourbon dynasty and declares that the first act of the revolutionary Junta of Toledo must be the issue of a declaration to the effect that "the house of Bourbon has ceased to reign in Spain."[3] We then hear how the Conde de Cerezuelo, driven almost insane by grief on account of Susana's association with Martín, comes to Madrid, where he dies, melodramatically, in the act of cursing his daughter.[4] Susana is torn between her love for Martín, whom she has at last promised to marry, and her duty to her family, who have arranged for her betrothal to one Don Lorenzo de Segarra.[5] She decides in favour of Martín and goes to join him at Toledo, where the Junta is holding its first meeting.[6] The rebels are, however, betrayed by one of their followers, Deza, whom Martín condemns to death in consequence of his treachery;[7] but the revolt is eventually crushed,[8] Martín is taken prisoner, and Susana commits suicide. Martín and

[1] Cap. xxiii.   [2] Cap. xxiv.   [3] Cap. xxiv., p. 267.
[4] Cap. xxv.   [5] Cap. xxvi.   [6] Cap. xxvii.
[7] Cap. xxviii.   [8] Caps. xxix.–xxx.

Rotondo are confined in the same cell with José de la Zarza, both eventually losing their reason.[1]

The struggle, begun in *La Fontana de Oro*, between Galdós the politician and Galdós the creative artist, is continued in *El Audaz*, which, however, as a work of fiction, is superior to its predecessor. Martín and Susana are real people, and one feels that Galdós is just as much interested in their psychology as he is in their politics. The minor characters, also, are excellently drawn, and the book abounds in types such as Galdós delighted to paint. If his aristocrats, like those of Balzac, smack at times of the novelette, and if the death-bed scene in chapter xxv., where the count curses Susana, is quite in the tradition of the serial story, the sketches of low life in Madrid are drawn in masterly fashion. With all its merits, however, *El Audaz* cannot rank as a great European novel; for Galdós still gives first place to what is ephemeral in human society and fails to concentrate upon those elements of permanent human interest which, in all great novels, must predominate over the merely local and transitory.

These two early novels, however, evince the boldness and originality of Galdós' genius, defining, as they do, his attitude towards the social problems of his day. Hereditary influences, on his mother's side,[2] inclined him towards conservatism—a temperamental inclination which his friendship with Pereda doubtless did something to strengthen—and the sentiment of the first series of the *Episodios Nacionales* is, as we shall see, traditionalist rather than radical in the religious sense. He

[1] Cap. xxxi.
[2] His mother's family came from Azpeitia, the land of traditionalism; and his maternal grandfather, Don Domingo Galdós y Alcorta, was, in the last years of the eighteenth century, sent to Las Palmas as secretary to the Inquisition.

came, however, to represent, more definitely than did any
other Spanish novelist of his age, the spirit of revolt against
tradition and convention. It is in the *Novelas Españolas
Contemporáneas*, the works which give him the best title
to European fame, that his "modernism" most strikingly
appears. Before dealing with these master-pieces of Spanish
realism, it will, however, be necessary to trace very briefly
the evolution of his genius in the *Episodios*, which, if they are
little read outside Spain, contributed much to enhance his
reputation in his own country.

(b) The "Episodios Nacionales"

IT would be without the scope of the present volume to make
more than a very brief reference to the *Episodios Nacionales*.[1]
They are hardly novels in the strict sense of the term,[2] and
their chief merit lies in the fact that they taught history to
many Spaniards who previously knew none.[3] Their interest,
in consequence, is local rather than European; national
rather than universal. No study of Galdós as novelist would,
however, be complete without some mention of the gigantic
monument to the energy, patience and erudition of their
author which these stories represent. Begun in 1873, they
embrace the entire career of Galdós. In them we can divine

---

[1] The writer wishes to acknowledge his indebtedness throughout this
section to "Andrenio's" excellent article on the *Episodios* in *Novelas y
Novelistas* (vide Bibliographical Note).

[2] Cf. González-Blanco, op. cit. cap. v., p. 385: "The *Episodios* . . .
are not novels. They are, as it were, historical narratives which effect a
work of popularisation rather than one of intense art." ["Los *Episodios*
. . . no son novelas. Son como narraciones históricas que realizan una
obra de vulgarización más bien que de arte intenso."]

[3] Cf. Menéndez y Pelago, *Discursos leídos ante la Real Academia
Española en las recepciones públicas del 7 y 21 de febrero de 1897.* p. 68:
"Han enseñado verdadera historia a muchos que no la sabían."

the general trend of his literary evolution, noting the changes wrought in him by the passage of time and his gradual progress to maturity. The twenty volumes of the first two series appeared at regular intervals of a year from 1873 to 1879, and in 1879 it seemed as though his work in this direction were concluded.[1] An illustrated *édition de luxe* of the *Episodios* was published,[2] while Galdós devoted his energies to the novel of contemporary life.

Nineteen years later, however, he returned to his old love, and the third series of *Episodios* appeared, to be followed immediately by a fourth. This new group was begun in 1898 and concluded in 1907—to be followed in its turn, by a "Serie Final."

The *Episodios Nacionales*, therefore, naturally fall into two great divisions which we may label, respectively, as "Episodes of the first period" and "Episodes of the second period."

The "Episodes of the first period" deal with the events of Spanish history from the battle of Trafalgar down to the death of Fernando VII. and the commencement of the Civil Wars. In the first series the War of Independence is in the foreground of the picture: in the second, the political upheaval which prepared the way for the constitutional régime. The plan, however, is not rigorously followed, for the first episode of the second series—*El Equipaje del Rey José*—takes us back to the battle of Vittoria, and in one of the volumes of the first series—*Cádiz*—greater stress is laid upon the debates in Cortes and

---

[1] Vide Foreword to *Zumalacarregui* (1898), the first volume of the third series, where Galdós tells us: "When, with *Un Faccioso más y algunos Frailes menos*, I had concluded the second series of *Episodios*, I swore that I would not for a third time put my hand to the historical novel." ["Al terminar con *Un Faccioso más y algunos Frailes menos* la segunda serie de los *Episodios Nacionales*, hice juramento de no poner la mano por tercera vez en novelas históricas," pp. 5-6.]

[2] 1885.

the political dissensions which foreshadowed the future struggles for the Constitution than upon the siege of the city. In the first series, comprising ten Episodes,[1] Galdós is, primarily, an historian, and the key to their "atmosphere" is to be found, as Alarcón Capilla remarks,[2] in the title of the first volume, *Trafalgar*. In them Galdós has given us the prose epic of modern Spain; moved as he is by the traditional spirit of patriotic fervour rather than by the modern demon of scepticism and irony. In the first two volumes of the first series he endeavours to picture the condition of Spanish society prior to the great struggle against Napoleon. Then he goes on to depict the several stages of that struggle—the heroic sieges, the popular risings,[3] and the political changes inaugurated in Cadiz. The hero of this series is an obscure veteran, Gabriel de Araceli, a native of Cadiz, who has been brought up in the lowest quarters of the town. He enters the service of a naval captain, Alonso Gutiérrez de Cisniega, and is present at the "glorious defeat" of Trafalgar. Then his adventurous temperament draws him to Madrid, where he forms an illicit union with an actress of the Teatro del Príncipe, Pepita González, and thus acquires an intimate

[1] *Trafalgar ; La Corte de Carlos IV. ; El 19 de Marzo y el 2 de Mayo ; Bailén ; Napoleón en Chamartín ; Zaragoza ; Gerona ; Cádiz ; Juan Martín, El Empecinado ; La Batalla de los Arapiles.*

[2] Antonio Alarcón Capilla: *Galdós y su obra* (Madrid, 1922), pp. 51-2.

[3] Nowhere is Galdós' profound sympathy with the masses more clearly illustrated than in his *El 19 de Marzo y el 2 de Mayo*. The tragic death of Pacorro Chinitas and his wife (pp. 258-9) in defence of Spanish independence is one of the most moving incidents in the whole of Galdós' works. Of this book Dendariena says: "I do not recollect ever having read any other description of this historical event which was so 'finished,' so masterly in its detail, its realism, its verisimilitude and its literary grandeur." ["No recuerdo haber leído ninguna otra descripción de este hecho histórico tan acabada, ni tan maestra en sus detalles, en su realismo, en su verosimilitud de sucesos y en su grandeza literaria."—*Galdós : su genio, su espiritualidad, su grandeza* (1922), p. 32.

knowledge of "La Corte de Carlos IV.," witnessing the gradual *rapprochement* between the various grades of society; the palace intrigues; the green-room scandals of the day. He becomes engaged to a poor girl, Inés, who eventually turns out to be the daughter of a countess, in the approved feuilleton style. In the love story of Gabriel and Inés we have, indeed, a typical feuilleton plot with its duels, rapes and abductions, corresponding, in the emotional sphere, to the stirring events of contemporary history. The fall of Godoy, the "Dos de Mayo," the heroism of generals, "guerrilleros," and the common people—all are brilliantly pictured. Subsidiary characters abound in the complicated action. In one of the Episodes of this series, Araceli, who has hitherto been the narrator of the story, gives place to his friend, Andrés Marijuan, who gives an account of the siege of Gerona, with a skilful mingling of comedy and tragedy in the thieves' den where the two children, Manolet and Badoret, are employed. The titanic conflict between stoic valour and the instinct of self-preservation makes this history sublime. True, the autobiographical form in which it is related has grave disadvantages. It is highly improbable that semi-educated vagabonds like Araceli or Marijuan would use the polished language in which the story is told, and the narrator must always be conveniently on the spot when anything stirring is afoot. In spite, however, of a certain atmosphere of artificiality, Galdós succeeds in gripping the reader; but it is in the history rather than in the fiction that we are interested. One quickly tires of such nonentities as Gabriel, Inés and Marijuan.

The second series [1] is dramatic rather than epic in character.

---

[1] *El Equipaje del Rey José ; Memorias de un Cortesano de 1815 ; La Segunda Casaca ; El Grande Oriente ; El 7 de Julio ; Los Apostólicos ; Un Faccioso más y algunos Frailes menos.*

The varying fortunes of revolutionaries and reactionaries are interwoven with the story of the bitter feud between Salvador Monsalud, the bastard son of Fernando Garrote, and his half-brother, Carlos; but here the historical element is subordinated to the fictional, and does not, as in the previous series, constitute the main interest of the tale. The violence of the struggle between tradition and "modernity" is individualised in the persons of Carlos and Salvador; and their hatred of one another on political grounds is intensified by the fact that both love the same woman, Jenara. This hatred between the two half-brothers is venomous and fatal; it poisons their lives, just as the deadly animosity between the two rival factions of reform and obscurantism poisoned the life of Spain. This stressing of the human element rather than the historical would have made this series far superior to the first if the character-drawing had been more convincing. The psychology, unfortunately, is poor. Monsalud is first presented as an intellectual doctrinaire who, while sympathising in a general way with liberal ideals, has no great belief in the ideas of any political party. Carlos, by contrast, is portrayed as a passionate fanatic, swayed by his emotions. Contrary to probability, it is Monsalud who risks his life for ideals in which he has no real faith, and behaves towards his vindictive enemy with heroic but incredible quixotry. Jenara, too, is unsatisfactory. After all allowance is made for the natural illogicality of her sex, her inconsistency of conduct in aiding revolutionaries to flee while professing an intransigent absolutism is quite abnormal. Her final conversion to radicalism also fails to convince.

In this series the plot is developed with greater rapidity than is the case in the first. The chief elements of the first series are, however, still present: the epic and the dramatic, the latter now predominating. The key, however, is lowered to suit the subject; for a civil war is neither so stirring nor so far-reaching in its effects as a national struggle against the foreigner. The objects for which men fought seem petty to the outsider, and the quarrels concern details rather than general principles. In the first series the story runs continuously from *Trafalgar* to *La Batalla de los Arapiles,* and is concluded in the latter. In the second the relation between the various volumes is not so close. The action of the individual volume is no longer, as in the first series, subordinated to the general theme; and the books can more easily be read as separate novels. This disintegration of the main action is continued in the Episodes of the second period [1] until, in the fourth and fifth series, the thread that connects the individual stories is almost severed.

These later *Episodios,* if inferior in technique to the earlier ones, are more interesting to the student of social history. They are more akin to the *Novelas Contemporáneas* than their predecessors, and bear witness to nineteen years of fruitful observation. The simple, direct, almost naïve language of the first series has given place to fuller, more rounded periods, rising at times to sublime heights of rhetoric. If, however, the *Episodios* of the second period share to some extent the merits of the *Novelas Contemporáneas,* they also, or especially those of the first series, exemplify the defects which mar the author's

[1] Third Series: *Zumalacarregui; Mendizábal; De Oñate a la Granja; Luchana; La Campaña del Maestrazgo; La Estafeta Romántica; Vergara; Montes de Oca; Los Ayacuchos; Bodas Reales.* Fourth Series: *Las Tormentas del 48; Narváez; Los Duendes de la Camarilla; La Revolución de Julio; O'Donnell; Aita Tettauen; Carlos VI. en la Rápita; La Vuelta al Mundo en la "Numancia"; Prim; La de los Tristes Destinos.* "Serie Final": *España sin Rey; España Trágica; Amadeo I.; La Primera República; De Cartago a Sagunto; Cánovas; Sagasta.*

later work in the novel of manners. In them we can trace the growth of that preoccupation with the abstract which gives a note of unreality to the productions of his declining years. In his desire to emphasise the spiritual significance of events he casts probability to the winds. We have seen how, in the early *Episodios*, he was in the habit of telling his story through the mouth of one of his characters, and how this method led to many unconvincing situations. In the later *Episodios* he introduces the marvellous element as "chorus." When the reader must be made to witness happenings outside the immediate field of the action one of the characters views them in an hallucination, or the "Muse of Spanish History" intervenes, or a spirit appears to supply the necessary information. This introduction of supernatural or mythological beings into modern historical fiction strikes a bizarre note; and in *La Primera República*, where Tito Liviano, who tells the story, journeys to Cartagena mounted upon a bull and attended by nymphs, the fantastic degenerates into the absurd.

The interest of the purely fictional element in the *Episodios* reached its height in the second series of the first period. In the adventures of Monsalud we were shown the history of an age as it was lived by a contemporary, and the fusion of the historical element with the fictional is complete. In the later Episodes the fictional element is rudimentary, with the exception of the first volume of the final series, *España sin Rey*, where Galdós plunges for the last time into romantic melodrama, with a story of tragic love. *España Trágica*, it is true, opens with a love intrigue—but we hear nothing more of it after the first few pages; *De Cartago a Sagunto* is almost devoid of plot, while *Cánovas* and *Sagasta* are studies in moral biography, glossed by the ubiquitous "Muse of Spanish

History," Mari-Clio. The judgment passed by González-Blanco upon the *Episodios* as a whole—"no son novelas"[1]—applies with especial force to these later works. In whatever *genre* they may eventually come to be classed, they are certainly not prose fiction in the ordinary sense of the word. Whether or no they are still living literature is open to question: but their popularity in Spain is undeniable, and it says much for Galdós' good sense and moderation that, dealing as they do with highly controversial matters, they have been of all his works the least subject to attack. It was in the *Episodios* that the Spanish "man in the street" gained sufficient knowledge of his country's history to enable him to take an intelligent interest in politics, and their reasoned, critical attitude was a valuable antidote to the verbal poison of the mob-orator. It is, indeed, difficult to overestimate the importance of their work in creating a sound, democratic public opinion in Spain. But they did more than create political opinion: they created what from our point of view is far more significant—an intelligent reading public. In the words of González-Blanco: "the merit of Galdós' work consists in this—that he drove into oblivion, and greatly improved upon, the historical, or rather pseudo-historical, novels of the romantic period."[2] They gave the modern "novel of chivalry," almost as fantastic in its extravagance as the ancient, its death-blow. They taught the average Spaniard of the last century his country's history, and to understand its spiritual significance; to know Spain and to know himself. History to Galdós was the "novel" of the human race

---

[1] Vide op. cit. cap. v., p. 384.
[2] " El mérito de la labor de Galdós consiste en esto: en que hizo olvidar y aventajó con creces a las novelas históricas, o mejor dicho pseudo-históricas, del período romántico " (vide op. cit. cap. v., p. 446).

—a thing inseparable from human passion, human laughter and human tears. In his own words: "The intimate entanglements and encounters between individuals, encounters which they never expected would be judged by posterity, are a branch of the selfsame tree which supplies the raw material of history wherewith we build up the structure of the external life of peoples—their princes, social changes, statutes, wars and peaces. With both materials, united as best we can, we erect the lofty scaffolding from which we see in clear perspective the soul, body and temper of a nation."[1] And again, at the conclusion of the illustrated edition of the *Episodios*: "That which is usually called history, to wit, the bulky volumes in which we read of the marriages of kings and princes, of treaties and alliances, of campaigns on sea and land, all the rest which makes up the life of peoples being forgotten, is not an adequate foundation for those relationships which are either nothing at all or else life itself, the feelings and very breath of a people."[2] That is the history of the *Episodios Nacionales*—the history of the soul of Spain—and no more fitting introduction to the history of the individual Spaniard as it is related in the *Novelas Contemporáneas* could be conceived. In the *Episodios* we can discern three distinct methods

---

[1] "Los íntimos enredos y lances entre personas, que no aspiraron al juicio de la posteridad, son rama del mismo árbol que da la madera histórica con que armamos el aparato de la vida externa de los pueblos, de sus príncipes, alteraciones, estatutos, guerras y paces. Con una y otra madera, acopladas lo mejor que se pueda, levantamos el alto andamiaje desde donde vemos en luminosa perspectiva el alma, cuerpo y humores de una nación;' (*España sin Rey*, p. 5).

[2] "Lo que comunmente se llama historia, es decir, los abultados libros en que se trata de casamientos de Reyes y Príncipes, de tratados y alianzas, de las campañas de mar y tierra, dejando en olvido todo lo demás que constituye la existencia de los pueblos, no basta para fundamento de estas relaciones, que o no son nada, o son el vivir, el sentir y hasta el respirar de la gente."

of approach to the author's great theme. In the early series the patriotic note predominates. Galdós burns with indignation at the treatment to which his country is subjected by the foreigner and sings the epic of Spanish bravery against the foe. Later, he concentrates upon the reaction of his characters to historical events of a purely domestic nature, the events themselves being frequently insignificant. It is now the characters which interest him, rather than the situation in which they are placed. Then, in the last phase, he loses interest not merely in the situation, but, to some extent, also in the characters, so far as their normal human qualities are concerned. He thinks only of the dominating ideals of the age as symbolised by the individuals. In the *Novelas Contemporáneas* we note a similar development. The early novels are prompted by the author's passionate desire to see his country emerge great and victorious from her misfortunes. But it is not here an external enemy which has brought her low. It is, so thinks Galdós, the "serpents in her bosom"—clericalism and political corruption. The disastrous effects of these, and other national evils, he deals with especially in *Doña Perfecta, Gloria* and *La Familia de León Roch.* Then, in the realistic masterpieces from *La Desheredada* to *La Incógnita*, he concentrates upon character-study and problems of psychology, especially abnormal psychology; and, finally, in the novels from *Realidad* to *La Razón de la Sinrazón*, he concerns himself with abstractions rather than with human beings.

IV

GALDÓS AND NATIONAL PROBLEMS. THE "UNHOLY TRINITY":
"DOÑA PERFECTA," "GLORIA," "LA FAMILIA DE LEÓN ROCH"

(a) *The Religious Problem. "Doña Perfecta"*

It is difficult for the modern reader to understand the storm
of indignation which was raised in the conservative camp by
the publication of *Doña Perfecta*—the first of the *Novelas de
la Primera Época*. Just as a modern audience now regards
Ibsen as verging upon the *gaga*, so Galdós appears to modern
readers as conventional, timid, even, at times, reactionary,
in his attitude towards the social problems of his day. That
a Catholic should be violently anti-clerical was, in the Spain
of 1870, scarcely conceivable; but in our own day the phenomenon is by no means uncommon. In order to understand the
mentality of Galdós it is essential to avoid being led astray by
literary critics such as El P. Blanco García (who almost writes
him down blasphemer!) and to remember that the author
of the *Novelas Contemporáneas* never openly renounced the
Catholic faith; while in nearly all his works the Christian ethic
is held up as the only possible solution of the problems of mankind. That in undermining, as he undoubtedly did, the
position of clericalism, he prepared the way for the Nietz-
scheanism of Pío Baroja and his school is possible; but there is
nothing but praise for Christianity in Galdós' work. In religious
sentiment he is, as González-Blanco admits, far more Spanish

than is generally believed [1]; and that his religious sympathies could accompany a faith in progress on democratic lines will easily be understood by liberal Englishmen of the Anglo-Catholic persuasion. Menéndez y Pelayo, who in his youth attacked Galdós on religious grounds, has admitted the fundamental idealism of the man,[2] and that idealism must be apparent to all unbiased minds. When *Doña Perfecta* appeared, Spain was agog with what were then revolutionary conceptions in philosophy and morals, and the spiritual unrest which accompanied the political upheaval of 1868 was, as we have seen, reflected in the literature of the time. A wave of incredulity had swept over Spain from across the Pyrenees, and many Spaniards of hitherto unimpeachable orthodoxy began to question their faith, especially in its dogmatic aspects.[3] In this, as in most things, Galdós was a man of his age; and he naturally conceived the idea of presenting the religious problem, as he saw it, in the form of a novel. In the early stages of his development that problem was inseparable in his mind from political questions, and through-

---

[1] Vide op. cit. cap. v., p. 428: "Even in his religion Galdós is more Spanish than is commonly believed. His attitude is that of Spanish liberalism, which proclaims the rights of the civil power and stands firm before Rome, without prejudice to the recognition of the supreme infallibility of the Pontiff, and fully recognises that the Catholic Church is our mistress and teacher throughout life, and that she watches with especial vigilance over her beloved children the Spaniards." ["Hasta religiosamente, Galdós es más español de lo que se cree comunmente. Su actitud es la del liberalismo español que reclama las prerogativas del poder civil y se mantiene fiero ante Roma, sin perjuicio de acatar la suprema infalibilidad del Pontífice, y reconocer que la Iglesia Católica es la maestra y doctora de nuestra vida, y que vela con especial protección por sus amados hijos los españoles."]
[2] "Galdós has been infected with the malady of his age; but his has never been either a sceptical or a frivolous spirit." ["Galdós ha padecido el contagio de los tiempos; pero no ha sido nunca un espíritu escéptico ni un espíritu frívolo."]—Op. cit., p. 75.
[3] Cf. Menéndez y Pelayo, op. cit., pp. 69-70.

out *Doña Perfecta* one feels that it is the claim of the Church to interfere in civil life which he is attacking rather than the fundamentals of Catholic doctrine. There is no suggestion in these early "anti-clerical" works of any attempt on the part of Galdós to formulate a faith of his own, in the manner of some of our contemporary English novelists. Such an attempt he made, at least some critics would have it so, in his later works; but in nearly all his "tendencious" novels it is with conduct rather than belief that he is concerned. In *Doña Perfecta*, which depicts the conflict of narrow dogmatism with religious "enlightenment," he does not condemn the hero's aunt for her beliefs but for her actions. The thesis which the book presents, interesting as it is, does not, however, constitute its principal claim to our consideration. It must stand or fall as a novel of European significance by reason of its literary qualities; and these, although its widespread popularity and the frequency with which it has been translated make the task seem almost superfluous, we shall endeavour to show are of the first order.

The chief objection to the majority of "novels with a purpose" arises out of the fact that the author allows the didactic element to oust the main business of story-telling. This fault we have remarked in *La Fontana de Oro* and *El Audaz*, and it appears frequently in Galdós' works. Not so, however, in *Doña Perfecta*. Here the author has succeeded in effecting an admirable fusion of the three literary forms whose evolution we have briefly traced—the novel of customs, the "thesis novel," and the novel of character. He has produced a work which is of lasting interest not merely to the sociologist and the historian but also to the lover of great literature. As a novel of customs it marks an extraordinary advance upon anything which had hitherto been attempted in that *genre*, while as a novel of character it has a profoundly human appeal— dealing, as it does, with the conflict of two fundamental instincts, the religious and the maternal. It is, indeed, the first Spanish novel of the nineteenth century which can be read with enjoyment by those who have no special knowledge of or interest in "the things of Spain"; and if it is not quite a European classic it is a close approach to one. One feels after reading *Doña Perfecta* that Galdós has definitely made up his mind to become a *novelist*. The wearisome digressions which mar *La Fontana de Oro* and *El Audaz* are no longer present. The "thesis" arises naturally out of the situation and it is put forward without undue obtrusion of the author's personal opinions. A brief analysis of the novel will show how far Galdós had progressed in technique since the publication of his first two works.

In *Doña Perfecta* we are straightway plunged *in medias res*. The train which is bringing Pepe Rey upon a visit to his aunt, Doña Perfecta Polentinos, has stopped at the tiny station of Villahorrenda—the "halt" for Pepe's destination, Orbajosa. This picture of an early morning arrival at a remote Spanish railway station is admirably drawn, and the reply of the porter when he is asked if there is a waiting or refreshment room— "There is nothing here" [1]—is one that Galdós must have heard very frequently when on his travels through Spain! There is a vigour, an alert directness about the opening chapters of this book which is in striking contrast with the prosiness and theorising of the initial pages of *La Fontana* and *El Audaz*.

Pepe Rey, a young engineer of Madrid, "modern," "enlightened," scientifically educated, a type of which Galdós is

[1] Vide *Doña Perfecta* (5th ed., Madrid, 1886), cap. i., p. 6.

F

especially fond, is met at Villahorrenda by his aunt's servant, Pedro Lucas—"El tío Licurgo," as he is nicknamed. Pepe inquires after his aunt and his cousin, Rosario—with whom, as we learn from a hint dropped by Pedro Lucas, there is a possibility of Pepe's making a match. Pepe is eagerly looking forward to his meeting with Doña Perfecta and her daughter, but is somewhat depressed by the gloom and aridity of the countryside—"this country which is a paradise to the tongue and hell to the eye" [1] and his gloom is not relieved when he hears from his guide that the best tracts of land, which he, Pepe, has inherited from his mother, have been appropriated by others. A meeting with Caballuco, the savage "guerrillero" who hates all strangers, also casts an ominous shadow over his approach to Orbajosa. The picture which Galdós draws of this miserable town—"the city which grows the best garlic in Spain"—provides a fine illustration of his descriptive powers.[2] Pepe is, to put it mildly, unfavourably impressed by the view,

[1] Vide op. cit., cap. ii., p. 11.
[2] Op. cit. cap. ii., pp. 21-2: "After half an hour's journey . . . there appeared before the eyes of both travellers, rising from the hilly slope upon which it was set, an ancient hamlet from which, at its highest point, there stood out a few sombre towers and the decaying fabric of a ruined castle. A mass of irregular walls and hovels of clay, gray and dusty as the soil, formed the base of the tower, together with some fragments of tessellated ramparts in the shelter of which a thousand wretched hovels raised their miserable façades of mud, like pale and hungry faces begging an alms of the passer-by. A mean little river encircled the town, like a tin belt, irrigating, as it flowed by, two orchards, which supplied the only touch of leafy green to cheer the eye." ["Después de media hora de camino , . . apareció a los ojos de entrambos apiñado y viejo caserío asentado en una loma, y del cual se destacaban algunas negras torres y la ruinosa fábrica de un despedazado castillo en lo más alto. Un amasijo de paredes deformes, de casuchas de tierra pardas y polvorosas como el suelo, formaba la base, con algunos fragmentos de almenadas murallas, a cuyo amparo mil chozas humildes alzaban sus miserables frontispicios de adobes, semejantes a caras anémicas y hambrientas que pedían una limosna al pasajero. Pobrísimo río ceñía, como un cinturón de hojalata, el pueblo, refrescando al pasar algunas huertas, única frondosidad que alegraba la vista."]

and, somewhat injudiciously, makes no attempt to conceal his thoughts from "El tío Licurgo." The latter is obviously nettled, but holds out hopes of better things within the "city" itself. There, for a moment, the cloud is lifted, for, as they pass by the wall of his aunt's garden, Pepe catches a glimpse of Rosario, a glimpse which more than confirms his brightest hopes.

This brings us to chapter iii., which is mainly devoted to Pepe's family history. He is the son of Don Juan Rey, a celebrated Madrid lawyer, who is obsessed by that idyllic conception of country life [1] which is not uncommon among those who have never resided for long outside a large town. We hear of his friendly relations with his sister-in-law, Doña Perfecta, and of his projects with regard to Rosario and Pepe. Then follows a short eulogistic commentary upon the latter's personal character—from which one gathers that he represents the author's ideal type of manhood. As it would apply with a few alterations of detail to several of Galdós' heroes, it is perhaps worth quoting at length here: "This excellent young man was nearly thirty-four years old. He was of a sturdy and somewhat Herculean build, admirably proportioned, and so proudly did he carry himself that had he worn uniform he would have had the most soldierly bearing and appearance imaginable. His hair and beard were fair, but there was nothing of Anglo-Saxon phlegm and imperturbability in his expression. The latter was, on the contrary, so vivacious that his eyes seemed black although they were not really so. He might well have passed for a beautiful and perfect symbol, and, if he had been a statue, the sculptor would have engraved upon its pedestal the words ' intelligence ' and ' force.' If not in visible

[1] Vide op. cit., cap. iii., p. 30.

characters, these were vaguely expressed in the fire of his glance, in the powerful magnetism which was the especial feature of his personality, and in the sympathy which his bearing cordially invited. He was not much given to talking: for only unstable mentalities and those of unbalanced judgment are inclined to verbosity. The acute moral sensibility of this excellent youth caused him to exercise restraint in the use of words during the course of those arguments upon various matters in which the men of our day are constantly becoming involved. In polite conversation, however, he could use a piquant and discreet eloquence which was founded upon good sense and a just and careful appreciation of affairs. He had no patience with double-dealing or humbug, nor with those sophistries of thought which certain minds, tainted with Gongorism, find amusing; and in order to vindicate the claims of truth Pepe Rey would employ, not always mildly, the weapons of irony. This, in the opinion of a great many of his admirers, almost constituted a defect in his character, because our youth seemed a little lacking in respect when faced with a multitude of facts taken for granted by the world at large. It must be stated, even though he may lose prestige in consequence, that Pepe Rey was untouched by the easy-going tolerance of the indulgent age which has manufactured peculiar veils of language and circumstance to cover that which might appear disagreeable to ordinary eyes." [1]

[1] "Frisaba la edad de este excelente joven en los treinta y cuatro años. Era de complexión fuerte y un tanto hercúlea, con rara perfección formado, y tan arrogante, que si llevara uniforme militar, ofrecería el más guerrero aspecto y talle que puede imaginarse. Rubios el cabello y la barba, no tenía en su rostro la flemática imperturbilidad de los sajones, sino por el contrario, una viveza tal, que sus ojos parecían negros sin serlo. Su persona bien podía pasar por un hermoso y acabado símbolo, y si fuera estátua, el escultor había grabado en el pedestal estas palabras: *inteligencia, fuerza*. Si no en caracteres visibles, llevábalas

In chapter iv. we are introduced to two other important characters in the story: the pompous, narrow-minded canon,[1] and Rosario, one of the most delightful of Galdós' heroines.[2] Rosario has something of the charm and fragrance of Eugénie Grandet, and, like Eugénie, she immediately falls in love with her town-bred cousin—a worthier object of affection than was Eugénie's perfidious Charles. The cheerfulness which emanates from the personality of Rosario is, however, quickly dispelled by "el tío Licurgo," who hints mysteriously at "a small matter" of which he must speak as soon as possible to Rey. In chapter v. the first signs of discord appear. The canon seems determined to make an enemy of Pepe, who, however, bears the lash of his sarcasm with commendable restraint. We now see that the main interest of the story is destined to lie in the author's presentation of the conflict between the new order, as represented by Pepe Rey, and the old, as personified by the canon together with Doña Perfecta and her associates. There

él expresadas vagamente en la luz de su mirar, en el poderoso atractivo que era don propio de su persona, y en las simpatías a que su trato cariñosamente convidaba. No era de los más habladores: sólo los entendimientos de ideas inseguras y de movedizo criterio propenden a la verbosidad. El profundo sentido moral de aquel insigne joven le hacía muy sobrio de palabras en las disputas que constantemente traban sobre diversos asuntos los hombres del día; pero en la conversación urbana sabía mostrar una elocuencia picante y discreta, emanada siempre del buen sentido y de la apreciación mesurada y justa de las cosas del mundo. No admitía falsedades, ni mistificaciones, ni esos retruécanos del pensamiento con que se divierten algunas inteligencias impregnadas de gongorismo; para volver por los fueros de la realidad, Pepe Rey solía emplear a veces, no siempre con comedimiento, las armas de la burla. Esto casi era un defecto a los ojos de gran número de personas que le estimaban, porque nuestro joven aparecía un poco irrespetuoso en presencia de multitud de hechos comunes en el mundo y admitidos por todos. Fuerza es decirlo, aunque se amengüe en prestigio: Rey no conocía la dulce tolerancia del condescendiente siglo que ha inventado singulares velos de lenguaje y de hechos para cubrir lo que a los vulgares ojos pudiera ser desagradable." (cap. iii., pp. 31-2).

[1] p. 34.   [2] p. 35.

is no hint as yet, however, of the tragic issues which this conflict is eventually to involve. In chapter vi. we meet Doña Perfecta's brother-in-law, the bibliomaniac, Don Cayetano Polentinos,[1] who is one of the few sympathetic inhabitants of this Spanish Yonville. The canon, who, with a provincial's keen sense of inferiority, is always on the watch for indications of haughtiness on the part of Pepe, continues to make the latter the butt of his heavy sarcasm.[2] Pepe, at last thoroughly roused, determines to annoy the churlish priest. His reply is, however, excessively long, and one feels that Galdós is reverting here to his old habit of using a character as a medium for propaganda.[3] A brief but scathing retort would certainly have been more effective in crushing "El Señor Penitenciario"! The unfortunate Pepe has now reached the stage when every word and every action gives offence. He irritates Don Cayetano by expressing a contempt for the latter's one interest in life apart from books—to wit, archæological research—and again infuriates the canon by remarks derogatory to the legal profession, of which the canon's adored nephew, Jacinto, happens to be a member.

The one bright spot in a gloomy situation is Rosario, to whose charms Pepe, needless to say, has fallen a ready victim. The love scene between them is one of the best in the novels of Galdós. This, together with the description of the honeymoon in Fortunata y Jacinta,[4] provides a sufficient answer to the charges of frigidity and "cerebralismo" which have been brought against him. These charges, however, are not, as we shall see later, altogether unfounded; for, although he excels in depicting idyllic affection, he becomes rhetorical and

---

[1] Ibid, p. 46.   [2] Ibid, p. 48.
[3] Pepe's retort occupies more than two pages (vide pp. 50–3).
[4] Vide Fortunata y Jacinta, part i., cap. v.

artificial when he attempts to portray a *grande passion*. It is a serious limitation which would, in the opinion of some, disqualify his claim to rank as a great artist.

One of the most brilliant character-sketches in the book is that of the precocious scholar, Jacintito, whom we meet in chapter ix., and whose portrait, a Galdosian masterpiece, is worth reproducing here: " He was one of those precocious infants whom the indulgent Universities, causing them to think they are men because they are ' doctors,' launch prematurely into the arduous battle of the world. Jacintito had a cheerful, round face with cheeks as rosy as a girl's, and he was stocky in build, short, verging on the undersized, with no hair on his chin other than the soft down which heralds a first growth. He was scarcely more than twenty years of age, and had been brought up from childhood under the supervision of his excellent and discreet uncle; so it goes without saying that the tender little tree was not twisted in its growth. A severe moral discipline kept him firmly upon the straight and narrow path, and he had scarcely any trouble in fulfilling his scholastic duties. When he had concluded his university studies — in which he was amazingly successful, for there was no class in which he did not gain the highest marks—he began to work at his profession, bidding fair, with his power of application and his aptitude for legal studies, to perpetuate at the Bar the glowing verdure of the laurels which he had won in the class-room. Sometimes he was as naughty as a child, sometimes as grave and responsible as an adult. If, indeed, Jacintito had not had a little weakness, even a great weakness, for pretty girls, his good uncle would have believed him to be perfect." [1]

[1] "Era uno de esos chiquillos precoces a quienes la indulgente Universidad lanza antes de tiempo a las árduas luchas del mundo, haciéndoles creer que son hombres porque son doctores. Tenía Jacin-

We know at once after this that we have met Jacintito before, and in this ability to produce a perfect illusion of reality by means of a few telling phrases Galdós is not unworthy to rank with Balzac. His "portraits" are almost invariably excellent, and we remember the individuals long after we have forgotten the events in which they took part.

No one, we feel, could, under any conceivable circumstances, have kept their temper in an argument with Jacintito, and we are quite prepared for Pepe's last and most tremendous outburst. In it he makes a reconciliation with Orbajosa for ever impossible by disparaging the cathedral, and reaches the climax of his own discomfiture when he hears that the Infant Christ's embroidered pantaloons, which so excited his ridicule and contempt, were the work of his cousin Rosario! Fortunately the latter is gifted with common sense, and she admits to Pepe that she, too, thought the breeches were inappropriate!

This brilliant satire on provincial life is continued in chapter x., where we meet more local celebrities, including the dean of the cathedral and the judge, and in chapter xi., where Galdós delivers a scathing attack upon the narrow outlook

tito semblante agraciado y carilleno, con mejillas de rosa como una muchacha, y era rechoncho de cuerpo, de estatura pequeña, tirando un poco a pequeñísima, y sin más pelo de barba que el suave bozo que lo anunciaba. Su edad excedía poco de los veinte años. Habíase educado desde la niñez bajo la dirección de su excelente y discreto tío, con lo cual dicho se está que el tierno arbolito no se torció al crecer. Una moral severa le mantenía constantemente derecho, y en el cumplimiento de sus deberes escolásticos apenas tenía peso. Concluidos los estudios universitarios con aprovechamiento asombroso, pues no hubo clase en que no ganase las más eminentes notas, empezó a trabajar, prometiendo con su aplicación y buen tino para la abogacía perpetuar en el foro el lozano verdor de los laureles del aula. A veces era travieso como un niño, a veces formal como un hombre. En verdad, en verdad, que si a Jacintito no le gustaran un poco, y aun un mucho, las lindas muchachas, su buen tío le creería perfecto" (pp. 69-70).

and colossal arrogance of the small town. In chapter xii., Pepe, lonely and out of harmony with his surroundings, scrapes acquaintance at the local casino with a cheerful ne'er-do-well, Juan Tafetán.[1] Together they pay a visit to "Las Troyas"—the three orphan daughters of a Spanish colonel—who have gained a bad reputation in Orbajosa by reason of their fondness for practical joking, but whose only real fault is an inordinate love of mischief. While they are on this visit, the girls throw a stone at the canon's housekeeper—but hit the canon by mistake! Jacintito appears at the window of his study (the canon's house is opposite to that of "Las Troyas") and the situation is ripe for a scandal. To make matters worse, Pepe is subsequently ejected from the cathedral for sacrilege! Meanwhile María Remedios, the canon's housekeeper, has gone to Doña Perfecta with the story of Pepe's visit to "Las Troyas." His aunt has already shown her determination to get rid of him by using her influence in Madrid to relieve him of the official business which is the ostensible reason of his visit to Orbajosa. Her anger now develops into fanatical hate, and she confines Rosario to her room, on a pretext of illness, so that the girl shall have no opportunity of meeting her cousin. Pepe complains bitterly to Don Cayetano of this seclusion; and the latter gives it as his opinion that Rosario is suffering from a mental disorder which has in the past affected her family. Rosario, torn between her love for Pepe and her duty towards her mother, meets her cousin secretly and confirms his belief in her devotion. A sense of impending disaster now broods heavily over the story. Pepe, assured of Rosario's love, determines to marry her with or without his aunt's consent. The arrival of a regiment of soldiers at Orbajosa,

[1] Vide p. 112.

sent by the Government to check certain manifestations of local unrest, and captained by an old friend of Pepe's, Pinzón, suggests to him a means of bringing his plans to fruition. He confides in Pinzón, who agrees to help him in an attempt to elope with Rosario. Meanwhile, after a stormy scene with her nephew, Doña Perfecta also looks round for an ally. She finds one in Caballuco, the "guerrillero," and champion of Orbajosan independence, whom she urges on in his schemes for revolt against the authority of the impious capital. Pepe contrives to obtain another interview with Rosario by the traditionally Spanish device of changing cloaks with Pinzón, who has succeeded in bribing the servant, also in the traditional manner, to admit him to Rosario's room. The girl's realisation that she now hates her mother, and the consequent moral upheaval which she suffers, are finely depicted by Galdós in a chapter of great lyrical beauty.[1] Meanwhile, Doña Perfecta's hatred of her nephew and the ideas of which he seems to her to be the personification, is intensified into an almost maniacal obsession. She does not, however, lose her sense of dignity, and contemptuously rejects the suggestion of María Remedios that she should bribe Caballuco to attack Pepe and thus frighten him away from Orbajosa. The housekeeper, however, carries out her own plan of campaign, and persuades the "guerrillero" to spy upon the man whom she has come to regard as Jacintito's rival. Caballuco discovers that Pepe and Rosario are in touch with one another, and reveals the situation to Doña Perfecta, who succeeds in extracting a confession from her daughter. On the night arranged for the elopement, Caballuco is lying in wait for Pepe in the garden, and the climax of the tragedy is reached with

[1] Cap. xxiv., "La Confesión."

Perfecta's passionate cry to Caballuco, "Kill him!" when her nephew falls into his hands.[1]

On that note of wild fanaticism the book should really have ended; but unfortunately Galdós, conforming to the literary conventions of his age, winds up the story with a series of letters from Don Cayetano to a friend in Madrid. We learn from these that Pepe has been mysteriously shot and that Rosario has lost her reason; but this information is not supplied until Don Cayetano has specified in detail certain volumes which he requires for his library! This is a masterly touch, and it justifies to some extent the rather unnecessary epilogue.

That *Doña Perfecta* marks an epoch in the development of the modern Spanish novel is scarcely open to dispute. Upon the question of its rightful place in the Galdosian hierarchy critics, however, would seem to disagree. In our opinion, it is one of the finest of the *Novelas de la Primera Época*. The events, which hold our interest from the first page to the last, march logically to an inevitably tragic conclusion; and the reader is gradually and skilfully led up to the point at which he can expect almost any villainy from Doña Perfecta and her associates. It is in connection with his portrayal of Perfecta that Galdós has been subjected to the severest criticism. El P. Blanco García roundly accuses him of unscrupulous party bias. To this critic Perfecta is inhuman, "a monster, a mother who cares nothing for the happiness of her daughter,"[2] and so on. Here, surely, he is guilty of a strange misunderstanding, for however strongly Perfecta might desire Rosario to marry the man of her choice, El P. Blanco García must, as a Catholic, approve her action in placing before all things the welfare of

---

[1] Cap. xxxi., p. 277.
[2] "Un mónstruo, una madre que para nada tiene en cuenta la felicidad de su hija" (vide op. cit., part ii., p. 497).

her daughter's immortal soul. One must bear in mind that Perfecta is an intensely religious woman, religious to the point of fanaticism, before she is faced with the problem which strengthens her profound convictions. That to save, as she believes, a soul from damnation, she should, in a moment of intense passion, provoke a murder is to our mind perfectly natural. If she had killed Pepe herself our credulity would have been strained. Her instincts would have revolted against the physical act. One feels, however, that she is the type of woman who would be quite capable of ordering a holocaust in the name of religion; and who, with a woman's logic, would when in the grip of remorse, exonerate herself from all responsibility. As she utters that tragic cry, "Kill him!" she is passionately convinced that Pepe represents the principle of evil in the universe, and that principle she will combat by fair means or foul. The cry rings true, and there is no melo-dramatic quality in it, for at that moment Caballuco is to her a heaven-sent avenger.

If need be, however, the heinousness of her crime can be mitigated upon other grounds. We are told that there is insanity in her family, and at the fatal moment her reason may have been temporarily unhinged. An emotional, un-balanced woman is incapable of following a *via media*. Bearing in mind the effects of religious exaltation upon such a temperament, it is easy to comprehend the attitude of mind which would send Pepe to his death with absolute complacency. It is then, in our view, unfair to accuse Galdós of party bias in his drawing of Perfecta; although such bias undoubtedly led him astray in some of his works. Apart from its absorbing emotional appeal, *Doña Perfecta* is one of the most penetrating and witty satires upon self-satisfied provincialism that has ever been written; and as a satire alone it can claim to rank as a great European novel. In Spanish literature it marked the dawn of a new era in prose fiction.

(b) The Racial Problem. "Gloria"

THE joy with which *Doña Perfecta* had been received by the anti-traditionalist party was intensified into ecstasy upon the publication of *Gloria*.[1] There is nothing in the earlier work which should have given rise to consternation in the soul of even the most orthodox Catholic; for, as we have seen, Galdós limits himself in that novel to an attack upon perverted religiosity and ignorant fanaticism. He raises no question of fundamental principle, and confines himself strictly to the portrayal of a tragedy arising out of the wrong-headedness of an individual. Pepe Rey, who, as we have seen, personifies the "modern spirit" in the story, is still a Catholic. His scorn is directed neither against the Church as an institution nor yet against the principles for which she stands. He sneers at the crudities of the cathedral, while respecting the spirit in which it was erected. The narrow interpretation which the Orbajosans put upon Catholic doctrine excites his contempt; but nowhere does he express disbelief in the fundamental validity of these doctrines. His views are indeed very similar to those held by "broad" Churchmen of our own day, and he accepts Christian ethics unquestioningly. All this, although it is not expressly posited of him by Galdós, can easily be divined.

In *Gloria*, the conflict arises not between two interpretations of the same faith but between two mutually antagonistic religions, two distinct traditions, two widely different modes

[1] Vide El P. Blanco García, op. cit., part ii., p. 498.

of life and thought. It is one aspect of a conflict older than Christianity itself, a conflict which has been fraught with an incalculable amount of bloodshed throughout centuries, and which is still in progress to this day—the eternal struggle between East and West. The particular phase of this conflict with which *Gloria* deals—the mutual antagonism of Christianity and Judaism—was bound to stir profoundly the inhabitants of a nation which, perhaps, still regards Judaism as the supreme blasphemy. That Galdós should come forward as the apologist for heresy within the Christian fold was bad enough; but that he should exalt a Jew at the expense of Catholics was, in the view of many, unforgivable. Hence in the case of *Gloria*, even more than in that of *Doña Perfecta*, caution is necessary in accepting the views of Spanish critics, especially those of El Padre Blanco García.[1] Menéndez y Pelayo, it is true, pays a high tribute to the literary excellence of the novel which, indeed, we venture to suggest, he is inclined slightly to over-rate [2]; but, by way of compensation, he has a sly dig at the author in his *Historia de los heterodoxos españoles*.[3]

[1] "A book of impious propaganda" is his verdict (op. cit., part ii. p. 500).
[2] Vide Discurso cit., p. 76, where he says of *Gloria*: "It is, from the literary point of view, one of the best of Galdós' novels, not merely because it is written with more care and polish than others, but also on account of the weightiness of the thought, the pathos of the action, the psychological wealth of the principal characters, the slow, majestic march of the events, the skill and unexpectedness of the *dénouement*, and, especially, the lofty idealism of the whole work, which is unsullied even at moments of the liveliest emotion." ["Es literariamente una de las mejores de Galdós, no sólo porque está escrita con más pausa y aliño que otras, sino por la gravedad del pensamiento, por lo patético de la acción, por la riqueza psicológica de las principales figuras, por el desarrollo majestuoso y gradual de los sucesos, por lo hábil e inesperado del desenlace, y, principalmente, por la elevación ideal del conjunto, que no se empaña ni aun en aquellos momentos en que la emoción es más viva."]
[3] "*Gloria* has been translated into German and English, and I do not doubt that it will soon come to the notice of the Bible Societies,

Although the claim for toleration which Galdós makes in *Gloria* is far wider than that which he enunciated in *Doña Perfecta*, there is nothing in the later novel which strikes the English reader of to-day as being especially revolutionary. In order to appreciate its significance in modern Spanish literature we must, as in the case of *Doña Perfecta*, exert our imagination and cast our minds back into the period which saw its first publication. As a "novel of tendency," and it is, unlike *Doña Perfecta*, primarily a *roman à thèse*, *Gloria* is one of the most interesting in the Galdosian repertoire. The author makes his intention clear at the outset when he tells us that the scene of the events he is about to describe is laid in "Ficóbriga, a town which is not to be sought on the geographical, but rather on the moral map of Spain, where I have seen it," [1] and the novel might aptly be described as a "moral guide" to the age in which it was written. It abounds in dissertations upon love, marriage, politics, art, literature, education, religion—all the controversial topics which can be imagined. Gloria, the heroine, is a Spanish Ann Veronica born before her time; an "emancipated" young woman (emancipated, that is to say, so far as it was possible for a Spanish girl of her period to be), who insists upon "thinking for herself" and who claims "the right to work out her own salvation";

who will scatter it abroad in the form of tracts throughout our towns, together with *Andrew Dunn* (a novel of the same type as *Gloria*), *The Anatomy of the Mass and Salvation for the Sinner*." ["*Gloria* ha sido traducido al alemán y al inglés, y no dudo que antes de mucho han de tomarla por su cuenta las sociedades bíblicas y repartirla en hojitas por los pueblos, juntamente con el *Andres Dunn* (novela del género de *Gloria*), la *Anatomia de la Misa* y la *Salvación del Pecador*."]—Vol. iii., p. 812. (Quoted by El P. Blanco Garcia, op. cit. part ii., p. 499.)

[1] ". . . Ficóbriga, villa que no ha de buscarse en la Geografía, sino en el mapa moral de España, donde yo la he visto." Vide *Gloria* (1920 ed.), cap. i., p. 5.

a type, in fine, which European novelists of the first decade of the present century (inspired by Ibsen) delighted to honour. A complete study of the women in the novels of Galdós would demand a separate volume; it is sufficient here to note that Gloria represents one aspect of the author's "ideal woman." Her type appears constantly throughout the *Novelas Contemporáneas*, contrasted frequently with that other aspect of womanhood which is represented in *Doña Perfecta* by Rosario. Of these two types, the one sturdy, independent, educated, witty, and beautiful, the other retiring, modest, gentle, domesticated and, unfortunately, often ignorant, the novels of Galdós, like life, rarely present a synthesis; and this lamentable omission on the part of nature to provide in one woman both wife and companion, constitutes the theme of his greatest novel, *Fortunata y Jacinta*. Let us return, however, to *Gloria* and see how Galdós works out his second problem of passion and faith. In the early chapters we are introduced to Ficóbriga (a town similar in many respects to Orbajosa) and to the Lantigua family, of which Gloria is the one surviving child. Gloria and her father, Don Juan Crisóstomo de Lantigua, are eagerly awaiting the arrival of a distinguished visitor— Don Juan's brother, Angel Lantigua, the bishop. Then, in accordance with Galdós' usual plan, we are given in a separate chapter the "dossier" of Don Juan. He is a Catholic reactionary tinged with Erastianism, for he regards the Church as "un instrumento oficial y reglamentado." [1] We are told how he has educated Gloria in accordance with his own "enlightened" views, and in the pages devoted to an account of her training Galdós finds an opportunity to deliver a scathing attack upon the methods of contemporary education,

[1] Cap. iv., p. 25.

as a result of which Gloria left school stammering French without knowing Spanish.[1] She is, however, a girl of decidedly more than average intelligence, and she amazes her father by expressing her views upon the art, literature, morals and social organisation of Spain's "Golden Age," views unflattering to the latter and disturbing to Don Juan, who heartily disapproves of her precocity. There is an air of unreality about this episode which is doubtless due to the fact that Galdós has temporarily substituted his own individuality for that of his heroine. Her views have a maturity which it is difficult to associate with a girl of her years and upbringing. She sees in seventeenth-century Spain "a society artistic in its imagination, but feeble in its conscience" [2]; in the picaresque novel "a deplorable, immoral, irreverent, and, in fact, antireligious literature, because in it there is made an apologia for evil-living, the ingenious idleness of buffoons, and all

---

[1] Cap. v., p. 28. The passage is worth quoting in full: "After residing for some years at a college which derived its name from one of the most sacred titles of the Virgin Mary, Gloria came home completely mistress of the Catechism, Sacred History, a portion of profane history, and with many (but confused) ideas upon the subjects of geography, astronomy and physics; stammering French without knowing Spanish, and a very indifferent needlewoman. She knew by heart, to a single letter, the duties of man, and was an adept at playing the piano, being able to put her hands to any one of those horrible 'fantasias' which, a terror to the ear and a blot upon the art of music, are beloved of young pianists." ["Después de residir algunos años en un colegio, a que daba nombre una de las advocaciones más piadosas de la Vírgen María, volvió Gloria a su casa en completa posesión del Catecismo, dueña de la Historia Sagrada y de parte de la profana, con muchas aunque confusas nociones de geografía, astronomía y física, mascullando el francés sin saber el español, y con medianas conquistas en los dominios del arte de la aguja. Se sabía de memoria, sin omitir letra los deberes del hombre, y era regular maestra en tocar al piano, hallándose capaz de poner las manos en cualquiera de esas horribles *fantasías* que son encanto de las niñas tocadoras, terror de los oídos y baldón del arte musical."]

[2] "Una sociedad artista en la imaginación, pero caduca en la conciencia," (cap. vi., p. 35).

G

the nasty tricks and brutal escapades which degrade a people"; [1] and her final charge against the brilliant civilisation of the Great Age might almost be an extract from a speech by Castelar: "On the one hand I see a reality which is debased and vulgar, in which misery is endemic, upon whose ragged and empty bosom squirmed the mass of the people, begging from the king positions, from the nobles the remains of a meal, from the monks soup, and from the politicians new countries to despoil. On the other hand, I see only well-fed men dazzled by an ideal of glory and world-dominion which in the end fades away like an empty dream, leaving them with their fingers on the strings of their cross-bows ready . . . to kill birds. . . ." [2] *Gloria*, indeed, contains all the necessary material for a comprehensive radical manifesto, and it undoubtedly paved the way for the Spanish antitraditionalist propaganda of our own day.

After he has revealed the intellectual quality of his heroine, Galdós turns to the emotional side of her nature, which, we learn, is as yet unawakened. Eligible suitors are not lacking—the chief of them being Rafael del Horro, the lay brother who accompanies the bishop on his visit. Gloria's heart, however, remains unconquered. After meeting some of the more important citizens of Ficóbriga, including Don Juan Amarillo,

[1] "Una literatura deplorable, inmoral, irreverente, y, en suma, anti-religiosa, porque en ella se hace la apología de las malas costumbres, de la holgazanería ingeniosa y truhanesca, de todas las malas artes y travesuras groseras que degradan a un pueblo," (cap. vi., p. 34).

[2] "Por un lado se me presenta una realidad baja y común, compuesta de endémica miseria, en cuyo seno haraposo y vacío se agitaba la gran masa de la Nación pidiendo destinos al rey, a los nobles las sobras de sus mesas, a los frailes el bodrío, y a la política nuevas tierras que expoliar. Por otro no veo más que hombres bien alimentados, a quienes deslumbra un ideal de gloria y una dominación del mundo, que cual sombra vana se desvanece al fin, dejándoles con la mano puesta en las mechas de sus arcabuces para matar pájaros. . . ." (cap. vi., p. 39).

the mayor, and Don Silvestre Romero, the priest, we hear of Don Juan de Lantigua's projects with regard to his daughter's betrothal. Although he regards Rafael del Horro as the ideal *parti*, he tells Gloria that he has no wish to exert an undue influence upon her inclinations. His views on marriage are strictly Catholic and orthodox. It is "a sacred union for a lifetime, a sacrament instituted by God, the most delicate and difficult of the steps to be taken during the course of our existence," [1] and must not be entered upon in a spirit of frivolity. To all this Gloria listens with filial resignation, and we gather from her " Very well, Papa; I will always do as you tell me," [2] that she has not advanced as far along the road to emancipation from parental control as have her modern counterparts in real life! She has, however, for long cherished a dream, which obsesses her continually, of an "ideal lover" who will some day come into her life, and the nature of this imaginary individual she reveals to us in a somewhat rhetorical soliloquy.[3] Gloria is no mere bluestocking. Beneath her cloak of intellectualism lies the *âme sensible* of a romantic heroine *à la Nouvelle Héloïse*, and the sentimental passages in the novel are treated on conventional, romantic lines. There is indeed an artificiality about them which is in striking contrast with the idyllic simplicity of the love scenes in *Doña Perfecta*.

The "perfect knight" of Gloria's fantasy soon materialises in the person of Daniel Morton, a young man of Anglo-German extraction who is rescued from a ship-wreck by the bravery of the parish priest. It is characteristic of the author that,

---

[1] "Una piadosa unión por toda la vida, un Sacramento instituído por Dios, el paso más difícil y más delicado de la existencia" (cap. xi., p. 71).
[2] "Bien, papá: yo hapé siempre lo que usted me mande." (cap. xi. p. 75).
[3] Cap. xii., p. 81.

after the chapter which leads up to this thrilling event,[1] he should call a halt in the march of the action and devote several pages to the personality of the rescuer, for "His portrait," he remarks, "should precede an account of his exploits." [2] Galdós, indeed, never really attained a complete mastery over the technique of the novel, and his character-sketches are frequently amplified to an unnecessary degree. This is especially true of *Gloria*, a work in which we have an early indication of his tendency to treat his characters as symbols. The three ecclesiastics in the book—Don Angel, the bishop; Rafael, the lay brother; and Silvestre Romero, the parish priest—stand respectively for three types of religiosity: simple piety; cynical Erastianism; and what we nowadays describe as "muscular Christianity." Don Juan de Lantigua represents "enlightened orthodoxy"; Gloria, "broad Christianity"; and Morton is a Jew by upbringing who inclines towards the "religion of the heart," whatever that may be.

Morton, as a youth of wealth and family, soon becomes the main object of interest to the Ficóbrigans who, after watching over his physical welfare, turn their attention to the state of his soul. They at first imagine him to be a Protestant, and the bishop's resolve to convert him is related by Galdós with a touch of good-humoured irony.[3] Don Angel's naïve piety is contrasted with the worldly cynicism of Rafael del Horro, revealed in a conversation with Romero which Gloria overhears.[4] Religion, says Rafael, must at all costs be preserved, for "women find such consolation in it." This gives Gloria furiously to think. She is already half in love with Morton;

---

[1] Cap. xvii.
[2] "A su hazaña debe preceder su retrato" (cap. xviii., p. 121).
[3] Cap. xx., p. 143.
[4] Cap. xxi., pp. 153-9.

and Rafael's remarks cause her to speculate upon the reality of the "barrier" raised by their difference in faith. She does not, however, as yet suspect how fundamental that difference is. Meanwhile, Morton (like Pepe in *Doña Perfecta*) does not attempt to disguise his views upon Catholicism and the ethics of the Spanish social system. He has the bad taste to inform Don Juan that he regards Spain as "the blasphemous and sacrilegious country *par excellence*." [1] Then, having alienated her father's sympathies, he openly declares his love to Gloria! In a chapter entitled "The Rebel Angel" Gloria reflects upon the nature of true religion: "I ask myself: Is he not good? Does he not observe the laws of God? Would I love him if he did not? Is not he a privileged soul? What is the difference between us? Nothing: an empty name, an idle word invented by the wicked to conceal their hates. Ah! those who love one another have the same religion. Those who love one another cannot have different religions, and if they have, their love baptises them both in the same Jordan. Let the various sects remain for those who hate one another. Seeing the matter in its true light, I can distinguish two religions: the religion of the good and the religion of the wicked. Must I believe that Daniel is not on the side of Jesus, that Daniel's religion is not the religion of the good? It cannot be . . .!" [2]

The first stage in this conflict between dogma and passion

[1] Cap. xxiii., p. 176.
[2] "Yo pregunto: '¿No es él bueno, no practica la ley de Dios? ¿Le querría yo si así no fuera? ¿No tiene un alma privilegiada? ¿Qué le diferencia de mí? Nada: un nombre vano, una palabrota inventada por los malvados para encubrir sus rencores. ¡Ay! *Los que se aman son de una misma religión.* Los que se aman no pueden tener religión distinta, y si la tienen, su amor les bautiza en un mismo Jordán. Quédense las sectas distintas para los que se aborrecen. Mirándolo bien, veo dos religiones: la de los buenos y la de los malos. ¡Concebir yo que Daniel no está con Jesús, yo que Daniel no es de la religión de los buenos . . . eso no puede ser!" cap. xxvi., (p. 207).

reaches its climax in a chapter of great lyrical beauty [1] which describes a meeting of the lovers in a pine forest on the outskirts of Ficóbriga. Galdós does not as a rule excel in the description of nature, and his novels are not especially rich in such descriptions. When he does attempt a landscape he is apt to treat it as a mirror which reflects the dominant emotion of a character. [2] Natural beauty is rarely portrayed objectively. In the opening passages of this chapter, however, he succeeds in conveying the splendour of nature itself—apart from the beauty with which it is invested by the transitory emotions of a human observer: "To the west of Ficóbriga there is a solitary and deserted pine forest, adjoining the sea, and so exposed to all the winds that, however gentle the breeze, its branches always murmur a song. Very dense towards the centre, it grows clearer at its boundaries, where avenues are formed, and some pines, creeping apart from the main group, make off towards the beach or the mountain, as though they had quarrelled with their fellows. Through the forest there runs a rustic dyke, where stones and grass mingle, forming, so to say, one family. At the foot of the pines grow a thousand charming blue flowerlets of a rare species unknown to gardens, and they seem to glow amid the bracken like little pieces of sky snatched by a storm from the great vault of the world and scattered over the earth. Here Nature is alone, busy with her own affairs, happy in her leafy calm, and passers-by fancy that they hear the throbbing of that 'silent music' of which the poet speaks, and that in such a spot it says to them,

---

[1] Cap. xxviii.
[2] Cf. cap. xxix., p. 232. Gloria is melancholy on account of Morton's departure and "she projected her sadness upon all created things. If black light could exist, it would have been her sun." ["Proyectaba su tristeza a todo lo creado. Si pudiera existir luz negra, ella sería el sol de ella."]

'Don't disturb me.'" [1] In this passage—and in the one that follows, in which he describes Gloria as she awaits her lover [2] —Galdós shows that, in spite of his occasional lapses into rhetoric and affectation, he is a master of Castilian prose. What could express more vividly the reluctance of two lovers to say good-bye than this beautiful simile: "They were like the shore and the waves, which seem always to be tearing themselves apart, and yet always embracing?" [3] The one blemish upon an otherwise perfect chapter is the rather stilted attack upon religious intolerance which Gloria delivers before the ultimate "Adiós." [4] Her love for a heretic is regarded by her uncle as a deadly sin and when, during her confession, she

[1] "Al oeste de Ficóbriga hay un pinar solitario y abandonado, vecino a la mar, y tan expuesto a todos los vientos, que siempre, por leves que éstos sean, suenan con murmurante música las ramas. Espesísimo en el centro, se clarea en sus extremos formando anchas calles, y algunos pinos se separan del grupo corriendo hacia el arenal o hacia la montaña, cual si hubieran reñido con sus compañeros. Corre por medio una cerca de rústica arquitectura, donde piedras y hierbas se confunden, formando al parecer una sola familia. Al pie de los pinos crecen mil encantadoras florecillas azules de rara especie, que no son conocidas en los jardines, y parece que brillan entre los helechos como pedacitos de cielo que las tempestades arrancan de la gran bóveda del mundo, esparciéndolos por la tierra. La Naturaleza está allí sola, atenta a sí misma, regocijándose en su paz nemorosa, y los caminantes creen oir una vibración de aquella música callada de que habló el poeta, y que en tal sitio les dice: ¡no me turbéis!" (cap. xxviii., pp. 217–18).

[2] To the fond eyes of her lover, all the serene beauty of the still evening was concentrated in her person, and she was the blue sky, the deep sea, with its mournful music, the fresh earth, with its smiling furrows, the soft shade of the wood with its faint breezes, the light, which at intervals passed through the open spaces in the foliage as through the windows of a cathedral." ["Toda la hermosura de la tarde, templada y serena, se había concentrado en su persona, según la veían los ojos del cariñoso amante, y ella era el cielo azul, la mar profunda y llena de armonías patéticas, el suelo fresco y salpicado de sonrisas, la dulce umbría del bosque con su balsámico ambiente, la luz que a trechos entraba por los claros, semejantes a las ventanas de una catedral."] Cap. xxviii., p. 218.

[3] "Eran como la playa y la ola, que siempre parece que huyen la una de la otra, y siempre se están abrazando" (cap. xxviii., p. 229).

[4] Cap. xxviii., p. 225.

reveals her inclinations to the bishop, he refuses her absolution. This refusal provokes her to final inward revolt against the claims of the Church to exclusive revelation. "Rebel, rebel!" she exhorts herself, "you have a superior intelligence. Rise, lift up your head, clear your eyes of this dust which darkens them and look the sun of truth in the face."[1] Outwardly, however, she submits. "She did what nine out of ten Catholics do" (thus Galdós); "that is to say, she kept her heterodoxy to herself in order to avoid giving pain to old people."[2]

After a delightful chapter[3] in which we are given an account of a banquet at the house of Don Silvestre Romero, and in which we hear further views upon the "modern spirit" from Rafael del Horro, the crisis in the relations between Gloria and Morton is reached with the latter's confession that he is a Jew. The fundamental nature of the conflict is revealed, and Gloria's tolerance is stretched to breaking-point.

"Within Jesus," she cries, "I admit everything; outside Him, nothing!"[4] Each must now endeavour to convert the other to the "true" faith: but it is no longer a conflict of dogmas which holds them apart. It is the clash of two traditions; the instinctive antagonism of two civilisations; and Morton, in a spirited defence of his faith, reminds Gloria that a Jew also has his racial pride. . . . "I also have a family, parents, name, reputation—and although we have no common country, we make one of our households and of the Holy Law in which

---

[1] "¡Rebélate, rebélate! Tu inteligencia es superior. Levántate, alza la frente, limpia tus ojos de ese polvo que los cubre, y mira cara a cara el sol de la verdad." (cap. xxx., p. 246).

[2] "Hizo lo que hacen las nuevedécimas partes de los católicos, es decir, guardarse sus heterodoxías para no lastimar a los viejos" (cap. xxxi., p. 249).

[3] Cap. xxxiii.

[4] "Dentro de Jesús lo admito todo; fuera de El nada" (cap. xxxvii., p. 305).

we are born and die. Since the days of my distant ancestors, who were Cordovans driven out of Spain by an iniquitous law, down to the present time and throughout all these successive generations of honourable Israelites who form my family, not a single one has ever abjured the Law." [1] The tragic nature of this conflict is brought home to us when we learn that Don Juan de Lantigua, hearing of Gloria's love for Morton, dies from the shock.

In the opening chapters of the second part we are introduced to Buenaventura and Serafina de Lantigua, brother and sister of Don Juan, of whom brief mention was made in part i.

One feels at times that Galdós loses himself in a maze of characters and that he is not always sure, at the outset, of the part they are going to play in the story. We hear that the married life of Serafina has been "the sum of all ills without a single compensating advantage," [2] and it is probable that in his account of this wretched and incompatible union Galdós is deliberately attacking the conventional belief that the Church can make holy a marriage which brings nothing but misery to both parties concerned. There seems to be no other reason for his dwelling upon this marriage here, for Serafina has long been a widow. The thread of the narrative is taken up in a conversation between Serafina and her brother, who is accused by her of desiring a compromise with reference to Gloria's love affair—for Buenaventura has written inviting

[1] ". . . yo también tengo familia, padres, nombre, fama, y aunque sin patria común, la formamos en nuestros hogares y en la santa ley en que nacemos y morimos. Desde mis remotos abuelos, que eran de Córdoba y fueran expulsados de España por una ley inicua, hasta el presente y en todas estas sucesivas generaciones de honrados israelitas que constituyen mi familia, ni uno solo ha abjurado la ley" (cap. xxxvii., p. 307).
[2] . . . "el conjunto de todos los males sin mezcla de bien alguno" (part ii. cap. i., p. 9).

Morton to return to Ficóbriga. He still has hopes that the Jew will eventually be converted. Meanwhile, Don Juan Amarillo and his wife, Teresa, who are jealous of the prestige which the Lantigua family enjoys in Ficóbriga, are eagerly hoping that Gloria will be forced to retire to a convent. Teresa, a soured "devota," does all she can to injure Gloria's reputation, circulating a story to the effect that the image of the ass which is destined to bear an effigy of Our Lord through the streets on Palm Sunday kicked in violent protest when Gloria's offering of flowers was placed upon it. The description of the ceremonies of Palm Sunday supplies Galdós with an opportunity to dilate upon the value of ritual in the services of the Church.[1] Serafina, horrified by the story of the recalcitrant ass, endeavours to persuade Gloria to enter a convent, but the latter refuses to follow her advice. The procession, of which Galdós gives a fine description in chapter viii.,[2] is interrupted by the arrival of Morton on horseback. To ride through the streets of Ficóbriga on the day of a solemn religious procession is an act of sacrilege, and Morton is arrested and imprisoned. Eventually, however, the mayor, whose respect for wealth and position outweighs his religious scruples, obtains the Jew's release. Morton then wanders through the town in search of a lodging, but finds that no one will take him in, not even a poor family which he has in the past befriended. He then confides in Don Buenaventura, who dwells upon the gravity of the problem with which they are faced: "Here, sir, we are faced with a terrible problem, religion: religion which, in diverse forms, rules the world, nations, families. We can't dispense with it on any account. It's nearly always a consolation, a stimulating force, a power which impels; now it

---

[1] Cap. vi., pp. 60–1.   [2] p. 75.

stands in our way with an ominous solemnity, and it is, both for yourself and for us, an insurmountable obstacle—disunion, strife, a mountain which is falling upon us."[1] It is inconceivable that Gloria should embrace Judaism—"I can't become a Jew—that is too much"[2]—and yet Buenaventura admits that if *he* found himself in Morton's position with regard to a woman of the Jewish faith he would become a Jew. Morton thereupon accuses him of insincerity: "Señor de Lantigua . . . you have no religion; you are not a Catholic,"[3] and Buenaventura is somewhat abashed. He retorts by pointing out that Morton, who charges Christians with intolerance, is far more intolerant than he. Bigotry, he contends, is destined to disappear from all religions: "I believe that faith, as our parents understood it, is losing ground day by day, and that sooner or later all dogmatic forms of religion will inevitably lose their present vigour. I believe that good and charitable people can be saved, and that they will be saved, easily, whatever their religion. I believe that many things ordained by the Church, far from increasing faith, diminish it, and that in all religions, especially in our own, there are too many rules, regulations, practices. I believe that religions would last longer if they were to return to their primitive simplicity. I believe that if the ecclesiastical authorities persist in attempting to increase their influence

[1] "Aquí, señor mío, nos hallamos en presencia de un problema terrible: la religión: la religión que en diversidad de formas gobierna al mundo, a las naciones, a las familias. De ella no podemos prescindir para nada. Casi siempre es consuelo, estímulo y fuerza que impulsa; ahora se nos ha puesto enfrente con amenazadora gravedad, y es para usted y para nosotros obstáculo implacable, desunión, discordia, una montaña que se nos cae encima" (cap. xi., p. 115).
[2] ". . . eso de hacerse judío es demasiado fuerte" (cap. xi., p. 117).
[3] "Señor de Lantigua . . . usted no tiene religión: usted no es católico" (ibid., p. 118).

criticism will do away with them. I believe that a reconciliation between religion and philosophy is possible, and that
if it is not possible chaos will be the result. . . ." [1]

We have quoted at length here because the opinions
expressed by Buenaventura may be taken to represent those
of Galdós himself at this period of his religious development.
Faith, in his view, cannot be divorced from practical morality,
and with the mystical and emotional side of religious experience he appears to have little sympathy.

Morton, however, is not persuaded by these arguments. He
feels that to marry a Christian would be to trample his faith
into the mire, while to embrace Christianity himself would be
an act of cowardly treason to his forbears.

Meanwhile Teresa continues her campaign against Gloria's
reputation, and reveals to Serafina her belief that secret
meetings are taking place at night between Morton and
Gloria; for the latter has on several occasions been seen to
leave the Lantigua mansion after dark. The rumours come to
Morton's ears, and, spurred by jealousy, he determines to
solve the mystery. One night he lies in wait for Gloria, and,
in a passionate interview, asks her why she has been trying
to avoid him. Reaffirming her love, she swoons in his arms,
and, with the help of his servant, Morton carries her back

---

[1] "Yo creo que la fe religiosa, tal como la han entendido nuestros
padres, pierde terreno de día en día, y que tarde o temprano todos
los cultos positivos tendrán que perder su vigor presente. Yo creo que
los hombres buenos y caritativos pueden salvarse, y se salvarán fácil-
mente, cualquiera que sea su religión. Creo que muchas cosas estable-
cidas por la Iglesia, lejos de acrecentar la fe, la disminuyen, y que en
todas las religiones, y principalmente en la nuestra, sobran reglas,
disposiciones, prácticas. Creo que los cultos subsistirían mejor si
volvieran a la sencillez primitiva. Creo que si los poderes religiosos
se empeñan en acrecentar demasiado su influencia, la crítica acabará
con ellos. Creo que la reconciliación entre la filosofía y la fe es posible,
y que si no es posible, vendrá el caos . . ." (ibid., pp. 119–20).

to her house. There she reveals to Serafina the fact that she has had a child by her lover. Serafina, appalled by this crowning shame, tells her that she must abandon her son and enter a convent immediately. In the religious life lies her only hope of salvation.

Meanwhile, Morton, to whom Gloria has confided her secret, yields to the persuasions of Buenaventura and resolves, outwardly, at any rate, to adopt the Catholic faith. His resolution is, however, shaken by a visit of his mother, Esther Spinoza Morton, to Ficóbriga. Esther is a fanatical Jewess, and she exhorts Daniel, in the name of all that he holds most sacred, not to abjure the faith of his fathers. Morton admits that he can never sincerely accept the Christian religion, but feels that his duty to Gloria demands his conversion. Esther, however, is inexorable, and will stop at nothing to avert what she regards as an act of disgraceful treachery on the part of her son. As he is about to be received into the Church, she charges him publicly with a terrible crime for which, she alleges, he was on the point of being arrested prior to his leaving England. Morton frantically denies the accusation; but his protestations are useless. No one, with the exception of Gloria, can conceive it possible that a mother would falsely blacken the reputation of her son, and even Gloria's faith appears to be shaken, for she refuses to live with him as his wife. Esther explains to Daniel that her action was devised merely for the purpose of gaining time. She is confident that Gloria, who is about to leave Ficóbriga with her aunt, will not return. The true motive of Gloria's renunciation of Morton is revealed to him later when she surprises him in an attempt to carry off their child. "My conscience," she says, "would not allow me to deprive you of your mother. I saw her as a lioness whose cubs have been stolen." [1] And then, by her reply to Morton's protestations that his mother's fanaticism is not religious but racial, she lays bare the full significance of the author's purpose in writing this novel. "It is the same thing," she answers; and defends Esther's action in endeavouring to prevent her son's marriage with a woman of an alien faith. She would do the same, says Gloria, if her own son wished to marry a Jewess. The maternal instinct, the racial instinct, the religious instinct—against these combined of what avail is the power of human reason? This seems to be the conclusion to which Gloria leads us here, so far as this world is concerned. The book ends upon a note of despair. Gloria dies unreconciled to Daniel who, two years later, meets his end in a lunatic asylum. ". . . He wore himself out in meditation, he lost his reason, and at last he died, extinguished as the flame of a lamp." [2] And then Galdós sounds a final note of hope in a passage which affirms his belief in a life beyond the grave, in which all varieties of human belief shall be resolved in a divine synthesis of faith and love: ". . . Will he attain his ideal there where someone awaited him impatiently, perhaps bored with Paradise until he should come? We must answer categorically—'Yes'—, or regard this book as unwritten. . . ." [3]

That *Gloria*, as a work of self-revelation, is one of the most interesting of the *Novelas Contemporáneas* can scarcely be denied. In it Galdós has pronounced weightily upon funda-

[1] ". . . Mi conciencia no me permitía privarte de tu madre. Yo la ví como una leona a quien han robado sus hijos" (cap. xxxii., p. 341).

[2] "Meditando se consumió, perdió la razón, y al fin apagóse como una lámpara a la cual dan un soplo" (cap. xxxiii., p. 365).

[3] "¿Encontraría su ideal allá donde alguien le esperaba impaciente, quizás con hastío del Paraíso mientras él no llegase? . . . Es forzoso contestar categóricamente que *si* o dar por no escrito el presente libro." (ibid.).

mental problems of life and morals, hinting at, if not expressly stating, his own solution of them. That it is a good novel is more open to question. It is, in the first place, far too long. The tragedy of the conflict would have been brought home to the reader more poignantly if the story had been confined within the limits of one volume. Our interest flags at times, and we lose the thread of the narrative in a maze of digression.[1]

The numerous purple passages in the romantic vein give an air of artificiality to the book, especially to the love scenes, which are unconvincing to a modern reader. Many of the situations put an excessive tax upon our sense of probability. Why should Morton at first conceal the fact that he is a Jew? He is represented as being proud rather than ashamed of his race when he makes his origin known. The death of Gloria is insufficiently accounted for. There appears to be no adequate physical reason for the mortal illness with which she is seized during her last interview with Morton. The most preposterous incident in the book, however, is Esther Spinoza's concoction of a charge against her son. If it is inconceivable that Morton should have been detained by the mayor on such vague grounds, it is even more unlikely that, however fanatical, a woman of Esther's pride and moral integrity could ever have been guilty of such perjury. One feels that Galdós is getting himself out of a difficulty by means of the first device which enters his head. The novel, which was commenced on the spur of the moment without any definite plan, bears, in fact, all the signs of hasty and ill-considered work. It is, nevertheless, one of the most interesting of the *Novelas de la Primera Época*

[1] The story of the peasant Caifás and his unhappy marriage is, for example, allowed to encroach too far upon the main theme (vide part i. cap. xxv.).

by reason of the thesis it sustains, a thesis which, at the time the book appeared, was to Spanish readers revolutionary in the extreme.

(c) 1. *The Sex Problem*   2. *The Class Problem* "*La Familia de León Roch*"

IN *Doña Pecfecta* Galdós shows how a narrow interpretation of religious dogma brings about the separation of two lovers. *Gloria* deals with a similar situation—but the barrier here is one which is erected by the mutual hostility of two races. In *La Familia de León Roch* the conflict arises out of the incompatibility of two temperaments and the instinctive antagonism of two classes.

Indications of Galdós' interest in the sex problem are already to be found in *Gloria*—where he touches upon the unhappiness caused by two unfortunate marriages—that of Caifás and that of Serafina. *La Familia de León Roch* might in a sense be regarded as a sequel to *Gloria*, for it describes the unhappy married life of two lovers whose attitude towards religion causes a breach between them. One feels, however, that here the breach is one which could never be healed by the "conversion" of either party; and that Galdós is concerned rather with the difference between the individuals themselves than with the conflict of their beliefs. This subordination of the didactic element to the study of character, together with the fact that it is the first novel of a long series in which Galdós chooses, as a background for the study of social problems, the life of the capital in all its varied aspects, brings *La Familia de León Roch* into closer relationship with *Las Novelas Contemporáneas* than with *Las Novelas de la Primera Época*—of which group it forms part.

In *Doña Perfecta* and *Gloria* the field of the action was a restricted one, and the plot, well-defined, was worked out on conventional "romantic" lines.

In *La Familia de León Roch*, as in the majority of *Las Novelas Contemporáneas*, the plot is slender and there is comparatively little incident. León Roch, an intellectual of agnostic tendencies, marries a simple, devout Catholic, María Egipciaqua Sudre, who embodies all the traditional Spanish virtues. He was attracted to her by reason of her great beauty, and while his senses remain enslaved they are tolerably happy together. Their essential incompatibility is, however, soon revealed—for María, a mental weakling completely under the control of her confessor, insists upon León's observance of religious ceremonies. She has no sympathy with the vague humanitarianism which constitutes León's "religion," and by her attitude towards his belief (or lack of belief) she reveals a total misunderstanding of his character. The rift between them grows wider—until León finally decides to leave his wife, with whom, he begins to realise, he has never been genuinely in love. We hear, in the letter from María to León which forms the first chapter in the book, of another woman—Pepa, daughter of the Marqués de Fúcar—with whom León has once been in love. In the remote country district to which he has retired, León meets Pepa—now unhappily married to a dissolute roué by whom she has had a daughter, Monina. León pays frequent visits to Pepa's house and grows very fond of her child. Soon he realises that Pepa is "the only woman he has ever really loved." Although we are given to understand that their relationship is entirely innocent, his

H

renewed intimacy with her provokes an unpleasant scandal. María's jealousy overcomes her dignity, and she visits León in order to charge him with his alleged infidelity. After a violent scene, she is taken ill and, falling into a "decline," eventually dies. Her death, however, does not solve the problem for León, for Pepa's husband, who has deserted her and whom she supposes to be dead, turns up at the critical moment. Pepa implores León to accept her as his mistress but, in spite of all his theorising on "true marriage" and the "law of the heart," he lacks the courage of his convictions and refuses to defy the censure of the world. This, in brief, is the plot of *La Familia de León Roch*—a psychological study rather than a novel of incident. It is, however, more than a study of the conflict between two individual wills. It is also the story of the struggle between two classes—the new bourgeois aristocracy, typified by León Roch and the Fúcar family, and the ancient aristocracy of birth, typified by María's reprobate father, the Marqués de Tellería; his spendthrift wife; and the voluptuous dilettante, Federico Cimarra. This particular aspect of the novel appears to have escaped the notice of those critics who regard it as a mere sequel to *Doña Perfecta* and *Gloria*. It is, in our opinion, as a comprehensive study of the social problem in a modern, democratic society that the book is especially interesting. The "background" of the story and the sketches of social types in which it abounds are, we think, the two most important elements in it.

After the letter from María to León,[1] which serves as an introduction to the "love interest" of the story, we are given a vivid picture of life at a fashionable Spanish health-resort—"which Spaniards frequent in the summer in order that they

[1] Vide supra.

may reproduce in the country the narrow, incommodious and unhealthy life of the towns." [1] We are introduced into "this anæmic, scrofulous world, made up of invalids who look healthy, healthy people who fancy that they are ill, individuals who are rotting away before one's eyes, eaten up with vice, and timid souls who would revolt against God if he were to decree universal health . . ." [2] and its follies and frivolities are laid bare to us by the scalpel of Galdós' inimitable irony.

Among its most important inhabitants are the Marqués de Fúcar—"one of the few oases of wealth situated in the midst of the barren waste of universal poverty"; [3] Don Joaquín Onésimo, the government official who "illuminates with his rays a Pleiad of Onésimos who, in various Government posts, eat up half a Budget" [4] and the dissolute Federico Cimarra—"this essentially Spanish and Madrilian type, a nightbird, weak, feverish, an embodiment of that national fever which burns and devours its way through editorial offices where work goes on all night, and casinos in which the lights are not extinguished until sunrise. . . ." [5] Their chief diversion is idle gossip, and chapter iii. is devoted to a conversation between them upon the affairs of their friend

[1] "A que concurren los españoles durante el estío para reproducir en el campo la vida estrecha, incómoda y enfermiza de las poblaciones" (La Familia de León Roch (1920 ed.), part i., cap. ii., p. 15).
[2] "Este mundo anémico y escrofuloso, compuesto de enfermos que parecen sanos, sanos que se creen enfermos, individuos que se pudren a ojos vistos carcomidos por el vicio, y aprensivos que se sublevarían contra Díos si decretara la salud universal . . ." (op. cit., ibid., p. 16).
[3] "Uno de los pocos oasis de riqueza situado en medio del árido desierto de la general miseria" (ibid., p. 20).
[4] "Ilumina con sus rayos a una pléyada de Onésimos que en diversos puestos del Estado consumen medio presupuesto" (ibid).
[5] "Este tipo esencialmente español y matritense, nocturno, calenturiento, extenuado, personificación de esa fiebre nacional que se manifiesta devorante y abrasadora en las redacciones trasnochantes, en los casinos que sólo apagan sus luces al salir el sol . . ." (ibid., p. 21).

León Roch. We hear of his projected marriage to the Marqués de Tellería's daughter, María, and gather that León's money will be a welcome source of relief to the impoverished house of which María is a member. The match, however, will, in the opinion of Cimarra, prove unsatisfactory. "It would be vastly entertaining," he remarks, "to see a freethinker caught at high tide with a bait of Our Fathers and Hail Marys." [1]

María has, nevertheless, the advantage of good looks— unlike her mother who is now "a total wreck." Onésimo thinks that she is too good for León, who, in his view, is a self-satisfied pedant—"one of these new-fangled savants, one of these products of the University, the Ateneo and the School of Mines in whom, damme, I've precious little confidence. A lot of German science which the devil alone can understand, a lot of obscure theories and ridiculous jargon; this air of despising all Spaniards for a mob of ignoramuses; a lot of conceit, and then all these infidel notions, which annoy me more than anything else. I'm not one of these people who call themselves Catholics and at the same time accept theories contrary to Catholicism: I'm a Catholic, a *Catholic*." [2] The marquis and Cimarra take up his defence, and the marquis gives it as his opinion that León is making the cardinal mistake of his career in uniting himself to a "badly disciplined

[1] " Sería cosa muy bufa ver a un librepensador de mares altos pescado con anzuelito de Padrenuestros y Avemarías " (cap. iii., p. 24).

[2] " Un sabio de nuevo cuño, uno de estos productos de la Universidad, del Ateneo y de la Escuela de Minas, que maldito si me inspiran confianza. Mucha ciencia alemana, que el demonio que la entienda; mucha teoría obscura y palabrejas ridículas, mucho aire de despreciarnos a todos los españoles como a un atajo de ignorantes; mucho orgullo, y luego el tufillo de descreimiento, que es lo que más me carga. Yo no soy de esos que se llaman católicos y admiten teorías contrarias al catolicismo: yo soy católico, católico " (ibid., p. 25).

and decadent family which will hopelessly ruin him." [1] He reveals the details of León's bourgeois origin, and how his father, Pepe Roch, the chocolate manufacturer, wanted to purchase a marquisate. He admires León for the latter's opposition to his father's ambitious schemes.

In the following chapter we are introduced to León Roch himself, and in a conversation which he has with Onésimo and Cimarra we hear something more of the Marqués de Fúcar and his ill-gotten millions, amassed, we are given to understand, by wholesale peculation. Later, in a chapter "in which something occurs which may well be a fresh manifestation of the national character," [2] the marquis gives us, in a conversation with Cimarra, his opinion of the country which has been the source of his fortune. The chief failing of Spain is "Laziness . . . the national idiosyncracy; I should say, rather, the national genius. Laziness, I say, thy name is Spain." [3] Cimarra agrees with him, but can suggest no remedy—"A question of race, Marquis . . . one of the few undeniably true facts: the fatality of caste: Here we shall never see anything but communism crowned with the lottery . . . that is our destiny." [4] And the chapter concludes with a digression upon games of chance. Such conversational asides abound in *La Familia de León Roch*, and they are the means by which Galdós conveys to his readers the views which he himself holds upon many

[1] ". . . una familia desordenada y decadente que le devorará sin remedio" (ibid., p. 27).
[2] "Donde pasa algo que bien pudiera ser una nueva manifestación del carácter nacional" (cap. v., p. 41).
[3] "¡La holgazanería! es decir, la idiosincrasia nacional; mejor dicho, el genio nacional. Yo digo: holgazanería, tu nombre es España" (ibid., p. 44).
[4] "Cuestión de raza, señor Marqués. . . . Esta es una de las pocas cosas que son verdad: la fatalidad de la casta. Aquí no habrá nunca sino comunismo coronado por la lotería . . . éste es nuestro provenir" (ibid., p. 45).

controversial topics. Although these conversational glosses upon social problems are preferable to homilies delivered by the author himself, they tend to encroach unduly upon the main theme. The book is, like so many of the *Novelas Contemporáneas*, far too long. Practically the whole of the first volume is devoted to arguments between various characters, together with Galdós' favourite portraits. The crisis in the relations between León and María does not occur until the last chapter of a volume of three hundred and seventy-five pages. Interesting as these discussions and character-sketches are, they become wearisome when they are developed at the expense of the action. One is made too conscious of the fact that Galdós has an axe to grind. In portraits *La Familia de León Roch* is especially rich. Let us take a stroll through this gallery of nineteenth-century Spanish types. Pepa we have already met under another name. She is a more fully developed and a wittier Gloria; especially "modern" in her abhorrence of sentimentality. Her philosophy of life might indeed be summed up in her own epigram: "To be supremely happy one should have a lot of money and marry a fool,"[1] were it not for the fact that beneath her cloak of worldly wisdom she is, like so many cynics, a confirmed romantic. León, however, does not divine this until it is too late. He is repelled by what he deems to be her heartlessness, and seeks consolation in the domestic virtues of the insipid María; for with all his learning he is unable to penetrate beneath the surface of Pepa's rather affected frivolity. True to his bourgeois origin, he detests the lack of serious moral purpose in the world around him. As he explains to Cimarra, he is not at home in "society": "By character and

---

[1] "La suprema felicidad consiste en tener mucho dinero y casarse con un tonto" (cap. vi., p. 53).

inclination I am drawn to an obscure and studious life. My father, who made a fortune by the sweat of his brow in the corner of a chocolate factory, wanted to turn me into an infinitely distinguished and aristocratic being, according to his mistaken ideas, and he said to me: 'Be a marquis, spend a lot, wear out horses, keep a carriage, seduce married women, have a mistress, marry into a noble family, be a minister, make a big splash, make your name known above all names.'"[1] All these things León hates from the depths of his soul. He does not want to marry a "woman of the world" —who would desire to shine socially. "I don't want a woman, he confesses to Cimarra, whose character is already formed—but rather one whose character has yet to be formed. I want her to have the fundamentals of character—keen feelings, profound moral rectitude, that is to say. . . ."[2] Cimarra laughs this notion to scorn: "This idea of marrying in order to play the schoolmaster is in the worst of taste."[3] The main thing to consider when contemplating matrimony is the prospective bride's bank balance, and if *that* is satisfactory, and the girl not actually repulsive, there should be no squeamishness on the part of a man of the world in marrying her. León, however, is not to be shaken in his convictions. He is certain that he will have no difficulty in moulding his wife's character into

[1] "Mi carácter y mis gustos me inclinan a la vida obscura y estudiosa. Mi padre, que ganó una fortuna con el sudor de su frente en el rincón de una chocolatería, quiso hacer de mi un sér infinitamente distinguido y aristocrático, tal como él lo concebía en su errado criterio, y me dijo: 'Sé marqués, gasta mucho, revienta caballos, guía coches, seduce casadas, ten queridas, enlázate con una familia noble, sé ministro, haz ruido, pon tu nombre sobre todos los nombres" (cap. vii., p. 64).
[2] "No quiero una mujer formada, sino por formar. Quiérola dotada de las grandes bases de carácter, es decir, sentimiento vivo, profunda rectitud moral . . ." (ibid., p. 68).
[3] "Eso de casarse para ser maestro de escuela, es del peor gusto" (ibid., p. 69).

conformity with his own; and it is not until the first glamour of marriage has faded that he realises how fundamentally incapable María is of understanding him. Her character, he then comes to realise, is, in fact, already formed. Her early youth had been spent in a small village near Ávila, her sole companion being her twin-brother, Luís Gonzaga, a neurotic, ill-balanced boy of precocious religious instincts. His influence upon her early development was profound, and León finds that upon matters of religion she is adamant. She regards her husband as little better than an atheist, and makes it clear that she will never be satisfied until she has "converted" him. This antagonism on grounds of faith is, however, not the only source of dissension. León begins to realise that all the members of the Tellería family are profoundly antipathetic to him. They are of a class which he dislikes and despises: they represent all that he believes to be most worthless in Spanish society. In the marquess, his mother-in-law, he finds that empty volubility and extravagant love of display which characterise the type of woman he most detests—the leader of "smart society." The dissipated and hypocritical marquis is equally distasteful to him; and between the open profligacy of Leopoldo and the smug self-satisfaction of Gustavo (his brother-in-law) he finds little to choose. In his portrayal of the Tellería family Galdós has not been kind to that grade of society which, he believed, was destined to extinction—the aristocracy of birth. In *La Familia de León Roch* he represents the old aristocracy as already falling into irremediable decay. It has, he avers, lost all sense of dignity, and is perfectly willing to accept any upstart into the fold—provided that the newcomer's pockets are well lined. That Galdós was out of sympathy with the ideal of an aristocracy of lineage is not, in our opinion, apparent from his novels—although he is frequently referred to as the champion of the bourgeoisie against the nobility of rank. His remarks upon the decline of aristocracy are usually regretful rather than exultant. Take, for example, this passage from *La Familia de León Roch*: "Personal merit in some cases, and in others wealth, level, level, level with indefatigable zeal, and our society is marching with giant strides towards an equality of titles. There is no country, among those which possess a history, that is closer to the verge of being without an aristocracy than ours. To this end are working on the one hand business, which is turning all of us into plebeians and, on the other, the Government, which is turning all of us into aristocrats" [1]—in which the abolition of social distinctions is assuredly not contemplated with eagerness. Galdós, indeed, has, in common with most artists, a contempt for mediocrity which he is at no pains to conceal. His instinctive hatred of the second-rate goes hand in hand, however, with a belief in the equal rights of all human beings; a belief which led him to embrace the democratic creed. His reason told him that class distinctions are no longer valid because they have ceased to be true distinctions; and yet it is scarcely open to doubt that he instinctively revolted against democracy in practice. It led, he found, to the apotheosis of the second-rate—and yet what juster system was there to replace it? The problem is an old one, and Galdós, in the later stages of his career, seems to have discovered its equally ancient solution, which consists in the realisation that it is,

[1] "El mérito personal unas veces, y otras la fortuna, nivelan, nivelan, nivelan con incansable ardor, y nuestra sociedad camina con pasos de gigante a la igualdad de apellidos. No hay país ninguno entre los históricos que esté más próximo a quedarse sin aristocracia. A esto contribuyen, por un lado, el negocio, haciéndoles a todos plebeyos, y por otro el Gobierno, haciéndoles a todos nobles" (cap. viii., pp. 86–7).

indeed, insoluble in this world. Hence we find him growing more and more preoccupied with the spiritual side of life— for, as the mystics could have told him, equality in the sight of God is by no means the same thing as equality in the sight of man. We shall have occasion to revert to this aspect of Galdós' genius in dealing with the novels of the last phase. Meanwhile it is interesting to note that he confines himself, in *La Familia de León Roch*, to attacking the abuses of aristocracy as it is typified by the members of the obnoxious Tellería family. The majority of its failings are to be found united in the person of the marquis, who is not even an interesting sinner: "He was not a perverse man, being incapable either of open vice or of open virtue. He was an insipid compound of weakness and dissipation, corrupt by contact with corruption rather than by any evil-doing of his own; he was one of a crowd, an individual whom it would have been difficult to distinguish from any other member of his class—for the absence of individuality has, with some notable exceptions, turned the upper classes, as well as the lower, into an amorphous congeries which must remain without an adequate name until the progress of neologism allows us to speak of 'the aristocratic masses.'"[1]

That the marquis should rank as a true aristocrat in any social system is, to León (i.e. Galdós), a manifest absurdity. He is a man totally devoid of initiative and individuality; as incapable of thinking for himself as any clerk or shopkeeper.

[1] "No era un hombre perverso, no era capaz de maldad declarada, ni de bien: era un compuesto insípido de debilidad y disipación, corrompido más por contacto que por malicia propia; uno de tantos; un individuo que difícilmente podría diferenciarse de otro de su misma jerarquía, porque la falta de caracteres, salvas notabilísimas excepciones, ha hecho de ciertas clases altas, como de las bajas, una colectividad que no podrá calificarse bien hasta que los progresos del neologismo nos permitan decir *las masas aristocráticas*" (cap. x., pp. 102-3).

His philosophy of life is summed up in a series of catch phrases, among which, "this country is ungovernable"; "let the venerable beliefs of our forefathers be preserved"; "nothing good can exist here"; "this is a ruined country"; "Castilian gentility"; "the incomparable piety of the Spanish people"; "the materialistic tendencies of the age," [1] are the most cherished. From this stock of platitudes he produces a reply to any problem with which he happens to be confronted. He disapproves of León's studies in natural history: "A fine service you are rendering to the human race, depriving it of its "venerable beliefs" and giving it in exchange —what? . . . the famous hypothesis which makes us first cousins to the monkeys in the Retiro! " [2] And rebukes him for his unorthodox religious views: ". . . Remember that we are living in an 'eminently religious' country . . . remember that the lower orders need our example to prevent them from going astray. We're not in Germany. Oh, I swear I detest Utopias! The Spanish people may have many failings, but it will never outrage that which has been the cause of its fame, and of the respect which it has inspired 'at home and abroad.' 'Castilian gentility' will always rise above our misfortunes . . ." [3]

The smug hypocrisy of the marquis irritates León beyond endurance, and, unable to contain himself, he finally tells the

[1] Ibid., pp. 103-4.
[2] "Bonito servicio estáis haciendo al género humano, arrancándole *sus venerandas creencias*, para darle en cambio . . . ¿qué? . . . la famosa hipótesis de que somos primos hermanos de los monos del Retiro" (ibid., p. 106).
[3] ". . . Consideramos que vivimos en un pueblo *eminentemente religioso* . . . recordamos que las clases populares necesitan de nuestro ejemplo para no extraviarse. Aquí no estamos en Alemania. ¡Oh! te juro que aborrezco las *utopías*. El pueblo español tendrá muchos defectos, pero jamás ultrajará lo que ha sido causa de su gloria y del respeto que infundió *a propios y extraños*. Por encima de nuestras miserias descollará siempre la *hidalguía castellana* . . ." (ibid., p 111).

old roué exactly what he thinks of him. This does little to improve the situation—which is rendered more unbearable by the importunate Leopoldo, who regards León as an inexhaustible mine of riches. One morning, as León is working in his study, Leopoldo enters—"A shrivelled, emaciated figure, with the distorted mouth of a corpse upon which the process of internal decomposition has permitted a little skin to remain: two protruding eyes which gleamed with the unhealthy brilliance of delirium; a scraggy, purplish neck, whose blotchy skin looked as though it had been recently patched; a sharp nose, also of a purplish hue, and finely cut, but whose sharpness gave it the appearance of a beak, lending a definitely ornithological expression to the whole countenance . . ." [1] He broaches the question of the discord which has arisen between León and María, and represents himself as the champion of León against a malicious world. He agrees that an ultra-religious wife is a nuisance: but rather than argue about it he would, if he were León, accede to all her requests. His advice is "peace at any price"—"this idea of going to hell without first having a good time is the most stupid thing in the world." [2] And then, after a little judicious flattery, he reveals the chief object of his visit: "Do you know, my beloved, that you are going to lend me another four thousand reals?" [3] León is only

[1] "Una figura enjuta y macilenta, una mueca de calavera, en la cual la descomposición subterránea perdonara un poco de piel: dos ojos saltones con cierta viveza morbosa como la de los delirantes; un cuello delgado y violáceo, cuya piel, llena de costurones, parecía recientemente remendada; una nariz picuda y violácea también, de fina estampa; pero que por su agudeza iba tomando aspecto de pico y daba al rostro cierta fisonomía completamente ornitológica . . ." (cap. xi., p. 113).

[2] ". . . eso de irse al infierno sin pasar antes buena vida, es lo más tonto del mundo" (ibid., p. 118).

[3] "¿Sabes, querido, que me vas a prestar otros cuatro mil reales?" (ibid., p. 118).

too glad to be rid of him at the price, and Leopoldo departs—
"without concealing the joy which, in human beings,invariably
accompanies the acquisition of money." [1] León, however,
receives no thanks from the family for his financial backing
of Leopoldo. Gustavo, the eldest son, reads him a lecture upon
the subject. Gustavo—"a very proper and rather solemn
young man"—is the glory of the Tellería family. A successful
barrister, "he had adopted the most truly national and adventurous career of all, and leaving the University with no
profession was on the way towards becoming everything." [2]
He strongly disapproves of his brother, Leopoldo, and finds
the only possible excuse for the latter's conduct in the upbringing which he has had. "I believe," he says, "that it is the
fault of my parents. Our upbringing has been very slack.
It is foolish to pretend that my mother . . . she has been
unable to extricate either herself or us, in time, from the whirl-
wind of that society which thirsts for pleasure; she has
lived outside her home rather than in it. To-day . . . when
such inroads have been made upon our fortune (and in my
opinion the little that is left will soon be in the hands of our
creditors)—isn't it monstrous that my mother should run her
establishment upon a basis of luxury which is beyond our
means? . . . This damned vanity!" [3]

[1] ". . . no ocultando la alegría que en la raza humana acompaña
siempre a la adquisición de dinero" (ibid., p. 119).
[2] "Había seguido la carrera genuinamente nacional y aventurera por
excelencia, y saliendo de la Universidad sin ser nada, hallábase en
camino de serlo todo" (cap. xii., p. 123).
[3] "Creo que mis padres tienen la culpa. Nuestra educación ha sido
muy descuidada. Es tontería disimular que mi madre . . . no ha
sabido apartarse y apartarnos a tiempo del torbellino de la sociedad
sedienta de goces; ha vivido más fuera de su casa que dentro. Hoy
mismo . . . cuando nuestra fortuna ha mermado tanto, y según creo,
lo poco que resta será bien pronto de los acreedores, ¿no es monstruoso
que mi madre sostenga su casa en un pie de lujo que no nos corresponde?
. . . ¡Infame vanidad!" (ibid., p 125).

He confesses to León that the family is on the verge of absolute ruin. ". . . You don't know certain disgraceful domestic secrets, León: you don't know what it is to live in a house where money is owing for everything, from the carpets to the daily bread, nor have you experienced the shudders caused by the terrible bell which is perpetually announcing aggrieved or indignant tradespeople about to claim their money . . ."[1] and contrasts this gloomy state of affairs with León's happy condition, marred only by his estrangement from his wife. This, he thinks, is entirely due to León's obstinacy. At all costs, he says, a scandal must be avoided: "Your first duty is to avoid scandal and not to offer to the world the spectacle of a marriage disrupted and disturbed by religious differences,"[2] and he appeals to the "eleventh commandment"—"every deformity should be veiled, especially those of the conscience, so that public morality shall not be offended."[3] It is León's duty to submit to the will of his wife, and he, Gustavo, will support María to the end. León now realises that a breach with the family is inevitable—unless he is prepared to sacrifice his convictions. More bitter still is his realisation that his marriage is an utter failure: "I fell in love like a fool . . . and how could I have done otherwise? She is so beautiful." Only the sensual bond remains, but it is enough yet to hold them together. León "filled the void in his soul with the

[1] ". . . Tú no conoces ciertas interioridades vergonzosas, León; tú no sabes lo que es vivir en una casa donde todo se debe, desde las alfombras hasta el pan de cada día, ni conoces los escalofríos producidos por la campanilla del terror, anunciando perpétuamente a los industriales afligidos o furibundos que van a reclamer su dinero . . ." (ibid., p. 126).

[2] "Tu primer deber es evitar el escándalo y no dar al mundo el espectáculo de una unión descompuesta y perturbada por la disensión religiosa" (ibid., p. 127).

[3] "Toda deformidad debe ser velada, y las de la conciencia más, para no ofender a la moral pública" (ibid., p. 128).

evanescent passion inspired by a dazzling beauty. He was not indifferent to her; on the contrary he was flattered by the 'beati possidentes' with which the world hails the owner of a beautiful and devoted wife." [1] He feels, however, that his is no true marriage. . . . "The world," he reflects bitterly, "is ruled by words, not by ideas. See how in our case even matrimony can be equivalent to concubinage." [2]

He endeavours in vain to convince his wife that her excess of devotion is not truly religious. "I don't see," he says, "either in your actions or in your feverish enthusiasm for sacred things, a single one of the precious attributes of the Christian wife." [3] María, however, is obdurate: "Do you want me to deny God and His Church, to become a rationalist like yourself? Do you want me to read your perverted books, full of lies; to believe in all that about monkeys, materialism, the God of Nature and the God of Nothing—in all your detestable heresies? . . ." [4] This is her final word on the subject; and any step to secure a *modus vivendi* must now be taken by León.

He eventually agrees to accompany her to church and to promise her "respectful attendance and sincere attention" [5]— provided only that she will consent to leave Madrid and settle

[1] "Llenaba el vacío de su alma con aquella pasión temporal encendida por una pasmosa belleza. No le era indiferente, antes bien le vanagloriaba el *beati possidentes* con que la multitud obsequia al dueño de una mujer fiel y hermosa . . ." (cap. xiv., p. 147).

[2] "El mundo está gobernado por palabras, no por ideas. Véase aquí cómo el matrimonio puede también llegar a ser un concubinato" (ibid., p. 148).

[3] "No veo en tus actos ni en tu febril afán por las cosas santas ninguno de los preciosos atributos de la esposa cristiana" (ibid., p. 150).

[4] "¿Quieres que yo reniegue de Dios y de su Iglesia, que me haga racionalista como tú; que lea en tus perversos libros llenos de mentiras; que crea en eso de los monos, en eso de la materia, en eso de la Naturaleza-Dios, en eso de la Nada-Dios, en esas tus herejías horribles? . . ." (ibid., p. 151).

[5] "Una asistencia respetuosa y una atención sincera" (cap. xv., p 167).

in the country. He hopes that by removing her from the family circle he will be able to proceed with his task of moulding her character unhampered by parental interference. She, however, refuses to accept his condition—and he then tells her that they must live apart. She may remain in Madrid if she likes—but he will go into the country. His departure is, however, delayed by the illness of Luís Gonzaga, María's ascetic brother; and, in his portrayal of Luís, Galdós finds yet another opportunity to attack what he regards as a perversion of the religious instinct. Luís is an early example of the abnormal types which abound in *Las Novelas Contemporáneas*. Delicate in his boyhood, he has developed into an ill-balanced, neurotic individual whose only emotional outlet is "his feverish mysticism." [1] He is a bizarre figure, strangely out of place in the worldly Tellería household—"a dark and melancholy blot upon the gaily coloured and gilded furniture, upon the exotic ornaments in the Japanese style whose lonely, nightmarish figures seemed in keeping with the squalid figure of the collegian." [2] So self-effacing is he that the servants are scarcely aware of his presence; one only among them pays any attention to him—Felipe Centeno, to whose career Galdós devotes a later work.[3] He has no desire to recover from the illness which threatens to send him to his grave: "I do not fear death," he declares. "On the contrary, I yearn for it with all

[1] "Su febril misticismo" (cap. xviii., p. 191).
[2] "Una mancha obscura y triste caída sobre el mueblaje de colorines y oro, sobre los exóticos objetos de estilo japonés, cuyas aisladas figuras de pesadilla parecían armonizar con la persona del escuálido colegial" (ibid., p. 190).
[3] *El Doctor Centeno*. With reference to what has already been remarked concerning the relationship of *La Familia de León Roch* to *Las Novelas Contemporáneas*, it is interesting to note that many of the characters in this book appear in later works. In *La Familia de León Roch* the author has already embarked upon his scheme for a Spanish *comédie humaine*.

the ardour in my soul, as a healthy prisoner longs for liberty." [1]
He refuses to eat any food of which he is especially fond—"I
am not going to eat this," he would say, "because I like it" [2]
—and only yields to persuasion when María argues that it
would be a real mortification of the flesh to eat what he likes
when he does not like to eat it! His only frequent visitors are
"a few priests, mainly French, . . . courteous, polished,
urbane, clean . . ." [3]; and those who accuse Galdós of intolerant anti-clericalism should note the complimentary
reference to the few Spanish clerics who come to see the
invalid: "Rarely seen there were those grave Spanish
'curas' who, when they are good, are, so to say, the most
clerical of all the clerics which Christianity has produced
—true ministers of God by virtue of their genuine gravity,
their unaffected gentleness and healthy knowledge of the
world." [4]

Luís's illness takes so serious a turn that the doctor advises
his removal to León's house on the outskirts of the city, where
the air is purer and where he will not be disturbed by the noise
of the traffic. He does not, however, improve. Spurred by his
desire for self-mortification, he frequently leaves his bed and
spends the whole night asleep upon the floor. When awake, he
is tortured by conscientious scruples of every description. "If
for the space of a quarter of an hour his thoughts strayed from

---

[1] "Yo no temo la muerte. . . . Por el contrario, la deseo con todo
el ardor de mi alma, como un cautivo sano desea la libertad" (ibid.,
p. 192).
[2] "No como esto, porque me gusta" (ibid., p. 194).
[3] ". . . algunos sacerdotes principalmente franceses . . . corteses,
finos, mundanos, limpios . . ." (ibid., p. 195).
[4] "Rara vez se veía allí a los graves curas españoles, que cuando son
buenos, son los clérigos más clérigos, digámoslo así, de la cristiandad,
verdaderos ministros de Dios por la seriedad real, la mansedumbre sin
afectación y la sana sabiduría" (ibid., p. 195).

I

meditation upon death, as soon as he was aware of this distraction he felt uneasy and was violently angry with himself . . . he crushed down every thought and every emotion other than his passionate longing for salvation." [1] The infliction of physical suffering upon himself gives him acute spiritual pleasure—"physical suffering was accepted by him, subconsciously, with a delirious joy— the product of his vanity and his sybaritism" [2]—and when, in the end, his tortured body can no longer bear the burden of pain which is laid upon it, it is with a cry of ecstasy that he sinks into the ultimate unconsciousness: "I do not want health, I do not want to get better, I only want pain, grief . . . I want to stifle, to die in a convulsion. . . . Oh, this joy which I now . . . feel. . ." [3] Then, as Galdós so beautifully phrases it, "he died as a bird which falls asleep." [4] This portrait of Luís Gonzaga concludes the series in which Galdós introduces to us, one by one, the members of the "Familia de León Roch." [5] Of these portraits, all masterpieces, that of Luís Gonzaga is one of the most interesting. In it Galdós' early attitude towards mysticism is clearly defined. He does not accuse Luís of insincerity—indeed he expressly defends him against any

[1] "Si por espacio de un cuarto de hora estaba su pensamiento ausente de las meditaciones sobre la muerte, al caer en la cuenta de su distracción sentía inquietudes y un vivo enojo contra sí mismo . . . y . . . mutiló en su pensamiento y en su sentir todo lo que no fuera el ardiente prurito de salvarse" (ibid., pp. 196–7).

[2] ". . . los dolores físicos eran recibidos allá dentro con un júbilo delirante que tenía su vanidad y su sibaritismo" (ibid., p. 197).

[3] "Yo no quiero salud, yo no quiero estar mejor, yo no quiero sino dolores, ansiedad, ahogarme, estremecerme, y morir. . . . Este bienestar que ahora . . . siento . . ." (p. 239).

[4] ". . . se murió como un pájaro que se duerme" (ibid., p. 239).

[5] Part i. of volume i. is mainly occupied with these "retratos": Cap. viii. "María Egipciaca"; ix. "La Marquesa de Tellería"; x. "El Marqués"; xi. "Leopoldo"; xii. "Gustavo"; xiii. "El último retrato" (León himself); xviii. "El asceta" (Luís Gonzaga).

such charge.[1] The mystic, in Galdós' opinion, is the Don Quixote of Catholicism. He is striving after an impossible ideal and breaking himself in the process. This much Galdós states plainly—but we can also divine in this portrait of Luís Gonzaga an implication to the effect that the mystic is unconsciously deceiving himself. A modern student of abnormal psychology would describe Luís as a masochist—one who experiences a voluptuous delight in self-torture. There are, as we have already had occasion to remark, many such abnormal types in the novels of Galdós. Granted that he was influenced by Dostoievsky, it would, in our opinion, be unfair to accuse Galdós of deliberately aping the Russian. It is obvious that he had a genuine interest in such types, and his treatment of them is one of the most original and interesting features of his work. From *La Familia de León Roch* onwards there is scarcely a novel which does not include one or more "abnormals"—products of that "monstrous synthesis of the ages," [2] the nineteenth century.

After the death of Luís Gonzaga, the story is mainly concerned with María's efforts to win back her husband from Pepa. How these attempts fail and how María falls ill and eventually dies as the result of a jealous outburst has already been briefly related. The scene in which, dressed like a prostitute, she visits her husband in a final desperate attempt to regain his love, even though that love can only be grossly physical, is one of the most tensely dramatic episodes in the novels of Galdós. Not until then is the true motive behind

---

[1] Vide ibid., p. 201: "Some said that this saintliness was merely a part well acted; but this statement lacked foundation." ["Alguien dijo que aquella santidad no era mas que un papel bien representado; pero esto carecía de fundamento."]

[2] "Monstruosa síntesis de los tiempos . . ." (ibid., p. 202).

all her recriminations revealed. One does not know whether to pity or despise her as she hurls vulgar abuse at the woman who, in spite of the greatest temptations, has always remained virtuous. María, her cloak of self-righteous piety torn from her, stands revealed in all her moral nakedness. As she spits forth the base slander concerning the paternity of Pepa's child, she is primitive woman deprived of her mate—rage, hatred, and jealousy incarnate.

León, however, does not altogether scape whipping. The enlightened and, one would imagine, morally courageous philosopher cuts but a poor figure in the end. Daring in theory, he proves a coward in practice, and Pepa alone is honest enough and brave enough to defy the world for the sake of her convictions. That the chief character of the novel should be a *heroine* is an indication of Galdós' attitude towards a problem, one or another aspect of which he touches upon in many of the *Novelas Contemporáneas*. His views on the place of woman in society might alone suffice as a justification of his claim to be regarded as the apostle of "modernism" in Spanish fiction of the last century. It is clear from his novels that he regards the social problem and the "feminist" question as inseparable. Until the legitimate claims of woman are recognised and satisfied, the social system must, in his view, lack a genuine basis of stability. We shall see later how he develops this theme in *La Desheredada, Fortunata y Jacinta* and *La Incógnita*.

V

A LYRIC INTERLUDE: "MARIANELA"

Marianela is the third, in chronological order, of *Las Novelas de la Primera Época*, and its true place is between *Gloria* and *La Familia de León Roch*. In it, however, Galdós turns aside from the noisy highway of controversy which he has hitherto followed and leads us, for a welcome respite, into glades of romance almost, if not entirely, undisturbed by the shrill, insistent voices of the demagogue, the mob-orator, and the vendor of political nostrums for the moral infirmities of mankind.

The opening passages of the first chapter strike the lyrical note which predominates throughout the book: "The sun sank below the horizon. Hard upon the brief twilight came the night, dark and serene, in whose dusky bosom the last murmurings of the drowsy earth died away; and the traveller continued on his path, quickening his steps to keep pace with those of the oncoming night. . . ."[1] "The traveller" is one Teodoro Golfín who, while on his way to visit his brother, Carlos, at the tiny mining village of Socartes, has strayed from the beaten track. Although he believes himself to be hopelessly lost, he decides to take the situation philosophically, and, lighting a cigarette,

---

[1] "Se puso el sol. Tras el breve crepúsculo vino tranquila y obscura la noche, en cuyo negro seno murieron poco a poco los últimos rumores de la tierra soñolienta, y el viajero siguió adelante en su camino, apresurando su paso a medida que avanzaba el de la noche . . ." (*Marianela* (1921 ed.), cap. i., p. 5).

sits down upon a convenient stone to await the arrival of some chance passer-by, from whom he may inquire his way. His meditations are interrupted by the sound of a woman's voice singing a popular air. Then, shortly after the song has died away in the distance, he hears the shrill barking of a dog quite close at hand. Soon the animal appears and, as it is running towards Teodoro, is recalled by its master, who has now come into sight. Teodoro inquires the road to Socartes, and the stranger informs him that he is already among the mines on the outskirts of the village. He offers his services as guide; which services Teodoro gladly accepts. Although he has been blind from birth, the stranger experiences no difficulty in finding his way through the tortuous maze of the disused mines—and of one of these mines, "la Terrible" as it is called, Galdós gives us a graphic description: "It looked" he says, "like an orgy of gigantic demons turned into stone; their mowings, the grotesque movements of their deformed heads, were set in the immutable attitudes of sculpture. The silence which filled the supposed crater was terrifying. One might have imagined that a thousand voices, a thousand screechings, had also been petrified, and that they had remained stone for century upon century." [1] Teodoro, whose curiosity has been excited by the rare beauty of the voice he has heard singing

---

[1] "Parecía la petrificación de una orgía de gigantescos demonios; sus manotadas, los burlones movimientos de sus disformes cabezas, habían quedado fijos como las inalterables actitudes de la escultura. El silencio que llenaba el ámbito del supuesto cráter, era un silencio que daba miedo. Creeríase que mil voces y aullidos habían quedado también hechos piedra, y piedra eran desde siglos de siglos" (cap. ii., p. 16). In this description of the mines of Socartes, Galdós displays an amazing wealth of technical knowledge (vide, especially, cap. v., pp. 56–60). Like the French novelists of the naturalistic school, by whom he was, as we shall have occasion to remark later, to some extent influenced, he spares no pains to become well versed in the terminology of any profession or calling which he undertakes to describe.

in the distance prior to his meeting with the stranger, inquires
of the latter whether he knows anything of its owner. The
blind man explains that it was the voice of Nela, his guide—
and Teodoro's desire to make her acquaintance is soon satisfied
by her appearance in person. She is an orphan—the daughter
of a lamplighter who used, when she was a baby, to carry her
about with him, while in the pursuit of his vocation, in a
basket tied upon his shoulders. On one occasion she had a
serious fall, which left her permanently deformed. After the
death of her parents, she was adopted by a working-class
family, the Centenos.[1] Her childhood is spent in extreme
hardship and poverty, and, unable on account of her deformity
to do any ordinary work, she acts as guide to the blind youth,
Pablo Penáguilas, with whom she falls deeply in love. Her
naïve views of life, nature and the universe are revealed to
us in passages of great lyrical beauty. She undergoes, when
in Pablo's presence, a wonderful transformation: "That feeble
creature, whose soul was, as it were, imprisoned and fettered
within a wretched body, grew and developed amazingly when
she was alone with her master and friend. In his presence she
had spontaneity, intelligence, feeling, wit, elegance, an elfish
charm. When they parted it was as though the dark doors of
a prison closed upon her" [2]; and everything she sees around
her is glorified by the poetry of her unsophisticated imagination: "The flowers," she tells Pablo, "are the stars of the
earth." "And what, then, are the stars?" he replies. "The

[1] The son of the house, Felipe, we met (at a later stage in his career)
in *La Familia de León Roch.*

[2] "Aquella débil criatura, en la cual parecía que el alma estaba
como prensada y constreñida dentro de un cuerpo miserable, se ensan-
chaba, se crecía maravillosamente al hallarse sola con su amo y amigo.
Junto a él tenía espontaneidad, agudeza, sensibilidad, gracia, donosura,
fantasía. Al separarse, creeríase que se cerraban sobre ella las negras
puertas de una prision " (cap. vi., p. 68).

stars are the glances of those who have gone to heaven." [1] The blind youth, charmed by her innocence, imagines her to be "beautiful as the angels who surround God's throne" [2]; and when he asks her, "Tell me, Nela, what are you like?" she cannot bring herself to admit her deformity. A crisis in their relationship develops when Florentina, Pablo's beautiful cousin, visits Socartes. Marianela, who has caught a first glimpse of her in a wood where she is gathering primroses, believes her to be the Blessed Virgin herself! Florentina takes pity upon and befriends the orphan child, who becomes greatly attached to her. The climax of the story is reached when Pablo's sight is restored by Teodoro Golfín. When Marianela touches the hand of the man she loves, he is unable to conceal the disillusion in his eyes: "A thousand ideas raced through his mind, but he could not find expression for one of them. To do that he would have had to discover a new language, just as he had discovered two new worlds, the world of light and the world of love of form. He merely stared and stared, calling to mind that dark world in which he had lived, that faraway world in which the emotions, thoughts and errors of a blind man were lost in mist. Florentina, the tears pouring down her cheeks, came and gazed into Nela's face, and Golfín, who saw her with the eyes of a man and a philosopher, uttered these melancholy words: 'It has killed her—his accursed sight!'" [3]

[1] "Las flores son las estrellas de la tierra." "¿Y las estrellas, qué son?" "Las estrellas son las miradas de los que se han ido al cielo" (ibid., p. 72).

[2] ". . . hermosa como los ángeles que rodean el trono de Dios . . ." (cap. vii., p. 85).

[3] "Pasaron por su mente ideas mil; mas no pudo expresar ninguna. Era preciso para ello que hubiera descubierto un nuevo lenguaje, así como había descubierto dos nuevos mundos: el de la luz y el del amor por la forma. No hacía más que mirar, mirar, y hacer memoria de

Pablo, as one is led to expect, marries his cousin Florentina. The conception of Marianela, the simple girl in whom moral beauty and physical deformity are united, is, of course, not an original one. The tale may have been suggested to Galdós by the Mignon episode in *Wilhelm Meister*, and, like the latter, it "dates." The sentiment is piled on too thickly for our present-day taste, and the dénouement of the story is obvious almost from the beginning. In spite, however, of these defects, *Marianela* is, technically, one of the best of all Galdós' novels.

There are few digressions in it, and such as do occur are neither forced nor unduly prolix—with the possible exception of the long conversation in chapter ix. upon philanthropy, charity and suicide.[1] Here the brothers Golfín speak as though they were on a public platform rather than at a picnic party. It must be remembered, however, that the Golfíns are parvenus, and their self-importance is the outcome of long years during which they had struggled in vain to gain the recognition they deserved. Teodoro, especially, delights in recounting the story of his ascent: "I am not without my vanities," he informs the party, "and among them is my pride in having been a beggar."[2] After incredible hardships, he eventually succeeded in qualifying as a doctor. Then he devoted most of his earnings to helping his brother—whose ambition it was to become an engineer. Both attain eminence in their respective professions

aquel tenebroso mundo en que había vivido, allá donde quedaban perdidos entre la bruma sus pasiones, sus ideas y sus errores de ciego. Florentina se acercó derramando lágrimas para examinar el rostro de la Nela, y Golfín, que la observaba como hombre y como sabio, pronunció estas lúgubres palabras: '¡La mató! ¡Maldita vista suya!'" (cap. xxi., p. 259).

[1] Note, especially, Teodoro's defence of suicide (p. 117) and his solution to the problem of the orphan's place in society (pp. 119-20).

[2] "Yo no carezco de vanidades, y entre ellas tengo la de haber sido mendigo" (cap. x., p. 124).

—Teodoro as a surgeon in America and Carlos as a metallurgist in Spain. Of the two, Teodoro is the stronger character— "a man of coarse features, dark-skinned, with a face as intelligent as it was sensual, thick lips, black, frizzy hair, piercing gaze, tireless energy, and a constitution strong, if a little worn by the American climate. He looked, in fact, like a lion and, like the king of beasts, he disclosed at every turn the excellent opinion which he had of himself." [1]

Carlos is a quiet, comparatively unaggressive individual— "a very quiet man, studious, a slave to duty, passionately devoted to mineralogy and metallurgy—two mistresses who ranked a good deal higher in his affections than did his wife." [2] In Sofía, his wife, Galdós gives us a good-humouredly ironical picture of the sentimental organiser of charity bazaars who lavishes most of her practical benevolence upon a lap-dog. She has no children alive, and "she occupied herself mainly with piano-playing and the organisation of ladies' philanthropic associations for the benefit of alms-houses, hospitals and schools." [3] With the aid of one or two other ladies of the parish—"equally fond of their neighbour"—she had succeeded in organising more than twenty amateur dramatic performances, as many fancy-dress balls, six bull-fights and two cock-fights—"all for the benefit of the poor.[4] This conception of

---

[1] "Un hombre de facciones bastas, moreno, de fisonomía tan inteligente como sensual, labios gruesos, pelo negro y erizado, mirar centelleante, naturaleza incansable, constitución fuerte, si bien algo gastada por el clima americano. En efecto, parecía un león, y, como el rey de los animales, no dejaba de manifestar a cada momento la estimación en que a sí mismo se tenía" (cap. ix., p. 105).

[2] "Hombre muy pacífico, estudioso, esclavo de su deber, apasionado por la mineralogía y la metalurgia hasta poner a estas dos mancebas cien codos más altas que su mujer" (ibid., p. 107).

[3] "Su principal ocupación consistía en tocar el piano y en organizar asociaciones benéficas de señoras para socorros domiciliarios y sostenimiento de hospitales y escuelas (cap. ix., p. 108).

[4] Ibid.

charity is severely attacked by Teodoro. Sofía and her friends, he says, never attempt to understand the poor people with whom they come into contact: they do not realise that of misfortunes "there are some so poignant that they cannot be assuaged by petty almsgiving . . . nor even by the gift of a crust of bread."[1] Her view of the matter, essentially that of the conventional woman of fashion, is revealed by her remarks upon the case of Marianela: "I ask myself: 'What is God's purpose in allowing such creatures to live?' And I also ask: 'What can we do for her?' Nothing, nothing more than feed her, clothe her . . . to a certain extent. . . ."[2] She cannot conceive that the poor should have anything more than material needs. The thesis of *Marianela*, in so far as it has a .thesis, seems to be this: that the poor are men and women like ourselves, and that no charity is of value unless it is given in a sympathetic spirit. It would, it is true, be possible to read into the story of Pablo's blindness more than is, we think, intended by the author. Would Pablo not have been happier in the end if he had remained blind and in the company of Marianela, the "illusion," than he will be, cured of his deformity and married to Florentina, the "reality"? It is an interesting question; but we do not think Galdós intended any such symbolical interpretation of this idyll of "La Nela" and her tragic love. It is to be regarded in our opinion as a "lyrical interlude" in the controversial series to which it belongs. Let those who would deny to Galdós the

---

[1] "Hay algunas tan extraordinarias, que no se alivian con la fácil limosna del ochavo . . . ni tampoco con el mendrugo de pan" (ibid., p. 114).

[2] "Yo me pregunto ¿para qué permite Dios que tales criaturas vivan? Y me pregunto también: ¿qué es lo que se puede hacer por ella? Nada, nada más que darle de comer, vestirla . . . hasta cierto punto . . ." (ibid., p. 115).

power of evoking a landscape read the masterly description
of the mining village of Socartes: "The sky had cleared; the
sun shed his rays freely upon the earth, and all at once the
vast area of Socartes was suffused in a ruddy glow.

Red were
the sculptured crags, red the precious mineral, red the waste
earth piled up in the gigantic works, which looked like Baby-
lonian ramparts; red the ground; red the ruts and the
waggons; red all the machinery; red the water; red the men
and women at work throughout Socartes. Save a few variations
in shade, the bright, red-brick colour was uniform and could
be seen everywhere: on the earth and on the houses, the tools
and the clothing. The washerwomen looked like a Pleiad of
rather dubious nymphs moulded in raw, ferruginous clay.
Towards the river, in the glade below, flowed a brook of
crimson water. One might have fancied that it was the sweat
of that gigantic labour of men, machinery, iron, and muscle "[1];
or that of the wood in the opening pages of chapter vii.:—
"They walked on until they reached the entrance to the wood
which lies beyond Saldeoro. They halted amid a group of
ancient walnut-trees, whose trunks and roots formed a series
of steps, with mossy folds and hollows so well adapted for
sitting that art could not have improved upon them. From

---

[1] "El cielo estaba despejado; el sol derramaba libremente sus rayos,
y la vasta pertinencia de Socartes resplandecía con súbito tono rojo.
Rojas eran las peñas esculturales; rojo el precioso mineral; roja la
tierra inútil accumulada en los largos taludes, semejantes a babilónicas
murallas; rojo el suelo; rojos los carriles y los vagones; roja toda la
maquinaria: roja el agua; rojos los hombres y mujeres que trabajaban
en toda la extensión de Socartes. El color subido de ladrillo era uniforme,
con ligeros cambiantes, y general en todo: en la tierra y las casas, en
el hierro y en los vestidos. Las mujeres ocupadas en lavar parecían
una pléyade de equívocas ninfas de barro ferruginoso crudo. Por la
cañada abajo, en dirección al río, corría un arroyo de agua encarnada.
Creeríase que era el sudor de aquel gran trabajo de hombres y máquinas,
del hierro y de los músculos" (cap. v., p. 60).

the highest point of the wood there ran a thread of water, leaping from stone to stone until its weary body reached a tiny pond which served as a reservoir for the spring used by the peasants. The ground opposite sloped gently downwards, revealing a magnificent panorama of green hills dotted with woods and hamlets, and smooth meadows where wandering herds of cattle grazed in peace. In the background, two proud and distant hills, marking the extreme edge of the land, revealed a large segment of the limpid blue of the sea. It was a landscape which revealed to the contemplative soul its lofty kinship with the infinite." [1]

In *Marianela* there are many such passages as these— passages which show that Galdós possessed, in addition to the wit of the satirist and the intellectual keenness of the sociologist, the sensitive perceptions of the great artist.

In view of the magnificent passages of descriptive prose which abound in *Gloria*, *Marianela*, *Tristana*, and *Angel Guerra*, it is, indeed, difficult to understand the charge of arid intellectualism which has frequently been brought against Galdós.

[1] "Siguieron adelante, hasta llegar a la entrada del bosque que hay más allá de Saldeoro. Detuviéronse entre un grupo de nogales viejos, cuyos troncos y raíces formaban en el suelo una serie de escalones, con musgosos huecos y recortes tan apropiados para sentarse, que el arte no los hiciera mejor. Desde lo alto del bosque, corría un hilo de agua, saltando de piedra en piedra, hasta dar con su fatigado cuerpo en un estanquillo que servía de depósito para alimentar el chorro de que se abastecían los vecinos. Enfrente, el suelo se deprimía poco a poco, ofreciendo grandioso panorama de verdes colinas pobladas de bosques y caseríos, de praderas llanas donde pastaban con tranquilidad vagabunda centenares de reses. En el último término dos lejanos y orgullosos cerros, que eran límite de la tierra, dejaban ver en un largo segmento el azul purísimo del mar. Era un paisaje cuya contemplación revelaba al alma sus excelsas relaciones con lo infinito" (cap. vii., p. 78).

VI

NOVELS OF CHARACTER AND OBSERVATION. THE MASTERPIECES

OF SPANISH REALISM

WE have seen how, in the *Novelas de la Primera Época*, Galdós undergoes a process of purification from the didactic obsession,[1] until, in *La Familia de León Roch*, the last novel of the series, the tendencious element is almost entirely subordinated to the human aspect of the theme.

The appearance of *La Desheredada* marks the opening of a new phase in the author's career: for this work constitutes his first attempt to bring the Spanish novel of manners into line with its trans-Pyrenean rival. We shall have more to say later concerning the influence which Balzac and Zola exercised upon Galdós. Traces of that influence can already be discerned in the tendency, noticeable in *Las Novelas de la Primera Época*, to introduce a character from one novel into the pages of another.[2] This, however, is only a point of detail. The atmosphere of *Las Novelas de la Primera Época* is

---

[1] Cf. Salvador de Madariaga, *Semblanzas Literarias Contemporáneas* (Barcelona, 1924), p. 75: "The development (of Galdós' genius) from *Doña Perfecta* to *La Familia de León Roch* reveals a gradual purification of his ethical passion and an effort to raise the field of conflict above that of prejudice to the level of tragedy." ["La evolución de *Doña Perfecta* a *La Familia de León Roch* revela una purificación gradual de su pasión ética y un esfuerzo para elevar el conflicto por encima de los prejuicios hasta el nivel de la tragedia."]

[2] e.g. Felipe Centeno appears both in *Marianela* and in *La Familia de León Roch*, while Doña Perfecta is mentioned in the latter work.

thoroughly Spanish. In *Doña Perfecta* Galdós deliberately imitates the style of Cervantes, while the plot, as we have seen, is marked out on conventional romantic lines. *Doña Perfecta, Gloria, Marianela*—all three novels have that strong flavour of the soil which is characteristic of Spanish literature as a whole. One feels that only a Spaniard could have written them. In *La Familia de León Roch* we sense for the first time that "European" atmosphere which distinguishes the *Novelas Contemporáneas* from their predecessors; but *León Roch* is still in many respects typically Spanish.

Although *La Desheredada* is timid and reticent as compared with almost any French novel of the naturalistic school, it bears, nevertheless, clear evidence of the source of its inspiration.

The central figure of the story is one Isidora Rufete, daughter of a plebeian ne'er-do-well, Tomás Rufete, who sedulously fosters a rumour to the effect that she is in reality of noble birth, to wit, the illegitimate child of Virginia de Aransis, daughter of La Marquesa de Aransis. In the hope that from this rumour there may accrue some profit to himself, he forges a document which purports to establish its truth. He then attempts to interest his brother (a priest who has attained to the rank of Canon) on Isidora's behalf.

The novel is mainly occupied with Isidora's efforts to substantiate her claim—a claim which is obviously foredoomed to failure. Of its authenticity, however, she has no doubt; and soon comes to think of herself as entitled by right of birth to all the advantages and luxuries which the Aransis family enjoy. This firm belief in the nobility of her birth leads her into excesses of every description. When her wealthy lovers have deserted her, and her lawsuit has proved unsuccessful, she finds herself an outcast from society. Constitutionally incapable of settling down to any form of steady work, she at last sinks into the miseries of prostitution.

From the point of view of technique and construction *La Desheredada* is among the worst of *Las Novelas Contemporáneas*. Several chapters are written in dramatic form—foreshadowing the attempts which Galdós was to make later at a fusion of two *genres* [1]—and the novel is sadly lacking in coherency. It abounds, however, in character-studies of exceptional interest, and, as the first of a new series, merits a fairly close analysis here. Part I., a kind of prologue to the story, opens with the ravings of Tomás Rufete in a madhouse. He is shortly to be transferred to the pauper asylum—his family being unable to meet the expense incurred by his treatment as a private patient. This opens the way for an interesting digression upon lunacy and the treatment of lunacy in general. Galdós attacks, especially, the paupers' ward: "In those primitive places, as yet scarcely touched by administrative reform, in the long corridors with their long rows of cells, in the courtyards of bare earth, where the imbeciles grovel and the maniacs pirouette—here is revealed the full horror of this ghastly department of Public Welfare in which Christian charity and society on the defensive combine to establish the gloomy fortress known as a lunatic asylum—a hospital and a prison in one. Here the sane feel their blood run cold in their veins; here their souls are oppressed by the sight of that section of humanity which is imprisoned for being ill; here they see how the madness of the insane is aggravated by mutual example, how the lunatics refine upon their lunacy, how they perfect themselves in the terrible art of doing all

[1] In *Realidad, La loca de la Casa* and *El Abuelo*.

that is contrary to the dictates of common sense!"[1] And he expresses the opinion that there is, in all essentials, very little difference between normal and abnormal psychological states: "The ideas of these unfortunate creatures are our ideas, but unhinged, torn from that mysterious thread which holds them firmly together. These wretched lunatics are we ourselves, we who last night, in our sleep, revelled in the dazzling variety of all conceivable ideas and who to-day awake to the arid solitude of one idea only."[2] And yet the wretched inmates are subjected to every kind of indignity and entrusted to the care of brutal keepers—"the inquisitors of absurdity," as Galdós styles them: "There is no pity in their faces, no gentleness in their hands, no charity in their souls. Of all the officials which the guardian State has contrived to invent, none is so detestable as the lunatic-tamer."[3] The description of the horrors of the asylum is quite in the naturalistic vein; but the

[1] "¡En aquellos locales primitivos, apenas tocados aún por la administración reformista, en el largo pasillo, formado por larga fila de jaulas, en el patio de tierra, donde se revuelcan los imbéciles y hacen piruetas los exaltados, allí, allí es donde se ve todo el horror de esa sección espantosa de la Beneficiencia, en que se reunen la caridad cristiana y la defensa social, estableciendo una lúgubre fortaleza llamada manicomio, que juntamente es hospital y presidio! ¡Allí es donde el sano siente que su sangre se hiela y que su espíritu se anonada, viendo aquella parte de la humanidad aprisionada por enferma, observando como los locos refinan su locura con el mútuo ejemplo, como perfeccionan sus manías, como se adiestran en aquel arte horroroso de hacer lo contrario de lo que el buen sentido nos ordena!" (*La Desheredada* (1909 ed.), part i. cap. i., p. 12).

[2] "Las ideas de estos desgraciados son nuestras ideas, pero desengarzadas, sueltas, sacadas de la misteriosa hebra que gallardamente las enfila. Estos pobres orates somos nosotros mismos que dormimos anoche nuestro pensamiento en la variedad esplendente de todas las ideas posibles, y hoy por la mañana lo despertamos en la aridez de una sola" (ibid., p. 13).

[3] "No hay compasión en sus rostros, ni blandura en sus manos, ni caridad en sus almas. De todos cuantos funcionarios ha podido inventar la tutela del Estado, ninguno es tan antipático como el domador de locos" (ibid., p. 14).

K

high-sounding rhetoric of the apostrophe to dawn [1] suggests
Dickens rather than Zola, and in view of what will be said
later concerning the relationship between Galdós and Dickens
it will bear quoting here in full: "Even in a madhouse the dawn
is a joyous thing; even there the smile of day as she opens her
eyes, the first glances exchanged by earth and sky, trees and
houses, mountains and valleys, are things of beauty. The early
birds warble there just as they do above the heads of lovers
in the groves of the Retiro; the sun, father of all beauty, works
there the same miracles of form and colour as in villages and
cities, and the same exhilarating air which stirs the trees, fans
the meadows, urges men to work, carrying everywhere joy,
good appetites, and health, diffuses throughout the asylum
its life-giving breath. The flowers unfold, the flies begin their
endless buzzing, the pigeons embark upon their distant aerial
journeys; in heaven and on earth everything responds, each
according to its own nature, to the vivifying impulse. The
madmen emerge from their cells with their savage instincts
powerfully stimulated. In that hour of universal awakening
their normal eccentricity is intensified, and they talk in louder
tones, laugh more uproariously, grovel more wildly and grow
increasingly stupid. Some say their prayers, others express
surprise that the sun should appear during the night, one hails
the distant crowing of the cocks, another greets his keeper with
polished urbanity; one demands paper and ink to write a
letter, the indispensable daily letter! another takes to his
heels, fleeing from a persecutor who comes mounted upon the
steed of dawn; and all that motley world begins with vigour
its ordinary life." [2]

[1] Ibid. pp. 17–18.
[2] "¡La aurora!, aun en una casa de locos es alegre; aun allí son her-
mosos el risueño abrir de ojos del día y la primera mirada que cielo

After this introductory homily upon the social and psychological aspects of insanity, we hear of Isidora's visit to the asylum in search of Tomás Rufete and of her conversation with a man whom she believes to be the director's assistant, but who is, in reality, a harmless lunatic. She tells him what she imagines to be the true story of her birth and how she has been brought up and educated by Tomás Rufete—who, she reveals, was driven mad with grief by the death of his wife. He was, she says, an excellent foster-father—his only fault being that "his one aim was to cut a dash, cut a dash and be a person of importance. . . ."[1] The lunatic, who appears to have retained his common sense, warns her against a failing which brings so many recruits to the asylum: ". . . ambition, love of social prestige, the jealousy of the lower classes of those above them, and this desire to climb by upsetting those who are on top—not by the stair-way of merit and work but by the

y tierra, árboles y casas, montes y valles se dirigen. Allí los pájaros madrugadores gorjean lo mismo que en las alamedas del Retiro sobre las parejas de novios; el sol, padre de toda belleza, esparce por allí los mismos prodigios de forma y color que en las aldeas y ciudades, y el propio airecillo picante que menea los árboles, que orea el campo, que estimula a los hombres al trabajo y lleva a todas partes la alegría, el buen apetito, la sazón y la salud, derrama también por todas las zonas del establecimiento su soplo vivificante. Las flores se abren, las moscas emprenden sus infinitos giros, las palomas se lanzan a sus remotos viajes atmosféricos; arriba y abajo cada cual cede al impulso excitante según su naturaleza. Los locos salen de los cuartos o dormitorios con sus fieros instintos poderosamente estimulados. Redoblan, en aquella hora del despertamiento general, sus acostumbrados dislates, hablan más alto, ríen más fuerte, se arrastran y se embrutecen más; algunos rezan, otros se admiran de que el sol haya salido de noche, aquél responde al lejano canto del gallo, éste saluda al loquero con urbanidad refinada; quién pide papel y tinta para escribir la carta, ¡la indispensable carta del día! quién se lanza a la carrera, huyendo de un perseguidor que aparece montado en el caballo del día, y todo aquel carnavalesco mundo comienza con brío su ordinaria existencia" (ibid., pp. 17–18).

[1] ". . . no tenía más idea que aparentar, aparentar, y ser persona notable . . ." (ibid., p. 31).

ladder of intrigue or violence, pushing, so to say, always pushing. . . ." [1]

It is, however, a weakness which eventually proves to be Isidora's undoing. She is the first of the series of discontented, ill-balanced and extravagant women to whom Galdós introduces us in *Las Novelas Contemporáneas*. While she is unburdening her troubles to Canencia, the lunatic, Tomás Rufete is lying mortally ill in another part of the building. He dies before she can be summoned to his bedside, and the news of his death is brought to her by a friend of her childhood, now a medical student, one Augusto Miquís —who does not disguise his satisfaction at the renewal of the friendship.

Isidora returns to her godfather's house, where she is now living, and spends the night in restless anticipation of the visit she must pay on the following day to her aunt, Encarnación Guillén, "La Sanguijuelera," who is taking charge of her brother, Mariano. One of the most curious traits in Isidora's character is her abnormally vivid imagination: "Her imagination would, in a very vivid manner, call up events before they passed into reality. If she expected something interesting to happen at a given time—a call, an interview, a spectacle, an entertainment—these occurrences took on in her mind shapes of extraordinray clarity and colour, enacting themselves with their scenes, places, views, individuals, figures, attitudes and language" [2]; and, we are told, she lives an intense internal life

[1] ". . . La ambición, el afán de engrandecimiento, la envidia que los bajos tienen de los altos, y eso de querer subir atropellando a los que están arriba, no por la escalera del mérito y del trabajo, sino por la escala suelta de la intriga, o de la violencia, como si dijéramos, empujando, empujando . . ." (ibid.).

[2] "Tenía la costumbre de representarse en su imaginación, de una manera muy viva, los acontecimientos antes de que fueran efectivos. Si esperaba para determinada hora un suceso cualquiera que la

of her own which is quite independent of externalities.[1] She is also acutely sensitive and prone to exaggerate the significance of her impressions: "In addition to the gift of a vivid imagination, she had the faculty of intensifying her impressions and, at times, of exaggerating them enormously, so that those things which her senses pronounced to be large were immediately apparent to her mind as colossal. Anything small became infinitesimal; anything ugly, revolting; anything pretty, divine, and beautiful beyond conception."[2] She is in fact, on the border-line between the normal and the abnormal; a neurotic with a bad family record—a typical "naturalistic" heroine. She feels an intense aversion to the environment in which she has been brought up—and especially detests the low quarter of Madrid where her aunt carries on her hardware business: "It was neither a village nor yet a town; it was a rag torn from the capital, cut off and discarded in the interests of hygiene, that it might not corrupt the centre."[3] Encarnación Guillén has, however, seen better days. She blames the Rufete family for her misfortunes, and has no patience with

interesase, visita, entrevista, escena, diversión, desde medio día o media noche antes, el suceso tomaba en su mente formas de extraordinario relieve y color, desarrollándose con sus cuadros, lugares, perspectivas, personas, figuras, actitudes y lenguaje . . ." (cap. ii., p. 40).

[1] Vide cap. iv., p. 63. "It was a second life encased within her corporeal life, a life created by her imagination; vigorous, complete, not a single detail bring omitted." ["Era una segunda vida encajada en la vida fisiológica y que se desarrollaba potente, construída por la imaginación, sin que faltase una pieza, ni un cabo, ni un accesorio."]

[2] "Tenía, juntamente con el don de imaginar fuerte, la propiedad de extremar sus impresiones, recargándolas a veces hasta lo sumo; y así, lo que sus sentidos declaraban grande, su mente lo trocaba al punto en colosal; lo pequeño se le hacía minúsculo, y lo feo o bonito enormemente horroroso, o divino sobre toda ponderación" (cap. ii., p. 41).

[3] "Aquello no era aldea ni tampoco ciudad; era una piltrafa de capital, cortada y arrojada por vía de limpieza para que no corrompiera el centro" (ibid.).

her niece's aristocratic airs. When Isidora haughtily inquires
whether her brother Mariano has been put to school, "La
Sanguijuelera" is unable to contain her wrath. Mariano, she
says, is "a walking purgatory,"[1] and is far better out of
mischief, at work in her shop. When Isidora protests that she
is of noble birth and that it is not fitting for her brother to be
an uneducated boor, Encarnación gives her a good berating
for her pains![2] The scenes between Encarnación and her
niece are among the liveliest and most entertaining in Las
Novelas Contemporáneas. "La Sanguijuelera" is an undeniably
Spanish figure, owing nothing to any foreign writer.

Augusto Miquís, who has by this time fallen violently in
love with Isidora, is scarcely more sympathetic to the latter's
ambitions than is her aunt. He laughs at her defence of the
aristocracy—"The best people in the country, fine people,
decent people, rich people; the class which owns things; which
has power, knowledge"[3]—and her pretensions to noble birth.
His erratic genius inclines him towards all that is anti-tradi-
tional and subversive of the existing social scheme: "He was
attracted by all the very latest theories—especially when they
were in conflict with tradition. Transformism in the natural
sciences and federalism in politics won him over completely"[4];
and he never misses an opportunity, when on an excursion
with Isidora, to ridicule the snobbery which he sees around
them. His comment upon the crowds which gather in the
streets on a public holiday is typical: "Here, on public

[1] "Un purgatorio saltando" (ibid., p. 45).
[2] Cap. iii., p. 61.
[3] "La gente principal del país, la gente fina, decente, rica; la que
tiene, la que puede, la que sabe" (cap. iv., p. 89).
[4] "Todas las teorías novísimas le cautivaban, mayormente cuando
eran enemigas de la tradición, El transformismo en ciencias naturales
y el federalismo en política le ganaron por entero" (cap. iv., p. 71).

holidays, you will see every class in society. They come here to stare at one another, to size one another up and to mark the respective distances between each other for purposes of attack. It's a question of getting upon the next rung of the ladder. You will see many families of fashion who are on the verge of starvation. You will see people dressed up in their Sunday best—the cream of vulgarity—straining to appear something other than they are. You will also see careless people dressed in the fashion of six years ago. You will even see landladies disguised as persons of rank, and milliners' assistants trying to look like young ladies. All rub shoulders, all tolerate one another, for here equality reigns. People are no longer jealous of illustrious names, but rather of material comforts. As everyone is insanely anxious to get into a better position, they begin by looking as though they were in it already. Imitation whets the appetite. They want all that they haven't got, and there's not a single 'number one' but wishes he could be elevated to the rank of the 'twos.' The 'twos' want to look like 'threes'; the 'threes' make believe they are 'fours'; the 'fours' say 'But we are "fives,"' and so *ad infinitum*."[1] Isidora, however, does not heed this second warning as to the misery which awaits the

[1] "Aquí, en días de fiesta, verás a todas las clases sociales. Vienen a observarse, a medirse, y a ver las respectivas distancias que hay entre cada una, para asaltarse. El caso es subir al escalón inmediato. Verás muchas familias elegantes que no tienen qué comer. Verás gente dominguera que es la fina crema de la cursilería, reventando por parecer otra cosa. Verás también despreocupados que visten con seis modas de atraso. Verás hasta las patronas de huéspedes disfrazadas de personas de rango, y las costureras queriendo pasar por señoritas. Todos se codean y se toleran todos, porque reina la igualdad. No hay ya envidia de nombres ilustres, sino de comodidades. Como cada cual tiene ganas rabiosas de alcanzar una posición superior, principia por aparentarla. Las improvisaciones estimulan el apetito. Lo que no se tiene se pide, y no hay un solo número uno que no quiera elevarse a la categoría de dos. El dos se quiere hacer pasar por tres; el tres hace creer que es cuatro; el cuatro dice: 'Si yo soy cinco,' y así sucesivamente" (cap. iv., p. 90).

social climber. She is overjoyed when she receives a letter from "El Marqués viudo de Saldeoro" announcing his intention of calling upon her at an early date. He is one of the distinguished noblemen to whom her uncle, the canon, has written concerning her claim to the Aransis property; and upon the slender basis of this letter Isidora's vivid imagination builds a castle of romance.

Leaving Isidora to her dreams, we are now taken back to the domain of "La Sanguijuelera" and hear more concerning her incorrigible nephew—whom, on account of his naughtiness, she has nicknamed "Pecado." After a vivid description of his misdoings as a street-urchin and his games with "Zarapicos" and "Gonzalete," his two friends, we learn how, as the result of a brawl in which he wounds "Zarapicos," he falls into the hands of the Civil Guard. The news comes as a severe blow to Isidora—who, in view of the marquis' letter, has been deliriously happy: "Everything she saw appeared delicious, enchanting, magnificent, or, from whatever point of view, interesting. Even a hearse, which she saw as she was leaving the house, impressed her as being sumptuous rather than gloomy." [1] She is convinced that her claims will be recognised —"It couldn't be otherwise, for what is just is just, and God can't want injustice, and if I were not in the eyes of the world what I should be, or rather what I *am* in my own eyes, it would be an injustice, a barbarity . . ." [2]—and she puts any doubts

[1] "Nada veía que no fuera para ella precioso, seductor, magnífico, o por cualquier concepto interesante, y hasta un carro de muertos que encontró al salir de la casa, más que por fúnebre, le chocó por suntuoso" (cap. vii., p. 133).

[2] "No podía ser de otra manera, porque lo justo, justo es, y Dios no puede querer cosas injustas, y si yo no fuera ante el mundo la que debo ser, o mejor dicho, lo que soy ante mil, resultaría una injusticia, una barbaridad . . ." (ibid., p. 134).

to rest by reflecting that: "books are full of similar cases! How many times have I not read my own story!" [1] She must celebrate in some way her forthcoming social apotheosis; so she spends all the money she has upon a new outfit! As Galdós wittily remarks: "To her, as to all spendthrifts (whose mental organisation with reference to arithmetic marks them as a distinct species in the human genus), the figures on the credit side always appeared enormous, and those on the debit side excessively feeble and insignificant. This race of spenders would involve humanity in gigantic catastrophes if the race of misers, created by the law of equilibrium, did not counterbalance it." [2]

It is time, however, as the author reminds us, for us to meet "one of the chief figures in this truthful and analytical history" [3]—Don José de Relimpio y Sastre. His portrait is worth reproducing here: "His little melon-coloured moustache, of a clear, moist golden hue; his eyes like two grapes, bland and amorous; his round, fresh, smiling face, with its two faded, rosy cheeks; his complacent glance, his complacent bearing, his whole person cast in the mould of complacency itself (human clay for which the Creator has very little use) went to make up that lump of insipid futility, that packet of sweetmeats, which among men was labelled José Relimpio

[1] "Los libros están llenos de casos semejantes. Yo he leído mi propia historia tantas veces . . ." (ibid., p. 135).
[2] "Como todos los gastadores (cuya organización mental para la Aritmética les hace formar un grupo aparte en la especie humana), veía siempre engrosadas las cifras del activo, y atrozmente flacas e insignificantes las del pasivo. Este grupo de los derrochadores arrastraría a la humanidad a grandes catástrofes, si no lo contrapesara el grupo de los avaros, creado por las leyes del equilibrio" (ibid., p. 138).
[3] "Una de las principales figuras de esta historia de verdad y análisis" (cap. viii., p. 141).

y Sastre. . . . He was the best man in the world. He was an utterly useless individual." [1]

Don José is a constant source of irritation to his energetic wife, Doña Laura, whose slender patrimony "he spent in a variety of pleasing escapades." [2] His only interests in life are book-keeping and gallantry: both in theory rather than in practice. The Relimpio family subsist mainly upon Doña Laura's small income, together with the contribution which the two daughters, Emilia and Leonor, make to the general exchequer. Melchor, the son of the house, "fresh from the womb of *Alma Mater*, as devoid of knowledge as he was full of pretension," [3] does not contribute a penny, for he is not yet a wage-earner. The University has taught him only to spend money, and with this his parents, confident that Fame has marked him out for her own, supply him as often as they are able. For a time he cultivates spiritualism, and "he came to acquire those obstinate convictions found only in the devotees of the more preposterous cults." [4] Spiritualism, however, he soon abandons in favour of pursuits which hold out greater prospects of financial gain, for: "He was not rich, but he had to appear rich; he had, that is, to dress as a rich man, frequent the company of rich men. It is cruel that, while unequal in

---

[1] "El bigotito de cabello de ángel, de un dorado claro y húmedo; los ojos como dos uvas, blandos y amorosos; la cara arrebolada, fresca y risueña, con dos pómulos teñidos de color rosa, marchita; el mirar complaciente, la actitud complaciente, y todo él labrado en la pasta misma de la complacencia (barro humano, del cual no hace ya mucho uso el Creador), formaban aquel conjunto de inutilidad y dulzura, aquel ramillete de confitería, que llevaba entre los hombres el letrero de José Relimpio y Sastre. . . . Era el hombre mejor del mundo. Era un hombre que no servía para nada" (ibid).

[2] Gastó . . . en varias suertes de amabilidades (ibid., p. 142).

[3] ". . . recién salido del vientre de la madre Universidad, tan desnudo de saber como vestido de presunción . . ." (ibid., p. 145).

[4] "Llegó a adquirir esas convicciones tenaces que sólo se encuentran en los prosélitos de los sistemas más absurdos" (ibid., p. 161).

fortune, we are all obliged to be equals in matters sartorial."[1] He formulates all kinds of projects to obtain the money he requires, but forgets "the simplest way of all—to work at some craft, profession or trade that he might earn, peseta by peseta, a certain amount of money."[2] Isidora is the only member of the family who remains unimpressed by his fantastic schemes. She fancies herself to be out of place in the bourgeois Relimpio household, and offends her cousins by her airs of superiority.

After this glimpse of middle-class life, we are transported to the palace of the Aransis family—"a building vulgar in appearance, like all aristocratic houses erected during the seventeenth century; houses which seem to correspond to the idea that Madrid was a provisional capital,"[3] where the marquesa is spending a few days prior to her departure for Andalusia. She has decided to reopen her dead daughter's room (which has been closed for nine years) as a token that her child is now forgiven the dishonour which she has brought upon the house. For nine years the marquess, a *grande dame* —"forged on the Calderonian anvil with the hammer of social prestige by the horny hands of religion"[4]—has not mentioned her daughter's name. While, a prey to bitter memories, she gazes at her child's portrait, her grandson, a marvellous pianist, is playing a Beethoven symphony in a neighbouring

[1] "Él no era rico, pero era preciso parecerlo; es decir, vestirse como los ricos, tratar con ricos. Es cruel eso de que todos seamos distintos por la fortuna y tengamos que ser iguales por la ropa" (ibid.).

[2] "La más sencilla de todas, que era trabajar en cualquier arte, profesión u oficio, con lo que podía ganar, desde una peseta para arriba, cualquier dinero" (ibid., p. 163).

[3] "Un edificio de apariencia vulgar, como todas las moradas señoriles construídas en el siglo XVII., las cuales parecen responder a la idea de que Madrid fuese una corte provisional" (cap. ix., p. 165).

[4] ". . . Forjada en el yunque Calderoniano con el martillo de la dignidad social, por las manos duras de la religión" (ibid., p. 174).

room: "It was that elegy of human anguish which, now and then, by a queer caprice of style, uses the language of irony. Now the festive chords yielded to the most pathetic tones which the voice of despair itself could utter. A single idea, as simple as it was heartbreaking, was revealed in that whirlpool of a thousand subsidiary themes, losing itself in the most capricious variety of notes that phantasy could conceive, only to reappear, on the instant, transfigured. If, in the minor, that idea was clad in darkness, now, in the major, it appeared bathed in resplendent light. Day succeeded night, and light succeeded shadow in that outpouring in music of emotions whose very vagueness deepened their intensity . . ."[1] And, again, as she reflects upon the death of her daughter "at peace with God, saying her prayers and kissing the Sacred Image of Our Redeemer,"[2] the music seems to echo her inmost thoughts: "One might well have believed that a soul in anguish was querying its destiny from the hollow of the tomb, and that a celestial voice from the clouds was answering in accents of peace and hope. The *motif* was at rest upon soft chords, and the harmonious background had a certain elasticity which gently lulled the melodious phrase. To this succeeded repetitions, now faint, now lively; varying shadows

[1] "Era la elegía de los dolores humanos, que a veces, por misterioso capricho del estilo, usa el lenguaje del sarcasmo. Luego las expresiones festivas se trocaban en los acentos más patéticos que pudiera echar de sí la voz misma de la desesperación. Una sola idea, tan sencilla como desgarradora, aparecía entre el vértigo de mil ideas secundarias, y se perdía luego en la más caprichosa variedad de diseños que puede concebir la fantasía, para reaparecer al instante transformada. Si en el tono menor estaba aquella idea vestida de tinieblas, ahora en el mayor se presentaba bañada en luz resplandeciente. El día sucedía a la noche y la claridad a las sombras en aquella expresión del sentimiento por el órgano musical, tanto más intenso cuanto más vago . . ." (ibid., p. 172).

[2] "Reconciliada con Dios, recitando oraciones y besando la santa imagen de Nuestro Redentor" (ibid., p. 175).

cast on all sides by the theme in its solemn development. To this majestic simplicity succeeded the learned, labyrinthine forms of the canon, and thereafter the beautiful theme was multiplied, and out of so many patterns of the same thing there was formed a glorious tapestry which, saying much to the emotions and little to the reason, uniting the charm of pure mysticism with the learned subtleties of theology, produced a strange and unique effect. Suddenly a modulation, like the blow of an axe, changed—together with the tone—the number, the language, the meaning. An erotic strophe, instinct with pastoral simplicity, then followed, and was succeeded by a festive rondeau, bristling with difficulties, with the eccentricities of a juggler and the contortions of a gymnast. Donning a gay mask, it rattled a tambourine. As a monkey scrambles on to its perch, it ascended, with ludicrous contortions, the highest notes of the scale; it descended at one bound the abyss of solemn chords, where it mimicked the mutterings of an old man and the obscenities of a friar. It dragged itself painfully along the middle keys . . . gave a sudden leap, heralding pleasure, dancing, intoxication and forgetfulness of work and sorrow." [1]

[1] "Bien podría creerse que un alma dolorida preguntaba por su destino desde el hueco de una tumba, y que una voz celestial contestaba desde las nubes con acentos de paz y esperanza. Descansaba el motivo sobre blandos acordes, y este fondo armónico tenía cierta elasticidad vaga que sopesaba muellemente la frase melódica. A ésta seguían remedos, ahora pálidos, ahora vivos, sombras diferentes que iba proyectando la idea por todos lados en su grave desarrollo. Las sabias formas laberínticas del canon sucedieron a la sencillez soberana, de donde resultó que la hermosa idea se multiplicaba, y que de tantos ejemplares de una misma cosa formábase un bello trenzado de peregrino efecto, por hablar mucho al sentimento y un poco al raciocinio, juntando los encantos de la mística pura a los retruécanos de la erudición teológica. Bruscamente, una modulación semejante a un hachazo variaba, con el tono, el número, el lenguaje, el sentido. Estrofa amorosa, impregnada de candor pastoril, aparecía luego, y después el festivo rondó, erizado

Meanwhile Isidora, in the company of Augusto and Don José, pays a visit to the Aransis mansion—the lodge-keeper, Alonso, who is a friend of D. Pedro Miquís, acting as their guide. Isidora's head is completely turned by the splendours of the palace, and her ambition to establish her claim becomes henceforth an obsession. She can, however, do nothing without the support of some influential person, and she finds a partner in one Joaquín Pez, eldest son of Don Manuel José Ramón del Pez—"leading light in the Ministry, beacon of government offices, star of second magnitude in politics, father of judicial proceedings, son of his own works, brother of two confraternities, son-in-law of his father-in-law, Señor Don Juan Pipaón, indispensable on commissions, necessary at meetings, the best head in the world for speeding up or delaying negotiations, the best hand for drawing up a scheme for a loan, the keenest nose for scenting a deal, servant of himself and his fellow-men, encyclopædia of political jests, indefatigable apostle of that sacred routine upon which the noble edifice of our glorious national apathy is raised; a machine for making laws, devising regulations, issuing edicts, and fulfilling instructions; first milker, by hereditary right, of the udders of Budgets; a man, in fact, whom you and I know as we know the fingers of our own hands, because he is a generation rather than a man, an era rather than a person, a caste, a tribe, half Madrid,

de dificultades, con extravagancias de juglar y esfuerzos de gimnasta. Enmascarándose festivamente, agitaba cascabeles. Se subía, con gestos risibles, a las más agudas notas de la escala, como sube el mono por una percha, descendía de un brinco al pozo de los acordes graves, donde simulaba refunfuños de viejo y groserías de fraile. Se arrastraba doliente en los medios imitando los gemidos burlescos del muchacho herido, y saltaba de súbito pregonando el placer, el baile, la embriaguez y el olvido de penas y trabajos" (ibid., pp. 175-6).

a summary and compendium of half Spain rather than an individual." [1]

In the history of the Pez family and all its ramifications,[2] Galdós attacks with mordant irony the national evils of "caciquismo" and nepotism. "Influence is among us a second Providence; it is equivalent to what other and less discreet people call luck, good fortune " [3]—and Manuel José Ramón Pez is the arbiter of many destinies: "The magistrates, judges, and fiscal officials of Pez stock distributed throughout Spain were to be counted by hundreds. In order that there might be a member of this omniscient and blessed family in every hierarchy, there was also a pisciform bishop, and even twelve canons and beneficed ecclesiastics who fattened upon the banks of Church and Clergy." [4]

[1] "Lumbrera de la Administración, fanal de las oficinas, astro de segunda magnitud en la política, padre de los expedientes, hijo de sus obras, hermano de dos cofradías, yerno de su suegro el Sr. D. Juan de Pipaón, indispensable en las comisiones, necesario en las juntas, la primer cabeza del orbe para acelerar o detener un asunto, la mejor mano para trazar el plan de un empréstito, la nariz más fina para olfatear un negocio, servidor de sí mismo y de los demás, enciclopedia de chistes políticos, apóstol nunca fatigado de esas venerandas rutinas sobre que descansa el noble edificio de nuestra gloriosa apatía nacional, maquinilla de hacer leyes, cortar reglamentos, picar ordenanzas y vaciar instrucciones, ordeñador mayor por juro de heredad de las ubres del presupuesto, hombre, en fin, que vosotros y yo conocemos como los dedos de nuestra propia mano, porque más que hombre es una generación, y más que persona es una era, y más que personaje es una casta, una tribu, un medio Madrid, cifra y compendio de una media España" (cap. xii., pp. 195-6).

[2] Vide chapter xii., "Los Peces (sermón)"; the mock-heroic tone of this burlesque "sermon" is quite Dickensian.

[3] "La recomendación es entre nosotros una segunda Providencia; equivale a lo que otros pueblos menos expedientescos llaman suerte, fortuna" (ibid., p. 197).

[4] "Los magistrados y jueces y promotores fiscales del género Pez se contaban por centenares distribuídos en toda la España. Para que en todas las jerarquías hubiera algún miembro de esta omnisciente familia de bendición, también había un obispo pisciforme, y hasta doce canónigos y beneficiados, que pastaban en el banco del Culto y Clero" (ibid., pp. 197-8).

Joaquín Pez, Manuel's eldest son, is none other than "El Marqués viudo de Saldeoro"—of whom we have already heard as the writer of a letter to Isidora.

He is a sentimental Don Juan, thirty-four years of age; and he sees in the preposterous story of Isidora's birth an opportunity for a possible conquest. He calls upon her: "On the first day he thought her pretty, on the second, very pretty, and on the third, exquisite, whereupon he marked her down as his own." [1] His task, however, is by no means easy; and after one or two repulses he decides to attempt a *coup d'état*. He invites Isidora to visit him—and interviews her alone. After a few carefully veiled remarks as to the advisability of her taking a house in a better quarter of Madrid, he reveals his true intentions. A violent scene ensues, and Isidora threatens to scream for help if he does not open the door. He then allows her to go—with a word of abuse which cuts her to the quick, for she cannot help being in love with him—if only on account of his exalted social position!

Their quarrel, however, is soon patched up. Joaquín apologises for his conduct and promises to do all he can to persuade the Marquesa de Aransis into granting Isidora an interview. In this he eventually succeeds; but without profit to Isidora, who receives a severe rebuff from the marquesa. She resolves, however, to take the matter into the courts—with the help of Joaquín Pez, who now, when Isidora is smarting under a sense of injustice, is closer to victory than he has ever been.

Part ii. of this novel opens with a reference to the political changes of the period: "The Republic, 'Cantonalismo,' the *coup d'état* of 3 January, the Restoration—all these forms of

---

[1] ". . . encontróla guapa el primer día, el segundo muy guapa, y el tercero deliciosísima, con lo que la diputó por suya" (ibid., p. 210).

government, following one upon another like the pages of a history book idly turned, passed away before we had any information or news concerning the two children of Tomás Rufete." [1] The author, however, falling one day a victim to a bad attack of neuralgia, calls in Augusto Miquís, now a famous doctor, and from him learns that Isidora is living in the Calle de Hortaleza and that she has a son—"a kind of monster, what is called a macrocephalic, that is to say he has a huge, deformed head." [2] From the description which follows of her house—"bought *in solidum* by Joaquín at a liquidation"— we gather that the "Marqués viudo de Saldeoro's" victory has cost him dear! In a long apostrophe to Isidora,[3] Galdós reveals the extent of the latter's extravagance. She is incapable of appreciating the value of money, and is well on the way towards ruining her benefactor. After a desperate attempt to borrow from her aunt, "La Sanguijuelera," she is forced to abandon the house to the mercy of the bailiffs. Then, after a month of poverty at Don José de Relimpio's, she accepts the protection of another lover, Alejandro Sánchez Botín, in the hope that with his money she may eventually win her lawsuit and take what she conceives to be her right place in society. Botín, however, soon realises that he is being used as a convenience and, having discovered that Isidora is unfaithful to him, turns her, penniless, out of his house. She soon finds herself, her child, and Don José completely destitute, and decides to appeal to Miquís. The latter advises her to marry

[1] "La República, el Cantonalismo, el golpe de Estado del 3 de enero, la Restauración, tantas formas políticas, sucediéndose con rapidez, como las páginas de un manual de Historia recorridas por el fastidio, pasaron sin que llegara a nosotros noticia ni referencia alguna de los dos hijos de Tomás Rufete" (*La Desheredada*, part ii. cap. i., p. 5).

[2] "Es algo monstruoso; lo que llamamos un *macrocéfalo*, es decir, que tiene la cabeza muy grande, deforme" (ibid., p. 6).

[3] Cap. ii., pp. 19–22.

L

her brother's employer, one Juan Bou, a master-lithographer—
a vulgar, but well-intentioned individual who has fallen
violently in love with her and whose offer of marriage she has
already once refused.[1] Isidora, however, pins her faith to the
lawsuit—and when that fails, as it does, her belief in the justice
of the universe is lost. After a wild and fruitless attempt to
petition the king, she resigns herself to her fate and to the only
career which can supply her with the luxuries she has come to
regard as her birthright. "The prey was devoured, and shortly
afterwards all was calm upon the surface of the social waters." [2]
This is the epitaph which Galdós writes upon her death to
society.

In spite of its prolixity and incoherence *La Desheredada*
marks an advance upon *Las Novelas de la Primera Época*.
The character-drawing is brilliant; the humour almost
Dickensian in its drollery—but without the Dickensian
exaggeration—and the style, if occasionally affected, rounded
and mature. Nowhere have the alleged failings of the author's
country—"caciquismo," "abulia" and nepotism, been more
wittily satirised. Isidora's downfall is due mainly to the fact
that she lacks the will to *work*. She expects the sweets of life to
fall into her lap unearned; and when her time of disillusion
comes she has not the strength of character to build up her
life again upon a sounder basis.

In the Pez family are exemplified all those vices which have
been held up by the "generation of 1898" and their successors
as the cause of Spain's decay. Modern reformers could find no
better text upon which to base their gospel of energy and effort
than *La Desheredada*. Indeed, as we shall have occasion to

[1] Vide cap. ix., pp. 126–7.
[2] "La presa fué devorada, y poco después en la superficie social todo
estaba tranquilo" (cap. xviii., p. 279).

remark later, the modern "advanced" school of thought in Spain undoubtedly owes much to Galdós and *Las Novelas Contemporáneas.*

El Amigo Manso, which immediately follows *La Desheredada,* is, technically, a far better novel than its predecessor; but it is comparatively limited in scope. It suggests, indeed, *Las Novelas de la Primera Época* rather than *Las Novelas Contemporáneas* and is, in many ways, one of the most typically Spanish of Galdós' works. The hero, Máximo Manso, is cast in the now familiar mould which gave us León Roch and Pepe Rey. He is a cultured agnostic, a university teacher by profession, who sees in human reason the only trustworthy guide through life. He has spent most of his youth in the company of his mother—a woman of rank and education—who makes great sacrifices in order to give her son the academic training which eventually brings him the coveted chair. His mother's death upsets the equilibrium of an almost incredibly well-ordered existence; and Máximo, after a period of unrest, settles down to bachelor life in a house in the Calle del Espíritu Santo. Here he makes the acquaintance of a neighbour, Doña Javiera—an intelligent, vivacious and ambitious bourgeoise who keeps a tripe shop. The dialogue between Máximo and Javiera in chapter iii.[1] is brilliantly executed.

As an outcome of this acquaintanceship, Máximo undertakes the education of Javiera's son, Manuel Peña, a youth of great abilities who lacks, however, the power of application which alone can bring them to fruition. A sincere affection grows up between master and pupil. The cordiality of their relationship is, however, eventually threatened by the fact that both fall in love with the same girl—Irene, adopted daughter of

---

[1] *El Amigo Manso* (1910 ed.), cap. iii., p. 19

Máximo's aunt, Doña Cándida. Máximo, owing to his ignorance of life and human nature, is the loser in the contest for Irene's heart. He feels his loss bitterly; but eventually accepts his fate with philosophical resignation.

As a secondary theme, we have the story of the settlement in Madrid of a wealthy South American family—that of Máximo's brother, José María Manso—and of the latter's efforts to gain a footing in society. At the "reunions" in the home of José María Manso we meet many entertaining characters—including some old friends, the Tellerías, D. Ramón María Pez, Federico Cimarra and Miquís. El Amigo Manso is most remarkable as a novel of character. Apart from the interest of the main theme, which deals with the effect of a rude contact with reality upon a sensitive and scholarly temperament, the book is remarkable for many inimitable character-sketches. One of the most entertaining figures in the Galdosian hierarchy is Doña Cándida, widow of García Grande. When her husband was alive she outdid even the Marquesa de Tellería in extravagance; but now that he is dead, and his fortune spent, she has to be content with memories. She still talks as though she had limitlesss wealth at her disposal: "Twenty years after her husband's death, and at a time when, bereft of youth, beauty, property, income, she was practically living upon charity, Doña Cándida's bombastic vanity and pompous, boastful chatter was intolerable." [1] Máximo puts up with her on account of her quondam friendship with his mother; but she is indeed a thorn in his flesh. She is always offering to sell him worthless articles—"for his collection"—

---

[1] "Viente años después de muerto su marido, y cuando doña Cándida, sin juventud, sin belleza, sin casa ni rentas, vivía poco menos que de limosna, no se podía aguantar su enfático orgullo, ni su charla llena de pomposos embustes" (cap. v., p. 36).

at what she maintains is an absurdly low price: "Look here—
what do you think they'd give me for this? It's a fine piece.
I know the Marquesa de X. would give ten or twelve *duros*,
but if you'd like it for your collection you can have it for four,
and thank me. See how I sacrifice my interests to you . . .
it's atrocious!" [1] This is merely her way of asking him for a
loan which, she always asserts, she will repay when she has
sold her "property in Zamora"—a very special estate for
which she is always, according to her story, besieged with
munificent offers. Even Doña Cándida, however, with all her
snobbery and vulgarity, is preferable, in Máximo's eyes, to
the odious poet whom he meets at one of José María's reunions:
"He was one of those who, in the numerous class to which he
belonged, might, with great leniency, be given the eighth
or ninth place. Twenty-five years old, pert, easy in his bearing
(with a name ten words long, and a large and various repertory
of compositions scattered through the albums of the second-
rate), arrogance and rickets made up three-quarters of his
personality, which was completed by his high collar, yellowish
beard, and a voice, harsh and peevish, as though impious hands
were squeezing his windpipe. This distant connection of the
Muses (I do not hesitate to put it bluntly) exasperated me.
The absurdly high opinion which he had of himself, his total
ignorance, and the impudence with which he would talk upon
matters of art and criticism, nauseated me and made me feel
thoroughly ill. . . ." [2]

[1] "A ver, ¿cuánto te parece que darán por esto? Es hermosa pieza.
Sé que la marquesa de X daría diez o doce duros; pero si lo quieres
para tu coleccióncita, tómalo por cuatro, y dame las gracias. Ya ves
que por ti sacrifico mis intereses . . . una cosa atroz" (ibid., p. 37).
[2] "Era de estos que entre los de su numerosa clase podía ser colocado,
favoreciéndole mucho, en octavo o noveno lugar. Veinticinco años,
desparpajo, figura escueta, un nombre muy largo formado con diez

Máximo tells us how the man's personality was expressed in his visiting cards, which gave the impression that "Francisco de Paula de la Costa y Sainz del Bardal," for such was the poet's name, ruled the roost at the Government department in which, as a matter of fact, he was an insignificant and underpaid clerk.[1]

The book concludes strangely. After his death, Máximo Manso delivers, from the next world, a homily upon the fate of various characters in the novel. This, however, is quite in keeping with the whimsicality of the opening chapters—where Máximo assures us that he has no real existence but is merely a fictitious being called into shadowy life by an author who has " already written thirty volumes,"[2] and who has confided to him that he has in view "the idea of perpetrating a deliberate fictional crime in connection with the great question of education."[3]

El Amigo Manso is, however, more than a treatise upon education. It is one of the most subtle and brilliant novels of character in the Spanish language.

In *El Doctor Centeno*, its immediate successor, Galdós embarks upon what Blanco García accurately describes as "a study in psychological analysis which is at times so minute

palabras; un desmedido repertorio de composiciones varias, distribuídas por todos los álbums de la cursilería; soberbia y raquitismo componían las tres cuartas partes de su persona: lo demás lo hacían cuello estirado, barbas amarillentas y una voz agria y dificultosa, como si manos impías le estuvieran apretando el gaznate. Aquel pariente lejano de las Musas (no vacilo en decirlo groseramente) me reventaba. La idea pomposa que de sí mismo tenía, su ignorancia absoluta y el desenfado con que hablaba de cuestiones de arte y crítica me causaban mareos y un malestar grande en todo el cuerpo . . ." (cap. xii., pp. 80–1).

[1] Vide ibid., p. 81, where the visiting-card is reproduced.
[2] "Había escrito ya treinta volúmenes" (cap. i., p. 7).
[3] ". . . la idea de perpetrar un detenido crimen novelesco, sobre el gran asunto de la educación" (ibid.).

as to cause fatigue," [1] for the story is almost devoid of plot and action. In it we make a closer acquaintance with Felipe Centeno, whom we met in *Marianela* and *La Familia de León Roch*. He runs away from home to seek his fortune in Madrid, where he falls in with Alejandro Miquís (brother of the Augusto of *La Desheredada*) and his friends, then students at the university. They take pity upon the little urchin and introduce him to Don Pedro Polo y Cortés, a dissolute cleric who, in partnership with José Ido—"education's obscure and unknown martyr" [2]—runs (but on milder lines than Mr. Squeers) a Spanish Dotheboys Hall. All that concerns the "education" of the unfortunate "Doctor" Centeno (so called by way of ironical comment upon his stupidity) is of great interest as revealing the conditions prevalent in the educational world at this period. Polo has "drifted" into teaching because it is the only occupation which requires no previous training: "Any profession, however brief the preparation it demanded, and however easy, meant time and books, and family necessities did not admit of delay. There existed only one career or profession which he could attempt, and for which he could qualify in a short time. . . ." [3] In the early stages he finds his work arduous "for he had to learn at night what he was going to teach on the following day" [4]; and his mode of acquiring knowledge is as unintelligent as his method of imparting it:

---

[1] "Un dechado de análisis psicológico, que a veces se extrema hasta causar fatiga" (Vide Blanco García, op. cit., part ii., p. 502).

[2] ". . . el mártir obscuro y sin fama de la instrucción." *El Doctor Centeno* (1905 ed.), vol. i., p. 58.

[3] "Cualquier profesión, por breve y fácil que fuese, requería tiempo y libros, y la necesidad de familia no admitía espera. Una sola carrera o profesión existía que pudiera acometer y lograr en poco tiempo . . ." (ibid., p. 64).

[4] "Porque tenía que aprender por las noches lo que había de enseñar al día siguiente" (ibid., p. 67).

"He taught everything . . . according to the method which he had employed in learning it; to put it more accurately, he taught nothing. What he did was to insert into the heads of his pupils—by a process which one might describe as 'cerebral injection'—a number of formulæ, definitions, rules, generalisations and scientific recipes. These remained inside in an undigested and fossilised state, encumbering the intelligence without giving it one atom of sustenance, and hindering the play of ideas—just as stones obstruct the conduit of a fountain." [1]

He resembles Mr. Squeers in the obvious delight which he takes in torturing the unfortunate youths committed to his care: ". . . This savage education went hand in hand with the idea of making a hole through which the intellectual pabulum, lacking within, might be inserted. The pinches inflicted by his steel-like fingers were as punctures in the skin through which injections of alkaloid knowledge from the text-books were made" [2]; but he is more conscientious than the terrible Yorkshire dominie, and his cruelty is the fruit not or a demoniacal sadism but of an honest conviction as to the truth of the old Spanish proverb, "la letra con sangre entra."

The greater part of the first volume of *El Doctor Centeno*

[1] "Todo lo enseñaba . . . según el método que él empleara en aprenderlo; mejor dicho, . . . no enseñaba nada: lo que hacía era introducir en la mollera de sus alumnos, por una operación que podríamos llamar *inyecto-cerebral*, cantidad de fórmulas, definiciones, reglas, generalidades y recetas científicas, que luego se quedaban dentro indigeridas y fosilizadas, embarazando la inteligencia sin darla un átomo de substancia ni dejar fluir las ideas propias, bien así como las piedras que obstruyen el conducto de una fuente" (*El Doctor Centeno*, id., pp. 67-8).

[2] "Esta cruel enseñanza iba acompañada de la idea de abrir un agujero por donde a la fuerza había de entrar el tarugo intelectual que allí dentro faltaba. Los pellizcos de sus acerados dedos eran como punturas por las cuales se hacían, al través de la piel, inyecciones de la sabiduría alcaloide de los libros de texto" (ibid., p. 69).

is taken up with the story of Polo's pedagogic activities and his relations with the daughters of his cousin, Sánchez y Emperador—Amparo and Refugio—of whom we are to hear more in *Tormento* and *La de Bringas*. After a brilliant character-study of Miquís' friend Federico Ruíz—"a pure Spaniard in his inconstancy, his sudden enthusiasms and his longing for renown" [1]—the volume closes with an account of how Felipe Centeno leaves the Polo family and becomes the servant of Alejandro Miquís. The opening chapters of the second part are especially interesting, describing, as they do, the boarding-house life of Madrid which Galdós knew so well. It is possible that he put a great deal of himself into Alejandro Miquís, law student and would-be dramatist, whose early ambitions are so unhappily thwarted. He certainly resembles the Galdós of student-days in his hatred of the profession for which he is studying: ". . . he hated the law. In his opinion intelligent human beings had produced nothing more detestable than this *jus*, this suspicious, prosaic, stereotyped conception which rules our lives, a conception hostile to passion, . . ." [2] and in his single-minded devotion to his art. The moral crisis which he undergoes also has a parallel in the career of Galdós, who, like Alejandro Miquís, soon abandoned the life of cafés and "tertulias" for an almost hermit-like retirement.[3] There is something, also, of Galdós in Alejandro's friend Arias Ortiz ——". . . an ardent admirer of Balzac, he had read practically all of that author's works and knew the characters of the

---

[1] "Era español puro en la inconstancia, en los afectos repentinos y en el deseo de renombre" (*El Doctor Centeno*, p. 161).

[2] ". . . odiaba el Derecho. Para él, la humanidad inteligente no había echado de sí cosa antipática que aquel *jus*, idea suspicaz, prosáica y reglamentadora de la vida; idea enemiga de la pasión" (ibid., vol. ii., p. 41).

[3] Vide ibid., vol. ii., p. 42, and Biographical Note, p. 12.

Comédie Humaine as though he had been personally acquainted with them." [1]

El Doctor Centeno is, indeed, chiefly interesting on account of its autobiographical element and as a satire upon certain aspects of the educational question.

In *Tormento*, Galdós gives us the history of Amparo Sánchez y Emperador. She is now an orphan and is obliged to earn her own living—which she does by acting as housekeeper, or rather general drudge, to the Bringas family. Rosalía Bringas, wife of the ineffable Don Francisco, vents all her petty spite and vulgar snobbery upon the unfortunate girl, whose life is intolerable until the arrival in Madrid of a South American cousin of the Bringas family—one Agustín Caballero—who, to Rosalía's extreme annoyance, falls violently in love with Amparo. He sees in the latter the unspoiled, domesticated type of woman for which he has long been searching in vain. Amparo, however, has not escaped corruption. An old intrigue with the dissolute priest Pedro Polo [2]—who seduced her when she was a mere girl—is reopened by the latter, who writes passionate letters imploring his "Tormento," as he calls her, to return to him. She is led by her weakness of character and fear of exposure into leading a double life. As a study in the fatal effects of vacillation *Tormento* is admirable. Amparo lacks the courage to tell Agustín, her fiancé, the truth—nor can she persuade herself to break with him. In the end she attempts suicide, but is frustrated by a servant. Agustín eventually comes to know of her relations with Polo, and, although he would have been willing to pardon her if she had

[1] ". . . muy devoto de Balzac, lo tenía casi completo, y a los personajes de la *Comedia Humana* conocía como si los hubiera tratado" (*El Doctor Centeno*, vol. ii., p. 59).
[2] Vide ibid.

been frank with him, cannot now face the prospect of making her his wife. She eventually consents—much to the disgust and chagrin of Rosalía—to become his mistress.

Despite a certain lack of coherency [1] which, as we have remarked, is noticeable in nearly all the *Novelas Contemporáneas*, *Tormento* is, both in its technique and its psychology, one of the best of the series. It is, indeed, one of the few novels of this group which do not err on the side of inordinate length. Confining himself in it to the study of a restricted environment, Galdós is able to concentrate upon the delineation of a comparatively small number of social types—and in no other novel does he succeed in producing in the reader a greater sense of the reality of his characters.

In Don Francisco de Bringas, of whom we hear more in *La de Bringas*, Galdós has immortalised a familiar metropolitan type, the conscientious, hard-working, unimaginative clerk whose life is bounded on the one side by the office and on the other by the domestic hearth: "He didn't know what a debt was; he had two religions, that of God and that of economy, and, that all might be perfect in so blessed a man, he dedicated most of his spare time to various domestic tasks of indisputable utility, wherein he demonstrated at once the keenness of his intelligence and the dexterity of his fingers. He had been a clerk since his salad days; his parents and grandparents had

---

[1] Orlando Lara y Pedraja regards this lack of coherency as the outstanding fault of both *Tormento* and *La de Bringas*. "The first thing which we notice in both productions is the lack of cohesion between the parts and the absence of subordination to one fact, one character, a nucleus, to anything, in fact. . . ." [". . . Lo primero que se nota en ambas producciones, es la falta de cohesión en las partes y de subordinación a un hecho, a un personaje, a un núcleo, a algo, en fin. . . ."]—Vide "*Revista de España*" (1884), *Novelas Españolas del año Literario*, vol. c., No. 399, p. 437. In our opinion, however, the criticism is less applicable to these novels than to many others of the series—e.g. *El Doctor Centeno* and the novels of the "last phase."

been clerks, and it is even thought that his great-great-grand-parents and their ancestors served in the Government offices of the Old and the New Worlds." [1]

He is completely lacking in initiative, has no ambitions, and finds his chief interest in household hobbies: "He had no ambition and, having no vices, he didn't even smoke. He was so industrious that, without the least effort and with absolute contentment, he not only did his own work, but also that of his chief—who was a solemn lazybones. He lost no time at home, and his mechanical gifts were so numerous that it would be no easy task to recount them all. Nature had endowed him with a variety of useful talents which enabled him to repair every kind of broken object. He even dared to try his skill upon watches that wouldn't go and toys from which, in the hands of the children, the mechanical virtue had departed. He made Nativities out of cork for Christmas, and toothpicks for every season of the year." [2]

In personal appearance, we are told, he resembles the great French historian Thiers: "It was the same round face; the

---

[1] "No sabía lo que era una deuda; tenía dos religiones, la de Dios y la del ahorro, y para que todo en tan bendito varón fuera perfecto, dedicaba muchos de sus ratos libres a diversos menesteres domésticos de indudable provecho, que demostraban así la claridad de su inteligencia como la destreza de sus manos. Empleado fué desde sus verdes años; empleados fueron sus padres y abuelos, y aun se cree que sus tatarabuelos y los ascendientes de éstos sirvieran en la administración de ambos mundos" (*Tormento* (1906 ed.), cap. ii., p. 15).

[2] "No sentía ambición, y por no tener vicios, ni siquiera fumaba. Era tan trabajador, que sin esfuerzo y contentísimo desempeñaba su trabajo y el de su jefe, un solemne haragán. En su casa no perdía el tiempo, y sus habilidades mecánicas eran tantas que no nos será fácil contarlas todas. Naturaleza puso en él útiles y variados talentos para componer toda suerte de objetos rotos . . . atrevíase hasta con los relojes que no querían andar, y con los juguetes que en manos de los chicos perdieron la virtud de su mecanismo. . . . Hacía nacimientos de corcho para Navidad, y palillos de dientes para todo el año" (ibid., p. 16).

same hooked nose; the thick, grey hair with its pyramidal tuft; the same broad and pleasant forehead; the same ironical expression, originating in the mouth, the eyes or the tuft —one doesn't quite know which; the same Roman profile. It was, moreover, the same figure, the same sturdy build. Bringas lacked only the keen glance and all that is peculiar to the physiognomy of the spirit—that which distinguishes the man of superior intelligence who can make history and write it from the ordinary man who was born to repair a lock or lay a carpet." [1]

When we learn that Bringas "wore gold spectacles and was clean-shaven," the picture is complete.

Further (and somewhat unnecessary) details of his character are given in *La de Bringas*, which continues the study of bourgeois domesticity initiated in *Tormento*. Galdós had almost exhausted his theme in the latter novel, and its successor has, therefore, the air of a work of supererogation.

The account of Bringas' indefatigable industry is excessively long,[2] and the book abounds in wearisome digressions. There is indeed considerable justification for Orlando Lara y Pedraja's mordant comment, "The fact is that he wanted to write another book, and everything is sacrificed to that end." [3]

[1] "Era la misma cara redonda; la misma nariz corva; el pelo gris, espeso y con su copete piriforme; la misma frente ancha y simpática; la misma expresión irónica, que no se sabe si proviene de la boca o de los ojos o del copete; el mismísimo perfil de romano abolengo. Era también el propio talle, la estatura rechoncha y firme. No faltaba en Bringas más que el mirar profundo y todo lo que es de la peculiar fisonomía del espíritu; faltaba lo que distingue al hombre superior, que sabe hacer la historia y escribirla del hombre común que ha nacido para componer una cerradura y clavar una alfombra" (ibid., pp. 20–1).

[2] The first three chapters of the book are devoted to a minute description of his labours upon a memento which he is constructing for his friend Manuel María José Pez.

[3] "Es que se ha querido hacer un libro más, y a este propósito se ha sacrificado vils." Vide Orlando Lara y Pedraja, op. cit., p. 443.

One cannot, however, agree with this critic when he maintains that the theme of *La de Bringas* is identical with that of *Tormento*. It is so only in so far as the domestic background and Don Francisco are concerned. The central figure, as the title indicates, is Rosalía, the mistress of the household, and the story tells of her downfall through extravagance and love of display. She is an addition to Galdós' portrait-gallery of unbalanced women; a friend of the Marquesa de Tellería,[1] who shares her proclivities. Rosalía is continually frustrated in her efforts to achieve social distinction by the meanness of her husband—who counts over every penny expended upon housekeeping. An attack of temporary blindness, the result of eye-strain incurred during his work upon the memento, renders Francisco incapable of exercising his usual vigilance in domestic matters. Rosalía is quick to take advantage of the situation, and she embarks upon a series of extravagant projects, which she endeavours to hide from her husband by means of various petty subterfuges. She eventually degrades herself so far as to borrow money from a prostitute—the once despised Refugio Sánchez y Emperador, sister of "Tormento."

The scene in which Rosalía attempts to obtain the loan is admirably executed. Refugio is at last enabled to enjoy the sweets of revenge, and delights in keeping the once haughty Rosalía on tenterhooks. She is determined to spare her sister's old tormentor no humiliation, and Rosalía has to disguise her hatred and contempt under a cloak of ingratiating politeness. Refugio is her last hope; for if she cannot raise a certain sum within a few hours the Bringas home will be sold up. The conflict between her consciousness of superiority as a "virtuous" woman and her sense of inferiority as the seeker of a favour,

[1] Vide *La Familia de León Roch*.

is revealed in a scene of dramatic intensity. More than once she is on the point of leaving without attaining her object —unable to tolerate the mocking insults of Refugio: "any domestic catastrophe seemed preferable to the ghastly torment she was suffering."[1] But the picture of Don Francisco in the clutches of the inexorable Torquemada—the money-lender from whom she has borrowed the sum which has to be repaid—rises before her mind; and she steels herself to bear the humiliation. If only on account of these admirable chapters,[2] *La de Bringas* deserves a place of honour among *Las Novelas Contemporáneas*.

Its successor, *Lo Prohibido*, is evidently inspired by the French naturalistic school. The hero, who relates his own story, is one of Galdós' favourite "abnormals": "From my childhood," he tells us, "I had suffered from certain attacks of hypochondria, from nervous troubles the intensity of which had diminished in the course of the years. They took the form of a complete lack of appetite and a total inability to sleep, an inexplicable disorder which seems to be moral rather than physical, and whose chief symptom was an agonising terror such as one experiences when faced with immediate and un-avoidable danger. For this reason I would not receive any callers whatsoever, and my servant, who already knew, among my other failings, this particular weakness, would not allow so much as a fly to enter my presence. . . . This vigilance was, however, wasted upon my uncle, who, falling over the guard, dashed straight into my study. He first told me, in a cheerful exordium, that mine was the 'mal du siècle' which,

---

[1] "Halló preferible cualquier catástrofe doméstica al tormento horroroso que padecía." *La de Bringas* (1906 ed.), xlvii., p. 272.
[2] Caps. xlv.–xlviii.

by increasing cerebral activity, creates a constitutional neuropathic diathesis in the whole human race." [1] His uncle, Rafael Bueno de Guzmán, is, however, not entirely free from this same malady: "We all, more or less," he confesses to his nephew, "suffer from the effects of a slight nervous instability the origin of which is lost in the obscure chronicles of the first Buenos de Guzmán of whom I have any record." [2] He goes on to give details of the aberrations to which various members of the family have been subject, and remarks upon the fact that the hereditary curse seems to be operating less forcibly in the case of his three daughters, María Juana, Eloísa and Camila. María Juana, who at one time suffered from hysteria, has been practically normal since her marriage. Eloísa, it is true, suffers from what modern students of abnormal psychology would call a "phobia": "She is terrified of feathers, not of quill pens, but of birds' feathers, and hence of everything that flies. She goes into hysterics at the sight of a canary" [3]; but apart from this trifling peculiarity she is "an angel of goodness." Only Camila

[1] "Desde niño padecía yo ciertos achaquillos de hipocondría, desórdenes nerviosos, que con los años habían perdido algo de su intensidad. Consistían en la ausencia completa del apetito y del sueño, en una perturbación inexplicable que más parecía moral que física, y cuyo principal síntoma era el terror angustioso, como cuando nos hallamos en presencia de inevitable y cercano peligro. . . . Por esta razón no quería recibir a nadie, y mi criado, que ya conoce bien este flaco mío y otros, no dejaba que llegase a mi presencia ni una mosca. . . . Ni valían estos rigores con mi tío, el cual, atropellando la guardia, se colaba de rondón en mi gabinete. . . . Díjome primero en su festivo exordio, que aquello era el mal del siglo, el cual, forzando la actividad cerebral, creaba una diátesis neuropática constitutiva en toda la humanidad" (Lo Prohibido (1906 ed.), pp. 10–11).

[2] "Todos padecemos en mayor o menor grado . . . los efectos de una imperfeccioncilla nerviosa, cuyo origen se pierde en la crónica obscura de las primeros Buenos de Guzmán de que tengo noticia" (ibid.).

[3] "Tiene horror a las plumas, no a las de escribir sino a las de las aves, y, por tanto, horror a todo lo volátil" (ibid., p. 19).

appears to have inherited to any striking extent the family instability: "She seems to be mad, or, rather, empty-headed and superficial "[1]; but even she is very far from being a fool or a lunatic.

The novel deals mainly with the attempts of the hero, whose neurosis takes the form of a morbid sexuality, to seduce his three cousins; attempts which are unsuccessful only in the case of the (apparently) scatter-brained Camila—who despises conventions and rejoices in scandalising the outwardly respectable. Nowhere is the tendency of Galdós towards extreme prolixity more evident than in *Lo Prohibido*. As in the case of *El Doctor Centeno*, the psychological analysis is so minute as to become wearisome. *Lo Prohibido* brings no new figure of outstanding interest to Galdós' portrait-gallery of national types. It is, indeed, no more than an unsuccessful attempt at a fusion of the naturalistic novel with the *roman à thèse*; the thesis being the somewhat platitudinous one that "moderation is best in all things." [2] Also, in his portrayal of Camila, Galdós doubtless intended to tilt at the conventional conception of sexual morality which he had already denounced in *La Familia de León Roch*; and the contrast between the heroine's outward lack of decorum and her inward virtuousness is, therefore, strongly—perhaps too strongly—emphasised.

Lo Prohibido is, in our opinion, one of the least interesting and least original of *Las Novelas Contemporáneas*. It was destined, however, to precede his masterpiece—*Fortunata y Jacinta*—which has been described by Menéndez y Pelayo as "one of the great achievements of the Spanish genius in our

---

[1] (ibid., p. 20.)
[2] Vide vol. ii. xxv., p. 339, where the hero (now a reformed character) reveals his intention of writing a work upon the great advantages of moderation ["una obra sobre los inmensos bienes de la templanza"].

M

day." [1] If it possessed no other distinguishing qualities, it would be remarkable on account of its enormous length—for it runs into four volumes of, approximately, four hundred pages each. In this respect, indeed, it is typical of Galdós at his worst; and one can only say in defence of its prolixity that the digressions in which it abounds are almost always of exceptional interest.

As a novel of customs it excels in its graphic portrayal of the transformations which the Spanish capital underwent from 1868 to 1875. In no other of Galdós' works will the student of sociology find a greater wealth of fascinating detail concerning the fortunes of the Madrid bourgeoisie during the latter half of the nineteenth century. [2] No novel in modern Spanish literature conforms more closely to Stendhal's well-known definition of this literary form as "un miroir que l'on promène le long du chemin. . . ." Not a detail is missed, and in scrupulous accuracy of observation Galdós vies here with the most masterly trans-Pyrenean hewers of "slices of life."

Fortunata y Jacinta is a complete picture of Spain in her era of transition; the Spain in which traditional ideals and traditional standards were slowly crumbling into decay. We are, however, left to draw our own conclusions from the picture;

---

[1] "Uno de los grandes esfuerzos del ingenio español en nuestros días" (vide op. cit., p. 89).
[2] Vide *Fortunata y Jacinta* (1917 ed.), part i. cap. ii.—"Santa Cruz y Arnáiz; Vistazo histórico sobre el comercio matritense"—where Galdós writes the epic of the "mantón de Manila," tracing the gradual elimination of colour from the dress of fashionable society. The gay Spanish shawl is eventually relegated to the mob: "the last, devoted disciple of gay colours" ["último y fiel adepto de los matices vivos"] (p. 59). It is interesting to note that Galdós attributes this decline of colour to the influence of Northern Europe: "this accursed North foists upon us the grey tones of its smoky sky" ["ese maldito Norte nos impone los grises que toma de su ahumado cielo"] (ibid.), and that the ruin of the Spanish cloth trade is attributed to Britain.

and it is this absence of partisanship, this detached attitude towards the life it portrays, which distinguishes this novel from the majority of its author's works. It is, however, more than a "cuadro de costumbres." It is, primarily, a story; a story told with the sympathetic insight of a great artist. As the sub-title—"Dos historias de casadas"—indicates, the novel has a dual theme and is, in fact, "two stories"—both of which deal with the problem of an ill-assorted marriage. We have already seen how Galdós approached the matrimonial question in *La Familia de León Roch*—a work in which the strident didacticism of his early phase is considerably modified. Although the ostensible cause of the breach between León and his wife is their difference in religious belief, one is, nevertheless, led to believe that it has its real origin in something more fundamental—a radical incompatibility of temperament. Would León and María have been happy in their married life even if León had become an honest convert to his wife's religion? Such a question is, we think, suggested in *La Familia de León Roch*.

In *Fortunata y Jacinta* Galdós not only attacks by implication the orthodox Catholic view of marriage, but seems to suggest that monogamy is an unsatisfactory basis for the social system. We shall, however, have occasion to revert to this aspect of the novel at a later stage.

The story may be summarised briefly as follows: Juanito Santa Cruz, son of the wealthy bourgeois Baldomero Santa Cruz and his wife, Barbarita Arnáiz,[1] marries his cousin, Jacinta. Previous to his marriage he has, however, formed an

---

[1] The history of these two families forms the basis of the chapter to which we have already referred (part I. cap. ii., pp. 23-75): "Santa Cruz y Arnáiz. Vistazo histórico sobre el comercio matritense." Further details of the Santa Cruz family are given in cap. vi.

illicit connection with a girl of the people, Fortunata, whom he now abandons. He intends to keep this episode a secret from his wife, who, however, worms out the truth from him while they are on their honeymoon. When he appears to regret his confession, she assures him that she will never be guilty of retrospective jealousy, and that provided he is faithful to her now that he is married she will not inquire too closely into what his life was like before their union. Juanito is not, however, the stuff out of which good husbands are made. While he always preserves a very real affection for his wife, he quickly tires of undiluted domestic bliss. While his wandering habits are naturally a source of disquietude to Jacinta, she is even more perturbed by the fact that their marriage has remained childless. Her thwarted maternal instincts cause her to harbour the most extravagant suspicions, and she becomes convinced that Fortunata has had a child by Juanito. Once, while on a visit to her husband's family, Jacinta hears an old friend of theirs, José Ido (the unfortunate pedagogue whom we met in *El Doctor Centeno*), speak of his neighbour's adopted child, nicknamed "El Pitusín." Jealousy leads her to fancy that this may be her husband's child, and suspicion soon gives way to certainty. She determines to visit José Izquierdo, Ido's friend, with the object of persuading him to let her adopt the infant. Meanwhile Juanito, when taxed by Jacinta with infidelity, admits having seen Fortunata since his marriage but stoutly denies that he is the father of the child.[1]

We are then introduced to the second male protagonist of the novel—Maximiliano Rubín ("Maxí"), and his brothers, Juan Pablo and Nicolás. After the death of their father

[1] This brings us to the end of vol. i., which, to judge by the title of the last chapter—"Final, que viene a ser principio"—is intended as a kind of introduction to the novel proper.

Nicolás Rubín,[1] the goldsmith, they go to live with their aunt, Doña Guadalupe Rubín—"Doña Lupe, la de los Pavos."[2] Maximiliano, who (as we might expect) suffers from a neurotic disorder, is introduced to Fortunata by the mistress of a friend, and he conceives the idea of "reforming" her. He falls in love with her in the process, and eventually marries her. His inordinately jealous temperament and his ill-health make him, however, an unsatisfactory husband. After a violent scene in which he accuses Fortunata of infidelity, she leaves him and renews her relations with Juanito Santa Cruz, who, on the plea that their connection is becoming a public scandal, soon abandons her as he had already done before his marriage. She seeks the protection of one Evaristo Feijóo, who advises her to return to Maxí. This she does only when Feijóo is no longer able to support her. An attempt on the part of a friend, Doña Guillermina, to bring her to a sense of wrong-doing meets with no success. Fortunata pours scorn upon conventional morality—"A wife who has no children," she protests, "is no wife."[3] Juanito is the only man she has ever loved and, by the "law of nature and the heart," Juanito is her husband.[4] One of the most dramatic scenes in the novel occurs when wife and mistress are brought face to face. Jacinta's bitter cry of "Thief!" cuts Fortunata to the heart. "You are the thief—you . . . *you*,"[5] she screams defiantly—abandoning herself to a passion of rage and mortification in which all her primitive coarseness is revealed.

---

[1] The history of various members of the Rubín family is traced in part ii. cap. i.
[2] Vide cap. iii.
[3] "Esposa que no tiene hijos, no es tal esposa" (vide part iii. cap. vii., p. 370).
[4] Cf. Pepa's protest in *La Familia de León Roch.*
[4] "¡ La ladrona eres tú . . . tú!" (vide part iii. cap. vii., p. 379.)

Meanwhile the wretched Maxí, ravaged by a jealousy which he refuses to recognise as such, is seized by a strange delusion, a species of religious mania which involves a theory of "liberation" by death. The true nature of his obsession is, however, revealed to him by the crazy José Ido, and when he realises the cause of his insanity he is immediately cured. "It was all jealousy," he confesses to Fortunata—and at the same time informs her that Juanito Santa Cruz is making love to her friend Aurora. After a terrible scene with her rival, Fortunata falls seriously ill and, after giving birth to a child whose parentage is doubtful, eventually dies. Maxí never recovers from the blow, and is confined in an asylum.

This, in brief outline, is the plot of Galdós' greatest novel. It is not, however, by its plot that we remember it, but rather by the admirable "cuadros" and character-sketches which it contains. As González-Blanco puts it: "*Fortunata y Jacinta* is, rather than a novel, an alluvion of facts strung together by a common thread, facts which will enable future ages to know the character and personalities of the age immediately preceding our own." [1] In no novel is Galdós' failure to use the pruning-knife less to be regretted; for we could ill afford to lose such figures as Doña Lupe, Doña Guillermina, Mauricia la Dura, and Moreno-Isla—all of whom have little to do with the main action of the story. Any attempt at an adequate appreciation of this extraordinary work would demand a study apart. Here we can only try to indicate those features which distinguish it from the author's other novels and which entitle us to regard it as his greatest achievement in fiction.

[1] "*Fortunata y Jacinta* es más que una novela un aluvión de datos, enlazados por un hilo común, que podrán servir a los tiempos futuros para conocer el carácter y personajes de la época anterior a la nuestra" (op. cit. cap. v., p. 376).

Apart from excessive length, it has none of the faults which we have noted in many of his preceding works. In the words of Menéndez y Pelayo: "It is a book which gives the illusion of life," [1] and what higher praise than this can be afforded to any novel? *Fortunata y Jacinta* is entirely free from artificiality; and to those who would accuse Galdós of coldness and lack of feeling in his rendering of love passages, chapter v. of part i., "El Viaje de Novios," is a sufficient reply. What sympathy and understanding is revealed in his account of the young bride's conflicting emotions when she first finds herself alone with Juanito! "The joy in Jacinta's heart did not, however, exclude a certain fear which grew at times into actual terror. The rattling of the omnibus upon the uneven surface of the streets; the climb up a narrow stairway to the restaurant, the room with its ill-chosen, vulgar furniture, a medley of city cast-offs and village luxuries, intensified that unconquerable chilliness and that terror-stricken expectation which made her tremble. And she loved her husband so much! . . . How could one reconcile two such mutually antagonistic desires . . . that her husband should leave her and yet still be near her? For the thought that he might go away and leave her alone was like the thought of death, and the thought that he might come to her and hold her in his arms with passionate temerity also made her tremulous and fearful. She would have liked him not to leave her—but to be very gentle!" [2] This chapter

[1] "Es un libro que da la ilusión de la vida. . . ." (vide op. cit., p. 88).
[2] "En el alma de Jacinta, no obstante, las alegrías no excluían un cierto miedo, que a veces era terror. El ruido del ómnibus sobre el desigual piso de las calles; la subida a la fonda por angosta escalera; el aposento y sus muebles de mal gusto, mezcla de desechos de ciudad y de lujos de aldea, aumentaron aquel frío invencible y aquella pavorosa expectación que la hacían estremecer. ¡Y tantísimo como quería a sn marido! . . . ¿Cómo compaginar dos deseos tan diferentes: que su marido se apartase de ella y que estuviese cerca? Porque la idea de

abounds in such idyllic passages; passages which never degenerate into the sickly sentimentalism of the romantic tradition.[1] Juanito Santa Cruz is one of the great lovers of Spanish literature; and Galdós, in a telling phrase, comments upon that refinement of voluptuousness which binds the young roué to his wife and which can make a vice out of virtue itself: "Those who are most accustomed to an irregular life occasionally experience a violent longing to submit for a short time to the law. The law tempts them as caprice can tempt them."[2] Juanito, who is totally incapable of a sincere emotion, is, nevertheless, quite oblivious of his shortcomings: "He was satisfied, as though he had created himself and seen that he was good"[3]—and he does not reproach himself in the least for his infidelities, which he regards as the legitimate diversions of a man-about-town. "El Delfín," as he is nicknamed, is a spoiled child of the middle-class, a member of that "new" aristocracy which Galdós appears to have regarded with mixed feelings.[4] Like León Roch, Juanito is reaping the reward earned by the labours of his father, and the latter is perfectly satisfied with such vicarious enjoyment. He does not share his wife's apprehension as to the danger of Juanito's trip to

que se pudiera ir, dejándola sola, era como la muerte, y la de que se acercaba y la cogía en brazos con apasionado atrevimiento, también la ponía temblorosa y asustada. Habría deseado que no se apartara de ella, pero que se estuviera quietecito" (part i., cap. v., p. 121).

[1] In this chapter also Galdós has given us two of his finest landscapes (vide ibid. cap. v., p. 150 and p. 155).

[2] "Las personas más hechas a la vida ilegal sienten en ocasiones vivo anhelo de ponerse bajo la ley por poco tiempo. *La ley les tienta como puede tentar el capricho*" (part i., cap. v., p. 155).

[3] Estaba satisfecho, cual si se hubiera creado y visto que era bueno" (ibid. cap. viii., p. 247).

[4] Contrast the views expressed here, where Galdós writes of "the happy confusion of all classes" ["una la dichosa confusión de todas las clases"] (ibid. cap. vi., p. 179), with the opinions offered upon the same questions in *La Familia de León Roch*.

Paris: "The boy's sound at bottom," he says, "let him have his fling and sow his wild oats. The youths of to-day must keep their eyes open and see a good deal of the world. These are not like my own days, when no boy in business ever went on the loose, the days when they had us well under their thumbs until they got us married. How different our times are from those! Civilisation's a great thing, my dear." [1] His estimate of Juanito's character is, in a sense, correct. "El Delfín" is too much of a Laodicean emotionally to allow a "grande passion" to disturb the equilibrium of his foppish and self-centred existence. He most nearly approaches sincerity in his relations with Fortunata. His love for her, however, does not prevent him from abandoning her with the utmost cynicism on two occasions. Galdós effectively sums up this typical "señorito" in his inimitable phrasing: "There can exist in certain people a relationship between their pet-name and their destiny. There are, in fact, Manuels who are predestined to be 'Manolos' all their lives. Be this as it may, the lucky offspring of Don Baldomero Santa Cruz and Doña Barbara Arnáiz was called Juanito, and Juanito he is called, and will be called, in all probability, until his grey hairs and the death of those who knew him in his childhood gradually change the pleasing custom." [2]

In striking contrast with the urbanity and social adequacy

[1] "El chico es de buena índole. Déjale que se divierta y que la corra. Los jóvenes del día necesitan despabilarse y ver mucho mundo. No son estos tiempos como los míos, en que no la corría ningún chico del comercio, y nos tenían a todos metidos en un puño hasta que nos casaban. ¡Qué costumbres aquellas tan diferentes de las de ahora! La civilización, hija, es cuento cuento" (ibid. cap. i., pp. 17-18).

[2] "En algunas personas, puede relacionarse el diminutivo con el sino. Hay efectivamente Manueles que nacieron predestinados para ser Manolos toda su vida. Sea lo que quiera, al venturoso hijo de D. Baldomero Santa Cruz y de doña Bárbara Arnáiz le llamaban *Juanito*, y *Juanito* le dicen y le dirán quizás hasta que las canas de él y la muerte de los que le conocieron niño vayan alterando poco a poco la campechana costumbre" (ibid. cap. i., p. 13).

of Juanito is the shrinking timidity and hyper-sensitive emotionalism of Maximiliano Rubín: "His shyness, far from diminishing with the passage of years, seemed rather to increase. He thought that everybody made fun of him, and regarded him as insignificant and futile. No doubt he exaggerated his inferiority, and his lack of self-confidence caused him to avoid society. . . . Certain individuals would induce in him a feeling of respect which bordered upon panic, and when he saw one of them coming along the street he would cross over to the other side."[1] His one pleasure "consisted in giving free play to his thought and to his imagination, creating a reality for himself and flying unhindered through the airy spaces of the possible, even though it were improbable "[2]; and his one ambition is that he may some day win the love of "a virtuous woman." "A good woman. That a good woman should love me!' Such was his dream. . . ."[3] His idealistic passion finds an object in Fortunata, whom he persuades to enter "Las Micaelas,"[4] a convent for the redemption of Magdalenes. Fortunata, who, like Marianela, is an ignorant "child of nature," cannot, however, be made to realise the enormity of her conduct: "Maximiliano laid constant stress upon the matter of her dishonour, for this point was of great importance

[1] "Su timidez, lejos de disminuir con los años, parecía que aumentaba. Creía que todos se burlaban de él considerándole insignificante y para poco. Exageraba sin duda su inferioridad, y su desaliento le hacía huir del trato social. . . . Ciertas personas le infundían un respeto que casi era pánico, y al verlas venir por la calle se pasaba a la otra acera" (part ii., cap. i., p. 21).

[2] . . . consistía en pensar e imaginar libremente y a sus anchas, figurándose realidades y volando sin tropiezo por los espacios de lo posible, aunque fuera improbable" (ibid., p. 23).

[3] "'¡Una honrada! ¡Que me quiera una honrada!' Tal era su ilusión." (ibid.).

[4] In the chapters which deal with Fortunata's experiences in this convent, Galdós attacks the methods of the houses of correction at this period.

in the scheme for her redemption. The inspired and enthusiastic youth would insist upon the wickedness of "señoritos" and upon the need for a law, such as exists in England, for the protection of young girls against seducers. Fortunata did not understand one word of all this about laws. The only thing which she insistently maintained was that the said Juanito Santa Cruz was the only man whom she had ever really loved, and that she would always love him." [1]

This attitude she maintains until the end. Her marriage to "Maxí" means nothing to her; and when once again she meets her old lover she hails him as her true husband: "you are my husband, you . . . all the others . . . papas!" [2]

Maximiliano's subconscious realisation that his wife belongs in reality to another man, gives rise to a curious mental aberration on his part—with which aberration the final volume of the story is mainly concerned. The first sympton takes the form of a violent distaste for ordinary life, and a passion for solitude and meditation. . . . "If I were not married to you," he tells Fortunata, "I should devote myself wholly to the religious life. . . . You don't know how it attracts me, how it calls to me . . . to withdraw from everything, to renounce everything, to annihilate utterly the exterior life and live the interior life alone . . . that is the only positive good. Everything else is like turning a water-wheel from which no drop of water

[1] "Repetidas veces sacó Maximiliano a relucir el caso de la deshonra de ella, por ser muy importante este punto en el plan de regeneración. El inspirado y entusiasta mancebo hacía hincapié en lo malo que son los señoritos y en la necesidad de una lay a la inglesa que proteja a las muchachas inocentes contra los seductores. Fortunata no entendía palotada de estas leyes. Lo único que sostenía era que el tal Juanito Santa Cruz era el único hombre a quien había querido de verdad, y que le amaba siempre" (ibid. part ii., p. 59).

[2] "Mi marido eres tú . . . todo lo demás . . ¡papas!" (ibid. cap. vii., p. 398).

ever comes." [1] Then a "philosophy" [2] is evolved; an effort on the part of Maxí to rationalise the instinctive hatred of life which follows upon the shattering of his illusion. According to his new creed "Incarnation is a penitential state, a state of trial. Death is liberation, pardon; true life, that is. Let us try to attain it soon. [3] Fear of death is "fear of liberty and love of the dungeon." [4] He endeavours to convert Fortunata to the new gospel, suggesting that they should both commit suicide. When he learns that she is pregnant his worst suspicions as to her infidelity are confirmed. During a conversation with the crazy José Ido, the true nature of his perverted mysticism dawns upon him with startling suddenness. "I invented religions," he confesses, "I wanted the whole human race to commit suicide: I was expecting the Messiah. And here I am, so sane and well." [5] Later he explains the origin of his "philosophy of liberation" to his wife: "I was jealous! Ah! my jealousy made my life unbearable. 'My wife is deceiving me,' I said, 'she can't help deceiving me, it's inevitable.' And as I loved you so much and thought that death was the only remedy for your sin— there you have the explanation of how there grew up in my mind, just as moss grows on the trunk of a tree, this idea of

---

[1] "Si yo no estuviera casado contigo, me consagraría por entero a la vida religiosa. No sabes tú cómo me seduce, cómo me llama. . . . Abstraerse, renunciar a todo, anular por completo la vida exterior y vivir sólo para adentro . . . este es el único bien positivo; lo demás es darle vueltas a una noria, de la cual no sale nunca una gota de agua" (part iv., cap. i., p. 13).

[2] Galdós appears to have been familiar with the doctrines of modern "theosophy." With these the ideas of Maxí have much in common.

[3] "La encarnación es un estado penitenciario o de prueba. La muerte, es la liberación, el indulto, o sea la vida verdadera. Procuremos obtenerla pronto." (part iv., cap. i., p. 63).

[4] "Miedo a la libertad y amor al calabozo" (part iv. cap. i, p. 83).

[5] "Yo inventaba religiones; yo quería que todo el género humano se matara; yo esperaba el Mesías. . . . Pues aquí me tiene tan sano y tan bueno" (ibid. cap. v., p. 256).

liberation—deceits and whimsies of the mind to justify murder and suicide. It was a reflection of commonplace notions, vulgar ideas, changed and distorted by my diseased brain. Ah, how ill I was! I tell you that when I invented this ridiculous philosophy I was at my worst. I don't want to remember it. . . . Later I was attacked by what I call "Messiahitis." That was also a change in my brain wrought by jealousy . . . think carefully, and you will see that it was all jealousy, jealousy fermented and putrefying." [1]

How far Galdós anticipated in his portrayal of Maxí certain theories popularised by our modern psycho-analysts, only an expert in abnormal psychology could decide. The tracing back of Maxí's religious phantasies to a sexual source and the disappearance of his "complex" when the true cause of it is apprehended by the conscious mind does, however, suggest that the author had grasped in their essentials aspects of the problem of consciousness which have only recently been seriously investigated. This fact adds interest to the minute psychological study which Galdós gives us of his second hero—one of the most original figures in *Las Novelas Contemporáneas*.

Another "abnormal" is Don Manuel Moreno-Isla, an aged roué who falls sentimentally in love with Jacinta. He is one

[1] "Yo tenía unos celos ¡ay! que no me dejaban vivir. 'Mi mujer me falta, decía yo, no tiene más remedio que faltarme; no puede ser de otra manera.' Y como por lo mucho que te quería, y no encontraba a tu pecado más solución que la muerte, ahí tienes por qué me nació en la cabeza, lo mismo que nace el musgo en los troncos, aquella idea de la liberación, pretextos y triquiñuelas de la mente para justificar el asesinato y el suicidio. Era aquello un reflejo de las ideas comunes, el pensar general modificado y adulterado por mi cerebro enfermo. ¡Ay, qué malo me puse! Te digo que cuando inventé aquel sistema filosófico tan ridículo, estaba en el período peorcito. No me quiero acordar. . . . Después me atacó lo que yo llamo la *Mesianitis*. . . . Era también una modificación cerebral de los celos. . . . Examínalo bien, y verás que todo era celos, celos fermentados y en putrefacción" (ibid. part iv. cap. vi., pp. 308-9).

of those "cosmopolitan" Spaniards whom Galdós appears
to despise, while approving many of their views. While
he would certainly not endorse Moreno-Isla's" " Here there is
no police, no philanthropy, no manners, no civilisation! . . ." [1]
one gathers that he might not reject as altogether blasphemous
Isla's suggestion that Spain could be improved by "a crossing
with some Northern stock, by the importation of Saxon
mothers." [2] We can divine, indeed, in Galdós the germ of that
theory of "Salvation from the North" which has been advanced
by certain members of the younger generation of Spanish
intellectuals. Of this, however, we shall have more to say later.

To Moreno-Isla everything Spanish is anathema. "This is
not a country, this is not a capital, there's no civilisation
here." [3] The merest trifles—such as the habit which Spanish
servants have of singing at their work—infuriate him. "Do
you know," he says to Baldomero and Barbarita Santa Cruz,
"one of the things which aggravates me most in Spain? It's
the habit which the servants have of singing at their work.
The fact is that this miserable race, which has no conception
of the value of time, is equally ignorant of the value of
silence." [4] He is loyal, however, to Spanish women; and after
a career of *bonnes fortunes* in every city in Europe he finds
his last love in Madrid. Unhappily, however, for his peace of
mind, Jacinta proves unconquerable.

[1] "Aquí no hay policía, ni beneficencia, ni formas, ni civilización"
(ibid. cap. ii., p. 104).
[2] ". . . el cruzamiento con alguna casta del Norte, trayendo aquí madres
sajonas" (ibid., p. 105).
[3] "Ni esto es país, ni esto es capital, ni aquí hay civilización. . . .
(ibid., p. 125).
[4] "¿ Saben Vds cuál es una de las cosas que me cargan más en
España? La costumbre que tienen las criadas de ponerse a cantar
cuando trabajan. . . . Es que esta pícara raza, que no conoce el valor
del tiempo, tampoco conoce el del silencio" (ibid., p. 112).

Fortunata y Jacinta is rich in "originals" of both sexes: Estupiñá, the old servant of the Santa Cruz family, whose "chief boast was that he had seen the whole history of Spain in the present century" [1]; José Ido del Sagrario (whom we met in *El Doctor Centeno*); Nicolás Rubín, "el curita peludo"; [2] Moreno-Isla's aunt, Guillermina Pacheco "Vírgen y Fundadora" [3]; Doña Lupe, "La de los Pavos" [4]; Mauricia, "La Dura" [5]; Don Evaristo González-Feijóo [6] and his friends Basilio Andres de la Caña, Melchor de Relimpio, Leopoldo Montes and Juan Pablo Rubín—the arbiters of the "tertulia" —all these are depicted in Galdós' inimitable style.

Fortunata y Jacinta has been well described as "an agenda and compendium of notes upon life in the last third of the last century." [7] The book is as intricate and varied as was the life of the period it depicts; and, while it deals chiefly with the Madrid bourgeousie, no class is neglected in its pages. [8]

Although it is not a propagandist work, the political problems of the time are freely discussed [9]; while the implications contained in it as to the validity of conventional moral standards are far-reaching. [10]

[1] "Fundaba su vanidad en *haber visto toda la historia de España* en el presente siglo" (part i. cap. iii., p. 78).

[2] Vide part ii. cap. i., p. 13, and part ii. cap. iv., pp. 174–5.

[3] Part i., cap. vii.   [4] Part ii., cap. iii.

[5] Part ii., cap. vi., pp. 257 et seq.

[6] Part iii., cap. i., pp. 12–13.

[7] "Agenda y breviario de apuntes de la vida en el último tercio del último siglo" (vide González-Blanco, op. cit. cap. v., p. 395).

[8] Cap. ix. of part i.—"Una visita al Cuarto Estado"—gives us a brilliant description of the low quarters of Madrid.

[9] Vide especially cap. i. of part iii. which deals mainly with the "tertulia" led by Juan Pablo Rubín and Feijóo.

[10] Blanco-García actually writes of the book's "lethal and pornographic sensuality." There is absolutely nothing in the work to justify such an indictment; although to a priest Jacinta's apparent condonation of her husband's adultery would seem unquestionably immoral (vide Blanco-García, op. cit., part ii., p. 504).

In *Miau*, the novel which follows *Fortunata y Jacinta*, Galdós returns to a favourite theme—the struggle for existence among the shabby-genteel which provided a background for *Tormento* and *La de Bringas*; but *Miau* lacks the human interest of the earlier works, there is practically no action, and the analysis of the depressing household presided over by the three women, Pura, Milagros and Abelarda, nicknamed "Miaus" an account of their cat-like appearance, quickly becomes monotonous. *Miau* is in many respects one of the most depressing of the *Novelas Contemporáneas*, and as a portrayal of unrelieved wretchedness it occupies a place apart among the novels of Galdós. Don Ramón Villaamil, an ex-government official, finds himself out of employment and seeks in vain the patronage which can alone provide him with another position. His efforts to find work proving utterly fruitless, he commits suicide, a martyr to the national vice of "caciquismo," which prevents him from obtaining the only kind of work which he is fitted to perform. This, briefly, is the argument of *Miau*, and it scarcely provides adequate material for a novel of four hundred odd pages in length! There are, however, some interesting character-studies in the book, especially that of the unfortunate little Luisito Cadalso (dubbed "Miau" by his schoolfellows on account of his connection with the Villaamil household), son of Don Ramón's good-for-nothing son-in-law Victor, who exercises a sinister influence upon all with whom he comes into contact —and, more especially, upon the fortunes of the Villaamil household. The abnormal, solitary life of the small Luisito, who has been entrusted by Victor to the care of the "Miaus," and who spends the greater part of his time in delivering Don Ramón's begging letters, is depicted with remarkable insight into the mentality of a hyper-sensitive and lonely child. The scene in which Abelarda, who has conceived a crazy hatred for the little boy, makes a furious attack upon him, on account of some childish naughtiness, is intensely dramatic; [1] and all that concerns the activities of Luisito is excellent. It is, indeed, mainly as a study in child psychology that *Miau* is deserving of mention here.

In *La Incógnita* and *Realidad* Galdós returns to the over-emphatic didacticism of his first period; and in their treatment of a moral problem arising out of an unsatisfactory marriage they are more frankly revolutionary than either *La Familia de León Roch* or *Fortunata y Jacinta*. Both stories deal with the same incidents. In *La Incógnita* these are witnessed by one Manolo Infante, who reports them in a series of letters to his friend "Equis," while in *Realidad* Galdós presents them in dramatic form. Apart from the disadvantages of the epistolary and dialogue forms in which, respectively, they are cast, *La Incógnita* and *Realidad* are among the least interesting of *Las Novelas Contemporáneas*. To tell exactly the same story, first as it impressed one of the actors in it and then in dramatic form, was an ingenious notion which had the merit of a certain novelty. The experiment, however, proved a failure.

After reading *La Incógnita*, we are inclined to agree with Manolo Infante when he modestly remarks, in his first letter to Equis, "I do not possess the art of decking out in gay clothing the nakedness of reality, nor do my conscience and my sterile wit, both in perfect agreement, allow me to concoct stories which shall amuse you with entertaining deceits." [2] The

[1] *Miau* (1907 ed.), p. 369.

[2] Ni poseo el arte de vestir con galas pintorescas la desnudez de la realidad, ni mi conciencia y mi estéril ingenio, ambos en perfecto acuerdo, me han de permitir invenciones que te entretengan con graciosos embustes" (*La Incógnita* (1906 ed.), p. 7).

N

story as he writes it—interlarded with wearisome passages of self-analysis—fails altogether to hold our interest. The characters whom Manolo describes as he meets them in the fashionable circles of the capital lack individuality, and we have met the counterparts of many of them elsewhere in *Las Novelas Contemporáneas*. The "problem" situation is hackneyed: Federico Viera falls in love with Augusta, wife of his friend, Tomás Orozco, and, unable to accept with resignation the demands which loyalty makes upon passion, commits suicide.[1] In *La Incógnita* piquancy is added by the fact that the person who is telling the story is also in love with Augusta (his cousin). He strongly suspects her of infidelity to her husband; but she is an unfathomable mystery to him—hence the title of the novel. *Realidad* reveals, as its title indicates, the "reality." In the course of prolonged conversations and soliloquies—nearly all of which are stilted and artificial—the individuals whom we saw, as it were, externally, in *La Incógnita* now reveal their innermost selves. Infante and Viera discuss with complete cynicism the question as to whether or no Augusta is virtuous and whether either of them would be justified in attempting to seduce her. Infante inclines to the view that she is not virtuous—and for this he blames the social sphere in which she lives—but he believes that she will at all costs avoid a scandal:

Viera, on the contrary, insists that she *is* virtuous, and strongly condemns Infante's designs upon her honour. The latter, however, points out that such designs upon his part are more excusable than they would be upon that of Viera, who is under a definite obligation to Orozco. And so the argument

[1] We do not, however, learn this until *Realidad*. In *La Incógnita* mystery surrounds the manner of his death.

continues—occupying over ten pages! [1] Although it is written in the form of a drama, there is nothing truly dramatic about this extraordinary work—surely one of the strangest literary abortions of modern times! The artificiality and unreality of the whole thing (never did a book have a more inappropriate title!) reaches its climax in the concluding dialogue [2] between Orozco and the ghost of his wife's lover. He justifies the latter's suicide: "My view is that you were impelled to take your life by your sense of honour and your conscience. Your death is a sign of moral greatness." [3] After reproaching himself for giving way to jealousy: "Jealousy—what folly! the whims, fancies or passions of a woman! Is it seemly that the spirit of man should be troubled on their account? No; to bring such trifles before the bar of the universal conscience is as though, upon seeing an ant, two ants, four, or one hundred dragging away a grain of meal, we were to inform the Civil Guard and the Judge of the High Court. No; let us keep calm in the face of these microscopic disturbances that we may the more profoundly despise them! . . ." [4] and so on for three pages. He eventually decides that his wife is not so much to blame for her adultery as for having kept him in ignorance of it! *Realidad* foreshadows in many ways the last development

---

[1] *Realidad* (1916 ed.), pp. 91-103.
[2] (ibid., pp. 433-40).
[3] "Pues mi opinión es que moriste por estímulos del honor y de la conciencia; te arrancaste la vida porque se te hizo imposible, colocada entre mi generosidad y mi deshonra. . . . Tu muerte es un signo de grandeza moral" (ibid., p. 440).
[4] Los celos, ¡que estupidez! Las veleidades, antojos o pasiones de una mujer, ¡qué necedad raquítica! ? Es decoroso para el espíritu del hombre afanarse por esto? No; elevar tales menudencias al foro de la conciencia universal es lo mismo que si, al ver una hormiga, dos hormigas o cuatro o cien, llevando a rastras un grano de cebada, fuéramos a dar parte a la Guardia Civil y al juez de primera instancia No; conservemos nuestra calma frente a estas agitaciones microscópicas, para despreciarlas más hondamente. . . ." (ibid., p. 434).

of Galdós' genius—the development we are about to discuss in the next chapter. The healthy realism of *Fortunata y Jacinta* gives way here to a farrago of mysticism and rhetoric which is frequently not far removed from nonsense. Orozco is a "Maxí" "taken seriously"; and his anxiety to preach a "new morality" is reflected in many novels of the last phase. The introduction of the supernatural element is also typical of the period of decline.

VII

Angel Guerra is the swan-song of Galdós as a novelist of European significance. With the possible exception of *Misericordia* (which stands apart from the other novels of this last phase) it is the one novel of the final group which can rival his great realistic masterpieces. The plot of the story is extremely simple, and it can be summarised very briefly as follows: Angel Guerra, the hero of many quixotic political escapades, eventually espouses the cause of the Republic and by so doing alienates the sympathy of his family. He leaves home and plunges into a life of dissipation. Upon the death of his mother and, shortly afterwards, that of his daughter Encarnación (he is a widower), he falls violently in love with Lorenza ("Leré"), formerly the governess of his child. He cannot, however, persuade her to marry him—although, as a guarantee of good faith, he deserts his devoted and unselfish mistress Dulcenombre. Leré enters a convent at Toledo, to which city Angel follows her. He continues to visit her and treats her with extreme respect and deference. The religious atmosphere of Toledo and the earnest entreaties of Leré bring about a change in his philosophy of life—hitherto positivist and ultra-democratic—and he is converted to Catholicism. He decides eventually to enter the Church and found a new

185

"Brotherhood of Mercy." His old political associates regard this conversion as the basest treachery to their cause, and the more irresponsible among them organise a murderous attack upon him. He eventually dies from the injuries he receives. This, in bare outline, is the story. It has, however, multitudinous ramifications, and in this respect it resembles *Fortunata y Jacinta*, which it rivals in point of length, occupying three volumes of over three hundred pages each. Much space is devoted to the doings of the worthless Babel family of which Angel's mistress, Dulcenombre, is a member [1]; and also to the family life of Angel's relations in Toledo. The novel is, however, mainly concerned with the psychology of the hero, who, like "Maxí," is suffering from a delusion born of passion. Like "Maxí," also, he eventually realises the true cause of his obsession, which takes the form of a more or less orthodox mysticism. He comes eventually to understand that his conversion to Catholicism and his desire to found a new Order of Mercy—with Leré as its head—is merely the outcome of his frustrated passion for that lady. It is a situation which would rejoice the heart of a good Freudian; and one which Galdós develops much to the advantage of that form of "supernaturalism" which he especially disliked. One feels, however, that Angel would have distorted any creed. He is, indeed (like so many of Galdós' characters), a fit subject for the student of abnormal psychology. He has strange dreams—one, especially vivid, of a fall: "This dream, which bore no relation to actual life, would come to Guerra when his brain was excited by vivid and depressing thoughts; a very common occurrence, for every individual has his own peculiar way of dreaming and his own nightmare which

[1] Vide *Angel Guerra* (1920 ed.), part i., cap. ii. et passim.

may be called 'constitutional' . . ." [1] Another, which is
so clear as to amount at times to an hallucination, he
traces back to his boyhood days. He had witnessed, together
with a friend, the massacre of the sergeants after the revolt
at the barracks of San Gil,[2] and has never been able to
forget the sight. Galdós gives a powerful description of the
terrible incident as it appeared to the small boys who had
contrived to edge their way in among the crowd of spectators:
"It was impossible to be aware of or to realise anything other
than the ghastly spectacle which was being enacted before
their eyes. Fear itself set fire to the curiosity of our good little
Guerra, who, oblivious of the whole world in the face of such
a tragedy, stared at that rectangular space, stared at the
sergeants whom the adjutants lined up about one metre's
length from the wall. . . . Some were kneeling, some standing . . . Those who wished to look in front of them, looked;
and those who were afraid turned their faces to the wall. . . .
A priest said something to them, and withdrew. . . . Immediately the two files of troops who were to do the killing
advanced . . . the first file kneeled, the second remained on
foot. One could hear nothing. . . . An agonising silence. No
one drew a breath. . . . Fire!—and, instantaneously, the
dreadful uproar, the bodies falling amid smoke and dust. They
fell (and well did Guerra remember it) in strange attitudes and
with a heavy thud, like sacks, filled to the brim and cast down
from a great height. It was all a matter of seconds—legs in the
air, blue trousers, bodies at full length on the ground, others

[1] "Este sueño sin relación alguna con la vida real, solía tenerlo
Guerra cuando su cerebro se excitaba por vivas impresiones depri-
mentes, caso muy común, pues cada persona tiene su manera especial
de soñar, y su pesadilla que podríamos llamar constitutiva . . ."
(ibid., cap. iii., p. 108)
[2] 22 June, 1866.

doubled up, face downwards, others with their last glassy stare fixed upon the high heavens. A piercing shriek rent the dismal silence just before the discharge and the smoke dispersed itself in pale strands. . . . A smell of powder. . . ." [1] Then, with a wild cry of protest, a man starts out from the crowd, "his hair literally standing erect upon his skull." [2] For the first time in his life, Angel grasps the significance of the phrase concerning hair "standing on end." He cannot blot out from his mind the picture of that "face like a Greek mask and hair like spikes," [3] and it haunts him in nightmares throughout his life. "As the marks of smallpox subsist indelibly until old age in those who have suffered from this cruel disease, so there remained in the psychological make-up of Angel Guerra the traces of that vast upheaval." [4] After his "conversion" he is

[1] "Imposible apreciar ni sentir cosa alguna fuera del espectáculo terrible que se ofreció a los ojos de entrambos. El pavor mismo encendía la curiosidad del buen Guerrita, que olvidado del mundo entero ante semejante tragedia, miró el espacio aquel rectangular, miró a los sargentos, que eran colocados en fila por los ayudantes, como a un metro de la tapia. . . . Unos de rodillas, otros en pie. . . . El que quería mirar para adelante miraba, y el que tenía miedo volvía la cara hacia la pared . . . Un cura les dijo algo y se retiró. . . . Inmediatamente, las dos filas de tropa que habían de matar avanzaron. . . . La primera fila se puso de rodillas, la segunda continuaba en pie. No se oía nada. . . . Silencio de agonía. Nadie respiraba . . . ¡Fuegó! y sentir el horroroso estrépito, y ver caer los cuerpos entre el humo y el polvo, fué todo uno. Caían, bien lo recordaba Guerra, en extrañas posturas y con un golpe sordo, como de fardos repletos, arrojados desde una gran altura. Todo fué obra de segundos, piernas por el aire, pantalones azules, cuerpos tendidos de largo a largo, otros, en doblez, caras boca abajo, otras con la última vidriosa mirada fija en el alto cielo. Algún alarido estridente rasgó el silencio lúgubre, posterior a la descarga, y el humo se deshizo en girones pálidos. . . . Olor a pólvora" (ibid. cap. iii., p. 111).

[2] ". . . los cabellos literalmente derechos sobre el cráneo" (ibid., p. 111).

[3] "Cara de mascarón griego y cabellos como puas" (ibid. cap. iii., p. 113). The phrase may have been suggested to Galdós by Goya's famous picture of the massacre of "El Dos de Mayo."

[4] Como subsiste indeleble hasta la vejez la señal de la viruela en los que han padecido esta cruel enfermedad, así subsistió en la complexión psicológica de Angel Guerra la huella de aquel inmenso trastorno" (ibid., p. 113).

frequently subject to a strange hallucination in which he sees and talks with his "double"—robed in the habit of a priest.[1] We are given to understand that this phantom is the objectification of the image of himself which Guerra often contemplates mentally.[2] On one occasion it informs him that a friend of his, Don Tomé, the chaplain, is seriously ill. Guerra finds this to be correct, and indulges in some interesting speculations as to the possible explanation of so strange a phenomenon: " 'Then it is not a dream,' thought Angel, analysing the last apparition of his clerical ego. 'And the fact that this excellent man has been ill proves it. . . . Then I exist in another form, I am a double being, I am a projection of myself into futurity.' Soon, however, various doubts dawned in his mind—doubts which shortly defined themselves more clearly, for he began to suspect that Teresa Pantoja had told him of Don Tomé's grave illness the night before. 'There is within me, so to say, a faint echo of Teresa's voice telling me about it. I can't be certain, but neither can I deny it. It's quite possible that Teresa told me and that I listened but paid very little attention to her and didn't realise it. It remained, however, in my mind as an isolated fact, submerged, a fact which later, with the interplay of my thoughts, peeps out where one would least expect to see it, and one sees it and. . . . In some way I heard of the fact and I recalled it by means of this phenomenon of dualism.' . . ."[3] We venture to suggest that Galdós was

[1] Vide part iii., cap. i., pp. 66 et seq.
[2] Vide ibid. "Ya no era nuevo en él contemplar mentalmente su propia persona ya transformada. . . ."
[3] "'Luego no fué sueño,' pensaba Angel, razonando la última aparición de su yo clerical. 'Y lo demuestra el haber resultado cierta la enfermedad de este bendito. . . . Luego yo existo en otra forma, soy un ser doble, soy una proyección de mí mismo en el tiempo futuro. . . .' No tardaron en apuntar en su mente algunas dudas, que se diseñaron mejor al poco rato, porque dió en sospechar que Teresa Pantoja le

one of the first to advance this explanation (now a commonplace hypothesis) of apparent prevision.

After the transmutation (as he imagines) of his physical passion for Lorenza into an ideal and spiritual love, Angel is disturbed by more strange dreams. In one of them, so he tells his confessor, she appeared to him "surrounded from head to foot with a dazzling radiance, and her eyes gazed at me with a severity which made me tremble, and, placing her hand upon her breast, she tore off a piece of flesh. . . . I seem to see her now . . . a piece of flesh . . . yes, large and very white, oozing blood, and she flung it in my face, saying, more in pity than in anger, these words, which I shall never forget: 'Take it . . . for the poor beast.'" [1]

This rather disgusting piece of dream-symbolism might have been taken straight from the pages of a modern treatise upon psycho-analysis! However unattractive in certain of its aspects, the question of dream-symbolism is one of which the importance has now been admitted by orthodox psychologists. Whether or no Galdós actually anticipated certain recent developments in that branch of knowledge is open to question; but in view of the rôle which abnormal

---

había dado cuenta la noche antes del grave mal de D. Tomé. 'Hay en mí como un eco apagadísimo de la voz de Teresa contándomelo. . . . No lo puedo asegurar; pero tampoco puedo negarlo. Es fácil que Teresa me lo dijera, y que yo lo oyese con poca o ninguna atención. No me enteré; pero en mi cerebro quedó como un dato suelto, caído, que después, al revolverse las ideas, asoma por donde menos se piensa, y lo ve uno, y . . . De alguna manera tuve noticia del hecho, y me lo recordé mediante el fenómeno ese del dualismo" (ibid., p. 71).

[1] "Rodeada de pies a cabeza de una luz cegadora, y sus ojos me miraron con una severidad que me hizo estremecer, y echándose mano al seno, se arrancó un pedazo de carne . . . me parece que le estoy viendo . . . de carne . . . sí, grande y blanquísimo, chorreando sangre, y me lo arrojó a la cara, diciéndome con más compasión que ira estas palabras que nunca olvidaré: 'Toma . . . para la pobre bestia" (part iii. cap. ii., p. 123).

psychology plays in contemporary fiction his interest is significant.

Leré, also, is unbalanced and suffers from a nervous disorder which is attributed to pre-natal influences: "Her face was one of the most enigmatic that can be conceived, utterly puzzling or extremely expressive according to the point at which one started to decipher it. Her skin, white as marble, formed a contrast with her black hair and eyebrows, which looked like two small pieces of black velvet fastened upon her skin. Her nose, badly formed, her mouth, imperfect, her teeth, white and uneven, went to make up a dubious whole of the type which is destined to be delivered up to æsthetic individualism and the caprice of men. In addition to all this, her greenish eyes, which had golden sparks in them, were affected with a constitutional mobility, an oscillation in a horizontal direction, which gave her the look of one of those mechanical dolls whose eyes move from right to left on a swivel. It was rumoured that this nervous trouble had its origin in a great fright which her mother had suffered when pregnant, and that the child was born with this vibration of the optic nerve, called, in scientific terminology, 'rotatory nistagmus.' "[1] This peculiarity, how-

---

[1] "Era su cara de las más enigmáticas que pueden verse, ininteligible o expresiva por todo extremo, según por donde se empezara a deletrearla. El blanco marmóreo de su tez contrastaba con lo negro de su pelo y de sus cejas, las cuales parecían dos tiritas de terciopelo pegadas en la piel. Mal figurada la nariz y no muy correcta la boca, blancos y desiguales los dientes, resultaba un conjunto dudoso, de esos que deben entregarse al personalismo estético y al capricho de los hombres. Además, sus ojos verdosos con radiaciones doradas hallábanse afectados de una movilidad constitutiva, de una oscilación en sentido horizontal, que la asemejaba a esos muñecos de reloj, que al compás del escape mueven las pupilas de derecha a izquierda. Cuentan que la causa de tal afección nerviosa fué que, hallándose su madre embarazada, tuvo un gran susto y la criatura salió con aquella vibración de los nervios ópticos, que científicamente se denomina *nistagmus rotatorio*" (part i. cap. iii., pp. 92–3).

ever, only enhances her elusive charm, and Angel compliments her upon it. "Believe me," he says, "it is as though I were looking at the reflection of the sun in moving water."[1]

There is, indeed, nothing in the least revolting about the eccentricities of either Angel or Leré. It is otherwise with the latter's brother—who has the misfortune to be a monster![2]

Although this preoccupation with the abnormal is the most striking characteristic of the novel as a whole, *Angel Guerra* is not a mere "psycho-analytical" *tour de force*. While condemning the false mysticism—"la loca de la casa," as he calls it,[3] which leads Angel to think that he has a vocation, Galdós reveals a genuine interest in those realms of the human mind which have not yet been adequately explored. The effect which Toledo has upon the dessicated positivism of Angel is sympathetically described. After wandering through the streets of the old Jewish quarter he is permeated by the spirit of the place: "His enthusiasm for bygone ages was so great that he conceived a violent aversion to the vociferous hurly-burly of contemporary life"[4]—and as he walks in and out of the ancient churches he is conscious of "Vague temptations to pay greater attention to religion, even to practise it and philosophise about it, seeking in it a means of communication with the supra-sensible world. He already admitted a kind of provisional faith, a kind of 'we'll see,' a 'well possibly,' which was already a stimulus powerful enough to make

[1] "Créeme que es como si estuviese viendo el reflejo del sol en el agua movible" (ibid., p. 93).

[2] Galdós harrows us with a truly "naturalistic" description of this horrible creature (vide part ii. cap. i., p. 32).

[3] Vide part iii. cap. i., p. 86.

[4] "De tal modo le apasionaban las edades muertas, que se determinó en él una atroz aversión del gárrulo bullicio de la vida contemporánea" (part ii., p. 39).

him think with respect about things which had previously provoked him to laughter. He suddenly realised that in the world of ideas there are regions as yet unexplored, unknown, which are open to us at propitious moments, inviting us to enter them; gloomy paths which are suddenly made light; Atlantidae which, when one least expects it, lead us to continents never before seen or dreamed of."[1] This "other-worldliness," which has no connection with the afore-mentioned rather cold-blooded probing of pathological states, is also a pronounced feature of the book. One feels that Galdós himself shares that thirst for the supernatural of which Angel speaks in his confession to El Padre Casado: "One of the desires which torments me most acutely is the longing for the supernatural, the desire that my senses should be aware of sensations contrary to the physical laws which we all know. The monotony of everyday natural phenomena drives one to despair."[2]

We are moving here in a very different world from that of *Gloria*. In his early attacks upon mysticism Galdós reveals a lack of sympathy with "supernaturalism" in any form. The religious code of his favourite types is severely practical. In *Angel Guerra*, while he still roundly condemns what he regards as the unhealthy mysticism of the cloister, he appears, as we

[1] "Tentaciones vagas de poner alguna mayor atención en el culto, casi, casi de practicarlo, y de cavilar en ello, buscando como una comunicación honda y clandestina con el mundo ultra sensible. Admitía ya cierta fe provisional, una especie de *veremos*, un *por si acaso*, que ya era suficiente estímulo para que viese con respeto cosas que antes le hacían reir. Por de pronto reconocía que en el mundo de nuestras ideas hay zonas desconocidas, no exploradas, que a lo mejor se abren, convidando a lanzarse por ellas; caminos obscuros que se aclaran de improviso; atlántidas que, cuando menos se piensa, conducen a continentes nunca vistos antes ni siquiera soñados" (part ii. cap. i., p. 41).

[2] "Una de las ansias que más me atormentan es la de lo sobrenatural, la de que mis sentidos perciban sensaciones contrarias a la ley física que todos conocemos. La monotonía de los fenómenos corrientes de la naturaleza es desesperante" (part iii. cap. ii., p. 124).

have remarked, to sympathise to a certain extent with his hero's yearning for contact with a supra-sensible world. In his earlier years Galdós believed, as did Angel Guerra, his creation, that the ills of humanity could be cured by means of a political nostrum. Later, like Angel Guerra, he seems to turn aside in disgust from the panaceas of the market-place and seek a remedy for mankind's disease in the interior of the spirit-world. Once found, however, that remedy must be applied in practical fashion: and Angel Guerra's "Dominismo," which aims at "the meticulous practice of the laws which Christ Our Lord gave us," [1] is excellent in so far as it is sincere. Galdós returns to the question of social regeneration in *Nazarín*, which, like nearly all the novels of the last phase, resembles a tract rather than a work of fiction. He also falls into the clutches of "la loca de la casa"—the elusive sylph, phantasy, who leads reason astray.

In spite of its rather wearisome concentration upon abnormalities, *Angel Guerra* is entitled to a high place among the *Novelas Contemporáneas*. It contains some fine descriptive passages in which Galdós has caught the brooding melancholy of "that stern countryside which expresses the idea of meditation, of a tranquility favourable to spiritual florescence." [2] and one of the most delicious pieces of satire in the whole series.[3] It also supplies some interesting additions to the Galdosian portrait-gallery, notably D. Simón García Babel— "so expansive and tenacious in society that it was at times

[1] "La aplicación rigurosa de las leyes de caridad, que Cristo Nuestro Señor nos dió" (part iii. cap. iv., p. 310).
[2] "Ese paisaje severo, que expresa la idea de meditación, de quietud, propicia a las florescencias del espíritu" (part ii. cap. i , p. 36).
[3] Vide part i. cap. iii., pp. 130, et seq., where the three doctors— Carnicero, Moreno Rubio and Augusto Miquís—argue about the illness of Doña Sales. This is almost worthy of "The Doctor's Dilemma."

necessary to avoid him as one would the plague"[1]; "Pito Babel" (his brother), "a hard-boiled individual"[2]; Doña Sales' agent, Braulio—"He was fat and rubicund, wore gold-rimmed spectacles, and his cheeks were like two fresh roses bathed in dew"[3]; and Don Francisco Mancebo, "Tío Providencia," "fairly keen-lipped and the owner of a good set of teeth which he would show as a proof of his excellent health."[4]

In *Tristana* Galdós approaches from a different angle the problem with which he had dealt in *La Desheredada*: that which concerns the position in society of a young girl without resources. Tristana, daughter of Antonio Reluz, is left an orphan at an early age. She was entrusted by her mother on the latter's death-bed to the care of an intimate friend of the family—one Don "Lope" Garrido. Unhappily for Tristana, Don "Lope," who is absolutely devoid of conscience where his passions are concerned, falls a victim to her charms. Taking advantage of his position as her guardian, he seduces his charge who, confined to the society of himself and his servants, remains for long totally ignorant of her position in the eyes of the world. Eventually, however, she becomes intimate with one of the servants—Saturnia, a lascivious old woman who explains the true state of affairs. While rebelling inwardly against her position, Tristana lacks the moral courage to break with her "guardian" and face the world alone. She

---

[1] "Tan expansivo y pegajoso en sociedad, que a veces había que huir de él como de la peste" (part i. cap. ii., p. 48).

[2] "Hombre muy pasado por agua" (ibid., p. 58).

[3] "Era grueso y rubicundo, usaba gafas de oro, y sus mejillas parecían dos rosas frescas, bañadas de rocío" (ibid. cap. iii., p. 88).

[4] "Bastante aguzado de morros y con buena dentadura, que solía mostrar como indicio cierto de su excelente salud" (part ii. cap. ii., p. 43).

contrives, however, to vary the monotony of her existence by scraping acquaintance with a young artist, Horacio Díaz, who—after a laborious youth spent in the chemist's shop of an intransigent grandfather—is now enjoying the vagaries of a belated adolescence. Upon the idyllic relations between Horacio and Tristana the story hinges. Tristana develops into an Ibsenian heroine who looks upon marriage as slavery and regards freedom and independence as "every woman's birthright." A disease of the leg makes the fulfilment of her desire for a career impossible; so she spends a devout old age as the lawful wife of the satyr, Don "Lope," who marries her in order to gain the approval of his old aunts, two "devotas" from whom he has expectations.

It is curious that *Tristana* should have been passed over in silence by the majority of critics. Although extremely slight as compared with any other of the books we have discussed, it is, technically, one of the best of *Las Novelas Contemporáneas*. It is, indeed, one of the few in which matter is proportionate to length. It contains passages of great lyrical beauty—especially those which describe the love-making of Horacio and Tristana. Such phrases as—"The day I found you was the last of a long exile"[1]; and—"I knew you for my own, and you declared that I was yours. That is life—the rest, what is it?"[2] are instinct with genuine passion; and for limpid purity of style it would be difficult to match the Spanish original of the following: "As evening fell they gazed upon the magnificent horizon bounded by the Sierra, bright turquoise in colour with touches and transparencies of unequal intensity,

---

[1] "El día en que te descubrí fué el último de un largo destierro" (*Tristana* (1892 ed.), cap. viii., p. 57).

[2] "Te reconocí mía, y me declaraste tuyo. Esto es vivir; lo demás, ¿que es?" (ibid. cap. ix., p. 72).

as though the limpid azure had been poured upon crystals of ice. The contours of the barren earth, fading away into the distance in undulating lines which seemed to imitate the gentle rise and fall of waves, called to their minds that 'more, always more,' which expressed the insatiable longing of their thirsty souls. On certain evenings, as they walked along the banks of the little canal on the Eastern side—an undulating patch of oasis which encircles the arid contours of Madrid—they revelled in the pastoral tranquillity of that miniature valley, the crowing of cocks, the barking of dogs, the huts of workmen; the swirl of the fallen leaves which the faint breeze gently swept together, piling them up around the tree-trunks; an ass grazing with solemn deliberation; the faint trembling of the loftiest branches of the trees from which the leaves were gradually being stripped —everything was a source of enchantment and wonder, and they exchanged ideas, giving them and taking them as though it were a single thought which leaped from lip to lip and eye to eye." [1] Tristana is a perfect mistress: "She could express her love in ways eternally new; she could be tender without cloying; ingenuous, without being insipid; bold, without a trace of corruption; with sincerity always to the fore as the

[1] "Contemplaban al caer de la tarde el grandioso horizonte de la Sierra, de un vivo tono de turquesa, con desiguales toques y transparencias, como si el azul purísimo se derramase sobre cristales de hielo. Las curvas del suelo desnudo, perdiéndose y arrastrándose como líneas que quieren remedar un manso oleaje, les repetían aquel *más, siempre más'*, ansia inextinguible de sus corazones sedientos. Algunas tardes, paseando junto al canalillo del oeste, ondulada tira de oasis que ciñe los áridos contornos del terruño madrileño, se recreaban en la placidez bucólica de aquel vallecito en miniatura. Cantos de gallo, ladridos de perro, casitas de labor; el remolino de las hojas caídas, que el manso viento barría suavemente, amontonándolas junto a los troncos; el asno, que pacía con grave mesura; el ligero temblor de las más altas ramas de los árboles, que se iban quedando desnudos: todo les causaba embeleso y maravilla, y se comunicaban las impresiones, dándoselas y quitándoselas como si fuera una sola impresión que corría de labio a labio y saltaba de ojos a ojos" (cap. ix., pp. 73-4).

O

chief and most apparent of her infinite charms" [1]—and she emphatically refuses to change her condition for that of wife: "Long live independence! . . . provided that it doesn't interfere with my loving you and being yours for ever. I know what I'm about: I have my own little ideas. Don't talk about marriage—we don't want to quarrel about who is to wear the petticoats. I think you will love me less if you make me your slave; I believe I shall love you very little if I have you under my thumb. Virtuous freedom is my motto—or, if you like, my creed . . ." [2] and so on through all the specious arguments in favour of the *union libre*. Tristana, however, may possibly be allowed a certain laxity in view of her guardian's cynical conduct. Galdós gives us, in his inimitable style, an arresting portrait of the old satyr. His real name is D. Juan López Garrido, but he has adopted the more sonorous "Don Lope," for "It fitted so aptly his gaunt face with its firm and noble lines; and was so well suited to his slender, erect body, his arched nose, his open forehead and sparkling eyes, his grizzled moustache and short pig-tail, stiff and provocative, that such an individual could have no other name. One would either have to kill him or call him Don Lope." [3]

[1] "Sabía expresar su cariño en términos siempre nuevos; ser dulce sin empalagar, candorosa sin insulsez, atrevidilla sin asomos de corrupción, con la sinceridad siempre por delante, como la primera y más visible de sus infinitas gracias" (cap. xv., p. 120).

[2] "¡Viva la independencia! . . . sin perjuicio de amarte y ser siempre tuya. Yo me entiendo: tengo acá mis ideitas. Nada de matrimonio, para no andar a la greña por aquello de quién tiene las faldas y quién no. Creo que has de quererme menos si me haces tu esclava; creo que te querré poco si te meto en un puño. Libertad honrada es mi tema . . . o si quieres, mi dogma. . . " (cap. xiv., p. 114).

[3] "Tan bien caía en su cara enjuta, de líneas firmes y nobles, tan buen acomodo hacía el nombre con la espigada tiesura del cuerpo, con la nariz de caballete, con su despejada frente y sus ojos vivísimos, con el mostacho entrecano y la perilla corta, tiesa y provocativa, que el sujeto no se podía llamar de otra manera. O había que matarle o decirle D. Lope" (cap. i., p. 6).

It was very difficult to determine his exact age, for he never seemed to grow older: "He had halted at forty-nine as though an instinctive horror of the fifties were holding him upon the dreaded confines of the half-century" [1] —and he is eternally youthful in gallantry.

As a moral exemplar, Don Lope, who—"prided himself upon the fact that he had stormed more towers of virtue and captured more strongholds of purity than he possessed hairs upon his head," [2] left much to be desired.

It may be that the heterodox moral tone of this work has militated against its attaining due recognition by orthodox Spanish critics. Whatever the reason may be, *Tristana* seems to have missed its deserts at their hands.

In *La Loca de la Casa*, which followed it, Galdós returns to his now threadbare theme of pseudo-mysticism and its attendant evils. The novel is dull and commonplace in conception and execution. Don Juan de Moncada suffers, after the death of his wife, a series of financial reverses which brings him near to ruin. His troubles are intensified by the fact that one of his daughters, Victoria, has been attacked by "that terrible ravager of the human brain, the bacillus of mysticism." [3] She eventually abandons, however, her idea of entering a convent and decides, happily for Don Juan, to sacrifice herself for the sake of the family by marrying the vulgar parvenu José María Cruz. In this novel we have the first manifestation of that weariness and carelessness which is, unfortunately,

[1] "Se había plantado en los cuarenta y nueve, como si el terror instintivo de los cincuenta le detuviese en aquel temido lindero de medio siglo" (ibid.).

[2] "Se preciaba de haber asaltado más torres de virtud y rendido más plazas de honestidad que pelos tenía en la cabeza" (ibid., p. 7).

[3] "Ese terrible asolador del humano cerebro: el *bacillus mística*" (*La Loca de la Casa* (1915 ed.), p. 17).

characteristic of the later works. The presentation of two other characters, Daniel, Marqués de Malavella, and Doña Eulalia, Moncada's sister, as victims of the "mystical bacillus" weakens rather than strengthens the author's case. He "insists too much." *La Loca de la Casa* is, if the truth be told, a dull piece of propaganda unredeemed by literary merit of any kind.

The four subsequent novels—*Torquemada en la Hoguera*, *Torquemada en la Cruz*, *Torquemada en el Purgatorio* and *Torquemada y San Pedro*—deal with the social and spiritual evolution of that terrible figure—"that inhuman being who had destroyed, as by fire, so many unhappy human lives" [1]— concerning whose activities we have had dark hints in previous stories.[2] Don Francisco de Torquemada (nicknamed by his unfortunate victims "El Peor"), who started business as a small moneylender in a poor quarter of Madrid, has built up a vast fortune out of the miseries of his fellow citizens. Prior to the opening of the story, he has lived in modest comfort upon his disreputable gains, unmolested by outrageous fortune. In the first volume of the series we learn how the fires of sorrow, which he has so often kindled for the destruction of others, are lighted in his own house. First comes the death of his wife, who was, literally, worth at least part of her weight in gold to him, for "She not only ruled the household with masterly economy but also advised her husband in difficult questions of business, helping him with the light of her experience in the matter of loans. She, who stood guard over the *céntimo* in the house lest it should stray into the street, and he, who plied his broom so that everything which passed by might be drawn in, made a married couple to whom waste

[1] "El inhumano que tantas vidas infelices consumió en llamas" (*Torquemada en la Hoguera* (1920 ed.). p. 9).
[2] Vide especially *Fortunata y Jacinta*.

was unknown, a pair who might well serve as an example to the entire race of ants, below and above the surface of the earth." [1] For long it seems that he will never recover from this terrible loss, but time does its work and at length —"the sun in his soul arose, illuminating once again the various numerical combinations which existed therein." [2] He finds consolation in his two children, especially in Valentín, his son, who turns out to be a mathematical prodigy: "Already from his earliest years, when he acquired the rudimentary notions of the science of numbers, he would add and subtract from memory amounts running into two and even three figures. He calculated with infallible accuracy, and his own father, who was keen as an eagle in reckoning rates of interest in his head, would frequently consult him." [3] This is a source of keen delight to Don Francisco, who takes an academic and at times almost metaphysical interest in his calling. If he had lived a century earlier Torquemada would, the author tells us, have been one of those idealistic practitioners of the art of usury who "adored the most holy and ineffable God of Numbers, sacrificing their material existence to him as the mystic subordinates everything to the one idea

[1] "No sólo gobernaba la casa con magistral economía, sino que asesoraba a su pariente en los negocios difíciles, auxiliándole con sus luces y su experiencia para el préstamo. Ella defendiendo el céntimo en casa para que no se fuera a la calle, y él barriendo para adentro a fin de traer todo lo que pasara, formaron un matrimonio sin desperdicio, pareja que podría servir de modelo a cuantas hormigas hay debajo de la tierra y encima de ella" (*Torquemada en la Hoguera* (1920 ed.), cap. i., p. 13)

[2] ". . . despejóse el sol del alma, iluminando de nuevo las variadas combinaciones numéricas que en ella había . . ." (ibid).

[3] "Ya desde sus primeros años, al recibir las nociones elementales de la ciencia de la cantidad, sumaba y restaba de memoria decenas altas y aun centenas. Calculaba con tino infalible, y su padre mismo, que era un águila para hacer, en el filo de la imaginación, cuentas por la regla de interés, le consultaba no pocas veces" (cap. ii., p. 24).

of saving his soul." [1] He has not, however, remained unaffected by the materialism of the last decades of the nineteenth century; and instead of living in a hovel and sleeping upon "a rough mattress full of fleas and banknotes stuffed into the straw" [2] he occupies a respectable house and changes his shirt once a fortnight! During the years immediately preceding his wife's death, rapid social progress has been made: "Torquemada started to wear a silk hat which cost fifty reals; he sported two coats, one superfine, with red lapels. The children also were well dressed. Rufina, the daughter, had a washstand of the kind that are made to be looked at rather than touched, together with a jug and a basin of blue glass which were never used in case they should be broken. Doña Silvia decked herself out in a coat made, apparently, of rabbit fur, and left the whole of the Calle de Tudescos and the Callejón del Perro squinting when she went out with her reticule adorned with glass beads. Step by step, in fact, they were gradually elbowing themselves into the middle class; our good-natured middle-class, all poverty and pretensions, which is, alas, growing so rapidly, so rapidly, that we shall soon be left without a 'plebs.'" [3]

[1] "Adoraban la santísima, la inefable cantidad, sacrificando a ella su material existencia, las necesidades del cuerpo y de la vida, como el místico lo pospone todo a la absorbente idea de salvarse" (cap ii., p. 17).

[2] ". . . un camastro lleno de pulgas y de billetes de Banco metidos entre la paja . . ." (ibid.).

[3] "Torquemada empezó a usar chistera de cincuenta reales; disfrutaba dos capas, una muy buena, con embozos colorados; los hijos iban bien apañaditos; Rufina tenía un lavabo de los de míreme y no me toques, con jofaina y jarro de cristal azul, que no se usaba nunca por no estropearlo; Doña Silvia se engalanó con un abrigo de pieles que parecían de conejo, y dejaba bizca a toda la calle de Tudescos y callejón del Perro cuando salía con la *visita* guarnecida de abalorio; en fin, que pasito a paso y a codazo limpio, se habían ido metiendo en la clase media, en nuestra bonachona clase media, toda necesidades y pretensiones, y que crece tanto, tanto ¡ay dolor! que nos estamos quedando sin pueblo" (ibid., p. 19).

A few years after his bereavement, Don Francisco wakes up to find himself a fully-fledged bourgeois—"he tapped himself, and the sound informed him that he was a man of property and a gentleman of means."[1] With increase of material comfort there comes, however, the keenest grief of his life. Valentín falls seriously ill, and, in spite of Don Francisco's clumsy prayers to the Deity whom he has hitherto neglected, the boy dies.

After a period of bitter scepticism, Torquemada finds spiritual consolation in the belief—suggested to him in the first instance by the religious theories of his friend José Bailón [2]—that Valentín will reincarnate. He spends hours in meditation before a photograph of his son, which he has placed upon an improvised altar. On one occasion he fancies that the portrait speaks to him, saying: "Papa, I want to come to life again" [3]—and from that time onwards he seriously contemplates a second marriage. Doña Lupe, "la de los Pavos," [4] his old friend and colleague, had begged him on her death-bed to marry one of the Águila sisters—the sole survivors of a distinguished but impoverished family. Torquemada has called upon them once or twice, but, after one of his visits, he remarks sorrowfully to himself: "I haven't any manners, that's the truth of it. When I am in the presence of a person of importance I feel like a drone and don't know what to say, nor what to do with my hands." [5] He has hitherto been

---

[1] "... se tocaba, y el sonido le advertía que era propietario y rentista" (ibid., p. 21).

[2] Vide cap. iii., p. 31 et seq. Bailón professes a vague pantheism—with reincarnation as its central dogma. His account of his own previous life as an Egyptian priest is extremely entertaining.

[3] *Torquemada en la Cruz*, cap xiv., p. 106.

[4] Vide *Fortunata y Jacinta*.

[5] "No tengo política, no la tengo; en viéndome delante de una persona principal, ya estoy hecho un zángano y no sé qué decir ni qué hacer con las manos" (Torquemada en la Cruz, cap. iii., p. 23).

unable to summon up the necessary courage to approach one of them upon the delicate question; and, granted the courage —which one was it to be? Valentín's presumed desire to revisit the earth forces his hand, and he eventually decides upon Fidela del Águila. The latter, however, is dominated by her strong-willed sister Cruz—who determines to rule her brother-in-law's ménage in her own way. Hence the punning title of the second volume—"Torquemada en *la Cruz*."

From the time Cruz takes the reins of his household into her capable hands, Torquemada's life is a purgatory.[1] Cruz is determined that her sister's sacrifice in marrying this vulgar clown shall not be in vain. She exhorts him to take the position in society which his wealth entitles him to hold, urging him on from expense to expense until at length she succeeds in persuading him to purchase a marquisate. Every penny that is spent fans the flames of the purgatorial fire which is consuming the unhappy Don Francisco. The fire, however, does its work efficiently and, purged of avarice in its grossest forms, he is exhorted by the indefatigable Cruz to concentrate upon the salvation of his immortal soul.

Torquemada y San Pedro deals with this final phase of his spiritual evolution, "San Pedro" being the name which Torquemada gives to Father Gamborena, the chosen ally of Cruz in the formidable task which she has set herself. Whether or no these two succeed in their campaign is not made clear. The last word which Torquemada utters as he lies on his death-bed is "*conversión*." This, however, might apply either to the "conversion" of his soul or to that of the public funds—with which his mind had of late been occupied![2]

[1] *Torquemada en el Purgatorio.*
[2] This inability to disentangle his religious principles from those which he has acquired in his trade is amusingly brought out in his

There is hardly sufficient material in the Torquemada series to justify four volumes. The whole story of the usurer's social apotheosis and spiritual development could, indeed, have easily been compressed into one; and it is to be feared that Galdós has here laid himself open to the insinuation that the quartering was effected with an eye to sales. His reputation was established; a large public eagerly awaited the appearance of a new novel; and four new novels are a better financial proposition than one! Apart from the central figure of the series, no great personage is added to the hierarchy of Galdosian types. Don Francisco de Torquemada, as he is revealed to us in these stories, is the last masterpiece in the portrait gallery of *Las Novelas Contemporáneas*.

In *Nazarín* Galdós approaches the religious problem from a different angle. Torquemada had expressed in its crudest form the popular conception of religion as a system of rewards

conversation with El P. Gamborena (*Torquemada y San Pedro*, part ii. cap v., p. 144). He demands guarantees that his soul will be saved: "And, of course, when I am dealing with the question of how I am to invest this considerable capital (his soul!) and make it secure, I must discuss in detail the terms of the investment. I hand over to you, then, what you demand from me, my conscience. . . . Good. . . . But you must guarantee that, once my conscience is entirely in your keeping, the gates of eternal glory shall be opened to me. You, yourself, must see that I get through, for you have the keys for that purpose. There must be loyalty and good faith on both sides. Have a care! Because, frankly, it would be very unfortunate for me, my dear Mr. Missionary, if I were to hand over my capital only to discover in the end that there were no such gates, no such glory, no Christ who supplies it. . . ." ["Y naturalmente, yo, tratando de la colocación de ese saneado capital, y de asegurarlo bien, tengo que discutir con toda minuciosidad las condiciones. Por consiguiente, yo le entrego a usted lo que me exige, la conciencia. . . . Bueno. . . . Pero usted me ha de garantizar que, una vez en su poder mi conciencia toda, se me han de abrir las puertas de la Gloria eterna, que ha de franqueármelas usted mismo, puesto que llaves tiene para ello. Haya por ambas partes lealtad y buena fe ¡cuidado! Porque, francamente, sería muy triste, señor misionero de mis entretelas, que yo diera mi capital, y que luego resultara que no había tales puertas, ni tal Gloria, ni Cristo que lo fundó. . . ."]

and punishments—"el negocio del alma." Nazarío Zaharín ("Nazarín"), the Catholic priest who endeavours to reproduce with literal fidelity the life of Jesus, holds the humanitarian view of Christianity as a code of ethics. His attitude, however, is very far removed from that of the mere positivist; and, as we can divine from the opinions he expresses in his interview with a reporter, there is a great deal of the mystic in him. This interview forms a kind of prologue to the novel.[1] In it the journalist plays Sancho Panza to Nazarín's Don Quixote, putting forward the usual "common-sense" objections to the priest's idealistic theorising. The latter probably reflects something of Galdós' growing distrust of science, democracy and political "progress"; but the author is impartial, and makes us feel that there is much to be said for the reporter's point of view. An undiscriminating altruism may bring forth good fruit in certain individuals. Society, however, would be the loser if everyone practised it. At the conclusion of the book we are left in doubt as to whether Nazarín did service to the state by his indiscriminate charity. Why should he refuse to defend himself against the calumnies to which he is subjected on account of his protection of the prostitute, Andara? Rather than attempt to justify himself, he submits to the indignity of ecclesiastical censure and wanders as a beggar through the streets, accompanied by Andara and Beatriz, his two disciples, "the one militant, the other pacifist,"[2]—until they are all arrested by the Civil Guard.

He soon gains notoriety, and in *Halma*, the sequel to *Nazarín*, we hear how his fame as "an extraordinary man, an

---

[1] Vide *Nazarín* (1907 ed.), part i. cap. iii., p. 23 et seq. Galdós has obviously been reading Tolstoy, to whom he is almost certainly in indebted in his conception of Nazarín.

[2] "La una batalladora, la otra pacífica" (part v. cap. vii., p. 301).

innovator, who preaches with acts, not words, who proselytises
with the will, not the intelligence, and who is destined to . . .
make an indelible mark upon our age," [1] has reached the
exclusive circle in which the Condesa de Halma-Lautenberg
moves. "El nazarismo" is on the point of becoming a society
craze. Antonio Cánovas del Castillo himself has been heard to
remark: "It would be the greatest of crimes to punish
Nazarín," [2] When it is ascertained that Don Nazarío "only
knows Russian literature by hearsay," [3] early suspicions as to
the source of his doctrines are allayed, and he comes to be
regarded by many—including the Countess Halma-Lautenberg—as a kind of Messiah. Catalina de Halma's life has been
an extremely unhappy one and, after her crowning sorrow—
the death of her husband—she seeks consolation in the performance of good works. She forms the ambitious project of
founding a colony for the poor and outcast, and has aspirations
towards sanctity and the contemplative life. Her dreams,
however, are rudely shattered by Nazarín, who pronounces
her to be totally unfitted for such a spiritual existence: "You
will attain nothing," he tells her, "by purely spiritual means:
you will gain all by human means." [4] She should abandon her
Utopian schemes for the care of the poor: "To the poor I say
—suffer and hope: to the rich—return to God by the path of
repentance: to the good—live holy lives according to the laws
of God and man. And to you, who are good, noble, and

[1] "Un hombre extraordinario, un innovador, que predica con actos,
no con palabras, que apostoliza con la voluntad, no con la inteligencia,
y que dejará . . . un profundo surco en nuestro siglo" (vide *Halma*
(1923 ed.), part ii., p. 79).
[2] "Condenar a Nazarín sería la mayor de las iniquidades" (ibid.
part iii., p. 140).
[3] "No conoce la literatura rusa más que de oídas" (ibid., p. 143).
[4] "Nada conseguirá usted por lo espiritual puro; todo lo tendrá
usted por lo humano" (part v., p. 338).

virtuous, I say—do not seek perfection in spiritual isolation, because you will not find it there. Your life needs the support of another life that it may not go astray, that you may always walk uprightly." [1] He advises her, in short, to marry again. The alleged novelty of Nazarín's doctrines is, to use a picturesque Spanish term, "una mixtificación," for they are a patent hotch-potch of orthodox Christianity, positivism and Russian humanitarianism of the Tolstoyan school. Of this Galdós himself was clearly conscious. "Qui s'excuse, s'accuse" —and the remark, already noted, to the effect that Don Nazarío had not read the Russian novelists is tantamount to an admission that his creator knew them well!

If the author's object in writing *Nazarín* and *Halma* was to excite our sympathies for the poor and the oppressed, he comes nearer to achieving that object in *Misericordia*. There is an atmosphere of unreality about the two former works which is conducive to impatience on the part of the reader. Not so in *Misericordia*—which depicts the conditions among the poverty-stricken classes of Madrid with the intimate understanding of one who knew and loved them well.

The story concerns the vicissitudes of a woman of the middle class—one Doña Francisca Juárez de Zapata, who is brought to destitution by her thriftlessness.[2] The central

---

[1] "A los pobres les digo que sufran y esperen, a los ricos que amparen al pobre, a los malos que vuelvan a Dios por la vía del arrepentimiento, a los buenos que vivan santamente, dentro de las leyes divinas y humanas. Y a usted que es buena, y noble, y virtuosa, le digo que no busque la perfección en el espiritualismo solitario, porque no la encontrará, que su vida necesita del apoyo de otra vida para no tambalearse, para andar siempre bien derecha" (ibid., pp. 338–9).

[2] Vide *Misericordia* (1920 ed.), cap. vii., p. 49: "Large towns supply innumerable examples of such descents and Madrid more than any other, Madrid in which orderliness can hardly be said to exist; but of all such examples that unhappy plaything of fate, Doña Francisca Juárez, is the most striking." ["Ejemplos sin número de estas caídas nos ofrecen

figure, however, is her old servant Benigna ("Benina")[1]—who remains true to her throughout her misfortunes. Benina, when Francisca is reduced to the verge of starvation, is obliged to seek means of support for them both by begging in the streets. Her adventures, during which she comes into contact with beggars of every description, provide a vivid record of mendicity in the capital. Worse, however, than the comparatively cheerful destitution of the professional beggars is the resigned misery of the "déclassées"—Frasquita, Paca and Obdulia. There is in all this poverty a total absence of bitterness which is characteristically Spanish. The poor man is "somebody" in Spain; and even takes a quaint pride in the dignity which poverty confers upon him.

Misericordia is not a "thesis novel." Galdós confines himself in it to a sympathetic portrayal of the life of the poor, among whom Benina moves like an angel of charity and pity. She receives, however, no reward for her devotion and self-sacrifice. When upon one of her begging expeditions, she is arrested and taken to the workhouse. After her release, she finds that the fortunes of her mistress have been re-established. Francisca, however, exhibits no gratitude, and dismisses, with a wretched pension, the pathetic old woman, who has to seek consolation in the devotion of her old friend the blind beggar, Almudena.[2]

While *Misericordia* cannot rank with *Fortunata y Jacinta*,

las poblaciones grandes, más que ninguna ésta de Madrid, en que apenas existen hábitos de órden; pero a todos los ejemplos supera el de Dóna Francisca Juárez, tristísimo juguete del destino."]

[1] Vide cap. ii , p. 18: "She answered to the name of 'Señá Benina' (from which it may be inferred that she was called 'Benigna')." ["Respondía al nombre de la *señá Benina* (de lo cual se infiere que Benigna se llamaba."]

[2] Almudena (vide *Misericordia*, ed. cited, cap. iv., pp. 31–2) is a Moor, and talks a curious jargon of his own. Galdós reveals in this novel a wonderful knowledge of Madrid *argot* and beggars' slang.

Realidad or *Angel Guerra*, it is free from the didacticism, artificiality, and extravagance which mar so much of Galdós' later work.

In *El Abuelo*, "a novel in five acts," Galdós returns to the novel in dialogue—a *genre* which he attempts to vindicate in an interesting Prologue to this work. "In composing *El Abuelo*," he writes, "I wished to gratify my own taste and theirs (my readers') by developing the dialogue as fully as possible, and reducing to the smallest proportions the descriptive and narrative passages" [1]—and he proceeds to deal with its advantages over the orthodox novel form. After explaining how the dialogue "reveals to us expeditiously and in concrete form the make-up of the characters," [2] he goes on to express his views upon the relations between the novel and the drama: "In every novel in which the characters talk, a play lies hidden. The theatre is merely the condensation and union of all that constitutes action and character in the modern novel. . . . The chief works of the great dramatists seem to me to be 'spoken novels.'" [3] He sees, indeed, no real distinction between the two *genres*: "Although by its structure and by its division into scenes and acts *El Abuelo* has the appearance of a dramatic work, I have not hesitated to call it a novel, without giving an absolute value to this nomenclature; for in this, as in all that belongs to the infinite kingdom of art, it is most

[1] "En la composición de *El Abuelo*, he querido halagar mi gusto y el de ellos (los lectores) dando el mayor desarrollo posible, por esta vez, al procedimiento dialogal, y contrayendo a proporciones mínimas las formas descriptiva y narrativa" (vide *El Abuelo* (1912 ed.), p. 5).
[2] "Nos da la forja expedita y concreta de los caracteres" (ibid.).
[3] "En toda novela en que los personajes hablan, lata una obra dramática. El Teatro no es más que la condensación y acopladura de todo aquello que en la Novela moderna constituye acciones y caracteres . . . las obras capitales de los grandes dramáticos nos parecen *novelas habladas*" (ibid., p. 7).

prudent to avoid the pigeon-holing and cataloguing of kinds and forms" [1]—and his fondness for the dramatic form is, indeed, apparent throughout the *Novelas Contemporáneas*. It must be remembered in this connection that he only turned to the novel as a makeshift after he had failed to capture the public with his early dramatic works. So soon as his reputation was established he turned once again to the theatre. This Prologue removes all doubt as to where his sympathies really lay. It is, in a sense, fortunate that his early plays were unsuccessful: otherwise he might have confined his attention to the drama and the "dialogue novel," and some of his most brilliant and characteristic work would never have been produced.

El Abuelo is saved from banality by the majestic figure of "the Lion of Albrit"—as Don Rodrigo de Arista-Potestad, Conde de Albrit, Señor de Jerusa y de Polán, etc., is called. He represents the traditional type of Castillian nobleman, and appears in the novel as the vindicator of that old stern code of honour which can make no compromise with modern laxities. Like the code he symbolises, he has fallen upon evil days; and, at the end of his life, he returns to Spain from the New World —"poor as a rat, ailing and nearly blind, his only worldly burden his years, which already number more than seventy." [2] He is obliged to accept the hospitality of an old servant, Venancio, and his wife, Gregoria—now owners of La Pardina, an estate which once belonged to him. This, however, is by no means the worst humiliation he has to suffer. His son

---

[1] "Aunque por su estructura y por la división en jornadas y escenas parece *El Abuelo* obra teatral, no he vacilado en llamarla novela, sin dar a las denominaciones un valor absoluto, que en esto, como en todo lo que pertenece al reino infinito del arte, lo más prudente es huir de los encasillados, y de las clasificaciones catalogales de géneros y formas" (ibid.).

[2] "pobre como las ratas, enfermo y casi ciego, sin más cargamento que el de los años, que ya pasan de los setenta" (ibid. jornada i., p. 15).

Rafael, Conde de Laín, from the shock of whose recent death he has not yet recovered, had married an Irishwoman, one Lucrecia Richmond. The Condesa de Laín drags the family name through the mire of a society scandal, and it is whispered that the Count was not the father of both her children, Leonor and Dorotea, ("Nell" and "Dolly," as they are called). The disgrace which his daughter-in-law has brought upon the house is almost more than the old Conde de Albrit can bear. He is obsessed by the idea of discovering which of his two little grandchildren, to both of whom he is passionately devoted, is illegitimate; for he feels that his son's honour will be in some degree avenged by a family disavowal of the bastard.

The Countess refuses to divulge her secret, and the old man is forced to adopt various subterfuges in his attempt to discover the truth. His partial blindness prevents him from studying the children's faces in order to seek for hereditary traits, and their descriptions of one another (in response to his questioning) only add to his uncertainty. "Nell, Dolly! Which of you is my grandchild, heir to my blood and to my name?" [1] he bitterly soliloquises; but the solution to the problem continually evades him. It comes at length, quite accidentally, through a chance remark dropped by an old peasant woman, "La Marqueza," who has known the children since their birth. Dolly, it appears, has marked artistic ability; and the Condesa's lover, Carlos Eraúl, was an artist. The Conde de Albrit's suspicions are confirmed in the course of a conversation with Senén, a sycophantic "hanger-on" of the Condesa's suite. Knowledge of the truth, however, does not bring with it peace of mind; for Nell, the true daughter of Laín, prefers the society

---

[1] " ¡ Nell, Dolly! ¿ cual de vosotras es mi nieta, heredera de mi sangre y de mi nombre?" (ibid. jornada iii., p. 192).

of her mother to that of her grandfather and urges the latter to accept the invitation of the Prior of Zaratán, who wishes the "lion of Albrit" to end his days in a religious retreat. The old man is broken-hearted: "Nell has no heart," he cries, "her cold disdain belies her noble blood."[1] Dolly, daughter of the low-born artist Carlos Eraúl, and Don Pío Coronado, the feeble-minded old schoolmaster who had acted as tutor to the little girls, alone remain loyal to the now mortally wounded "Lion of Albrit," who crawls away into the wilderness to die.

The unctuous sentimentality and melodramatic rhetoric of *El Abuelo* render it distasteful and, at times, even grotesque to a modern reader. One of the grave disadvantages of the pseudo-dramatic form is that the descriptions and narrative elements of the orthodox novel have to be incorporated in the dialogue—and upon the latter there is laid, in consequence, a burden grievous to be borne. The characters must talk continuously; and the action is, as it were, drowned in a sea of verbiage. There are, in *El Abuelo*, the makings of a good melodrama [2]; but it is, in its novel form, far too long.

In *Casandra*, which followed it, Galdós retains the dialogue form,[3] but amplifies considerably the glosses and

[1] "Nell no tiene corazón; su frialdad desdeñosa desmiente la noble sangre" (ibid. jornada v., p. 417).

[2] It was played for the first time on 14 Feb., 1904, and had a *succès fou*.

[3] In a short Prologue to this work Galdós returns to his defence of the "novela teatral": "I must not hide the fact that I have grown fond of this sub-genre, the product of the crossing of the Novel with the Theatre, a pair who have explored the literary-social field seeking and experiencing their respective adventures, and who now, tired of going about alone in scornful independence, seem to want to enter into a more intimate and fruitful relationship. . . ." ["No debo ocultar que he tomado cariño a este sub-género, producto del cruzamiento de la Novela y el Teatro, dos hermanos que han recorrido el campo literario y social buscando y acometiendo sus respectivas aventuras, y que ahora, fatigados de andar solos en esquiva independencia, parece que quieren entrar en relaciones más íntimas y fecundas que las fraternales. . . ."] Vide *Casandra* (1906 ed.), pp. v.–vi.

P

"acotaciones" which are a feature of *Realidad* and *El Abuelo*. What in a normal drama would be stage directions are here developed into long parentheses which either describe the personal appearance, disposition etc. of a character or serve to fill in "background."[1] They amount, indeed, to a confession of failure so far as the *genre* is concerned; for in them Galdós reverts to the methods of the orthodox novel; which methods are, as it were, superimposed upon the normal technique of the drama. To make use of Galdós' own symbolism, a true "marriage" of the two *genres* was never effected; and *Casandra* is an example of the "novela teatral" at its worst. It aroused a great deal of opposition when it first appeared on account of its religious and political implications; and many critics who attacked it were, in consequence, accused of unfair bias. There can, however, be no question as to its inferiority as a work of art.

The theme is the abuse of bequests to the Church. A millionairess, Doña Juana Samaniego, Marquesa de Tobalina, widow of a contractor and "purchaser of Government stock," is an old devotee who is entirely ruled by her confessor. She is surrounded by a host of needy and greedy relations—to whom she doles out assistance in niggardly fashion. They are all anxiously awaiting her decease and their inheritance; one in order to exploit his rural properties; another to develop his inventions; another to live in comfort without working; another to take up business as a moneylender. Among these relatives is one Rogelio, an illegitimate child of Juana's late husband, who is living with his mistress Casandra. Rogelio is an "abnormal"—a humorous devil-worshipper who gives

[1] The portrait of Rosaura (jornada i. escena vii.), and the description of the sacristy (jornada iv. escenia vii.).

demon-names to the people he dislikes. The equanimity of her
connections is considerably upset when they hear that Doña
Juana is on the point of leaving all her wealth to the Church.
Casandra, however, gets them out of their difficulty by mur-
dering the old lady before she has time to alter her will! Doña
Juana, however, revenges herself upon them by reincarnating
as an old beggar woman! At least, so her niece, Clementina,
believes! *Casandra* is, indeed, an extraordinary farrago of
improbabilities; and its final excursion into the fantastic is
quite in keeping with the general tone of the work. In it, and
in its successors, the even more extravagant *El Caballero
Encantado* and *La Razón de la Sinrazón,* the genius of Galdós
reaches its nadir.

VIII

THE SIGNIFICANCE OF GALDÓS IN THE HISTORY OF MODERN SPANISH FICTION AND HIS PLACE IN EUROPEAN LITERATURE

WE have endeavoured in the preceding analyses of Galdós' principal novels to give some indication of the scope of his genius. It now remains to estimate the precise significance of his contribution to the national literature. To what extent is he indebted to his predecessors ? What do recent developments in Spanish fiction owe to him ? In what relationship does he stand to the great novelists of other European countries ?

As Menéndez y Pelayo has pointed out,[1] it was Galdós who first seriously embarked upon the task of redeeming Spanish fiction from the deplorable state into which it had fallen since the great age of Cervantes and the " gusto picaresco." It is true that Alarcón, Valera and Pereda were not unknown as writers prior to the appearance of *La Fontana de Oro*; but none of them had yet turned their attention to the novel proper. When Galdós entered the arena, he was faced with the task of creating the modern Spanish novel—and he met with such notable success in the performance of it that he has come to be regarded by many of those who are most competent to judge of

---

[1] Vide Menéndez y Pelayo, Discurso cit., p. 58: "There can be no doubt, then, that Galdós, the youngest of the eminent geniuses to whom we owed, twenty years ago, the restoration of the Spanish novel, was chronologically the first to undertake it." ["No hay duda, pues, que Galdós, con ser el más joven de los eminentes ingenios a quienes se debió hace veinte años la restauración de la novela española, *tuvo cronológicamente la prioridad del intento.*"]

such matters as the greatest Spanish novelist since Cervantes.[1] In all the types of fiction which had been crudely essayed by his predecessors—the historical novel, the novel of customs and the *roman à thèse*—he attained signal distinction. To these he added the novel in dialogue and that curious species of imaginative literature to which Menéndez y Pelayo has given the name of "novela simbólica" [2]—both of which forms are, in spite of their many inconsistencies and absurdities, of considerable interest and importance.

The early cultivators of the historical novel lacked, as we have seen, both the psychological insight and the sound basis of erudition which this *genre* demands.[3] In the majority of

---

[1] Vide González-Blanco, op. cit., cap. v., p. 270: "To talk of a national novel, in very truth Spanish, with the wide horizons of realism . . . is to name the author of *Doña Perfecta*." ["Decir novela nacional, de verdad española, con toda la amplitud de horizontes del realismo . . . es nombrar al autor de *Doña Perfecta*"]; also p. 373: "Among the modern writers of Spain, perhaps there is no single one who can vie with Galdós in creative power." ["Entre los escritores modernos de España quizá no haya uno solo que pueda competir con Galdós en fuerza creadora."] This view is supported by Menéndez y Pelayo (Discurso cit., passim), who speaks of Galdós in terms of the highest praise: "Galdós, brave designer of a monument which, possibly after the *Comédie Humaine* of Balzac, has no rival in copiousness and variety among all the edifices raised by the genius of the novel in our century" ["Galdós—artífice valiente de un monumento que quizá después de la *Comedia Humana* de Balzac, no tenga rival, en lo copioso y en lo vario, entre cuantos ha levantado el genio de la novela en nuestro siglo"] (p. 35); "To talk of the novels of Galdós is to talk of the Spanish novel during the last thirty years." ["Hablar de las novelas del Sr. Galdós es hablar de la novela en España durante cerca de treinta años" (p. 43).]

[2] Vide Discurso cit., p. 45.

[3] Cf. Menéndez y Pelayo, Discurso cit., p. 49: "There was lacking in almost all his imitators . . . that species of archæological second-sight with which Walter Scott made the domestic annals of his country familiar to Europe. There was plenty of genius among the Spanish romantics, but they knew little about their country's history, and what they did know they knew in a general and confused way. Hence their sketches of ancient customs were rarely effective æsthetically, nor did they so much as produce the illusion of life. . . ." ["A casi todos sus imitadores . . . les faltó aquella especie de segunda vista arqueológica con que Walter Scott hizo familiares en Europa los anales domésticos de

cases, they were content to reproduce, either in direct translation or in adaptation, the masterpieces of Scott and Dumas: and even those works for which originality is claimed bear obvious signs of foreign origin. The best of them are but pale reflections of a greater genius, and the worst of them are quite unreadable. These early novels of the Scott tradition are, however, with all their faults, preferable to the extravagant romances of chivalry seasoned to the taste of the modern palate which succeeded them; for the latter make no attempt to follow the dictates of common-sense. In the words of Menéndez y Pelayo: "If the works in the first manner were usually conducive to slumber, although well written, those of the second period, in addition to being clumsy and awkward in their diction, were monstrous in their construction and even crazy in their plot." [1]

The *Episodios Nacionales* of Galdós came, then, as a revelation to Spanish readers wearied of literary monstrosities; and they possessed, in addition to a firm basis of historical knowledge,[2] a profound human appeal. So far as Spanish fiction was concerned, they were something entirely new [3]—

su tierra. . . . Abundaba entre los románticos españoles el ingenio; pero de la historia de su patria sabían poco, y aun esto de un modo general y confuso, por lo cual rara vez sus representaciones de costumbres antiguas lograron eficacia artística, ni siquiera apariencias de vida. . . ."]

[1] "Si las obras de la primera manera solían ser soporíferas, aunque escritas muy literariamente, las del segundo período, además de torpes y desaseadas en la dicción, eran monstruosas en su plan y aun desatinadas en el argumento" (Discurso cit., p. 52).

[2] "With the data collected by Galdós in order to write one of his last *Episodios*, a well-documented 'History of the Moroccan War' could be published." [" . . . con los datos recogidos para escribir alguno de sus últimos Episodios por Galdós, podría publicarse una documentadísima 'Historia de la Guerra de África.'"] — González-Blanco, op. cit., cap. v., p. 385.

[3] It is, of course, possible that Galdós drew upon Mesonero and Flores for some of his historical "background." Vide section i. of this volume.

and they were hailed with intense enthusiasm by a public which has never been remarkable for intellectual curiosity. To his Spanish predecessors in the historical *genre* Galdós owes little or nothing; but the general scheme of the *Episodios* was almost certainly suggested to him by his reading of the brothers Erckmann-Chatrian.[1] The novels of the latter were popular in Spain when Galdós conceived his project; and between the two series there is a clear external similarity. The French writers have a distinct advantage so far as background is concerned, for the French Revolution and the Napoleonic campaigns are events of transcendental significance in European history, while those of which Galdós treats in the *Episodios* are, with one or two exceptions, purely local in their appeal. He makes, however, the best possible use of his material; and out of many unpromising situations he succeeds in extracting the maximum of human interest.[2] The *Episodios* are not, as we have seen, historical romances, in the orthodox sense of the term; but, inasmuch as they are an endeavour to interpret history in terms of the human spirit, they belong to the historical *genre*—of which, in modern Spanish literature, Galdós is, indisputably, the creator.

His position with regard to the novel of customs is not

---

[1] Cf. E. Martinenche, *Le Théâtre de M. Pérez Galdós : Revue des deux Mondes* (April 1906), pp. 819–20: "Que M. Galdós ait d'abord subi l'influence d'Erckmann-Chatrian et qu'on la puisse retrouver dans quelques-uns de ses procédés, c'est à quoi je ne contredirai point."

[2] Cf. González-Blanco, op. cit., cap. v., p. 385: "One must pay this tribute to Galdós: even if his best works are to be sought in the *Novelas de la Primera Época* and in the *Novelas Españolas Contemporáneas*, he got out of the *Episodios* all that an artistic soul and a born novelist could derive from such a hard and unpromising vein." ["Hay que hacerle este honor a Galdós; si bien sus mejores obras han de buscarse en las *Novelas de la primera época* y en las *Novelas españolas contemporáneas*, sacó de los *Episodios* todo lo que puede sacar de tan seca y dura veta un alma artista y un novelador de raza."]

so clear. So far as the regional novel is concerned, the premier place must be awarded to Pereda; and the work of the early "costumbristas," especially that of "El Solitario," Mesonero, and Larra, is by no means negligible. If, however, we interpret the term "novel of customs" in its broadest sense, then, surely, to Galdós belongs the honour of having created it. In the words of Salvador de Madariaga; "Pereda belongs to a region—the mountain; Valera, to a class—the aristocracy; Blasco Ibáñez is a cosmopolitan writer, if not a French one. Galdós is Spanish, and embraces the whole of Spain, all the colours and shades of her thought, and all the years of her nineteenth century." [1] Galdós, then, takes the whole of Spain for his province, and for him "the people" does not signify, as it did, usually, for Calderón and Mesonero, the "plebs" merely, but the whole people—especially the middle classes, which in Spain, as he points out, are a synthesis of all classes.[2] Although he has shown in many of his works that he is as much at home in the country as in the capital, he concentrates especially upon Madrid—where all types meet.[3] What

[1] Pereda pertenece a una región—la montaña; Valera, a una clase— la aristocracia, Blasco Ibáñez es un escritor cosmopólita, ya que no francés. Galdós es español y comprende a toda España, todos los colores y matices de su pensamiento y todos los años de su siglo XIX" (Salvador de Madariaga, *Semblanzas Literarias Contemporáneas*, p. 69).

[2] González-Blanco calls him "the Homer of our mesocracy." ["El Homero de nuestra mesocracia . . ."] vide op. cit., cap. v., p. 373.

[3] "From his first novel, *La Fontana de Oro*, we begin to see, unfolding itself beneath his pen, the dilapidated, irregular town with its excitable and good-natured mob, its vast aristocratic mansions, squat masses of granite and brick, its blocks of slums, with their densely peopled courts seething with strife and gossip; its irregular and badly paved streets which, like rivers which dry up into sandy beaches, radiate towards the desert of the plain above which, as our author says, 'the sky rises like the spiritual life above the arid wastes of asceticism." ["Desde su primera novela, *La Fontana de Oro* (1870), comenzamos a ver bajo su pluma la villa irregular y destartalada, con su gentío impresionable y bien humorado, sus vastas mansiones aristócratas, achatadas moles, de berroqueña y ladrillo; sus bloques de casas de vecindad con sus

sketch of local customs can compare in brilliance and human interest with the "Visita al Cuarto Estado" in *Fortunata y Jacinta*? Where is the atmosphere of an ancient Spanish city more realistically evoked than in the picture of Toledo in *Angel Guerra*? Where can we find more entertaining sketches of life in a small provincial town than those in *Doña Perfecta* and *Gloria*? It is true that Galdós has given us no "regional" novel in the conventional sense of the term; but he has infused into the "género de costumbres" a human interest which transcends the merely local appeal of the earlier sketches. One has only to contrast *Doña Perfecta* with *La Gaviota* to appreciate the extent of the advance which had been made. How jejune and stilted Fernán Caballero's masterpiece appears beside that of Galdós! With all its undeniable merits, the former dates. The latter stands outside time.

Sr. Salvador de Madariaga has defined the subject-matter of Galdós' work as "Human nature seen by an unprejudiced observer of nineteenth-century Spain." [1] It can hardly be maintained, however, that Galdós approached the national problems of his day without any preconceived notions as to the cause of his country's ills and the best remedy for them. According to his own admission, he regarded the novel as a means of propaganda; and all his novels are, in a sense, thesis novels. There is, however, a great difference between the "thesis novel" as it was cultivated by la Avellaneda and the "novel with a purpose" as it was conceived by Galdós. We

patios como aldeas hirvientes de grescas y hablillas; sus calles irregulares y mal empedradas, que, como ríos que van a morir en arenales, irradian hacia el desierto del llano sobre el cual, como dice nuestro autor; 'se alzan los cielos como la vida espritual sobre la aridez del ascetismo.'"]—Salvador de Madariaga, op. cit., pp. 69–70.

[1] "La naturaleza humana vista por un observador sin perjuicios del siglo XIX. español" (op. cit., p. 69).

have seen how he humanised the "género de costumbres"; and the didactic novel undergoes a similar process at his hands. The problem is not allowed, save in certain exceptional cases, to swamp the human interest of the work. In *Sab*, *Guatimozín* and *Espatolino* the "thesis is the thing"; while in *Fortunata y Jacinta*, for example, one feels that the story gives rise to the problem, not the problem to the story. It is, of course, true that *Fortunata y Jacinta* is one of the least blatantly controversial of Galdós' works, but even where the "thesis" is emphatically apparent, as in *Doña Perfecta*, *Gloria* and *La Familia de León Roch*, the author is interested in his characters as individuals. As we have seen, he falls at times into the error of using them as mouthpieces for his own opinions: but when he does so it is a lapse and nothing more. It is no exaggeration to state that Galdós is the greatest master of the novel of tendency in Spain. He purged it of its most objectionable characteristics and incorporated it into the novel of manners—which, in his view, must always have a "purpose." What, in Galdós' case, was that purpose?

It was, in the first instance, we venture to suggest, the diagnosing of the spiritual malady from which he conceived Spain to be suffering. It is, in our view, a mistake to regard even the earlier novels as nothing more than clever pieces of anti-clerical propaganda. Clericalism is attacked merely because, in the opinion of Galdós, it fosters a certain attitude of mind, and it is that attitude of mind against which his shafts of irony are really directed. Bigotry and prejudice are the outcome of a spiritual provincialism which, in its turn, arises from mental laziness, a deep-rooted disinclination to think for oneself if someone else will do the work for one. The parochial spirit and the spirit of intolerance are, as we all know, very closely allied. The latter, indeed, arises out of the former. The Orbajosans of this world accept their immediate surroundings as beyond criticism very largely because they are too lazy to criticise, too indolent even to take stock of the platitudes which constitute their mental equipment. New ideas involve thinking—they may possibly involve an expenditure of physical energy. That, say the Orbajosans, would be a bore —so let us go on in the old way as our fathers did before us. What was good enough for them is good enough for us, and so on. It was this irrational, unthinking conservatism which Galdós lashed with relentless irony and not, as some might suppose, the conservatism which is born of mature reflection.

The malady of Spain, like the "mal du siècle" as it shows itself in the individual, is, Galdós seems to indicate, the result either of sheer laziness, or of lack of will ("abulia") or of the misdirection of energy. One form of such misdirection is to be found in a certain type of mysticism which alienates those who indulge in it (for Galdós, like certain modern psychologists, regards it as a form of sensuous indulgence) from the practical affairs of life. With this, as we can divine from so many of his books, he has no manner of patience. Whether it takes the form of orthodox piety, as in the case of María Sudre [1] or Victoria [2] or of vague philosophising, as in the case of Maxí,[3] it is equally to be condemned; for it is invariably a means of self-deception. The key to individual, as to national, health is—action. This must not, however, take the form of a vague physical unrest, a mere pointless "hustle." Even when disguised as philanthropy,[4] this is pernicious. Energy is a valuable commodity,

---

[1] *La Familia de León Roch.*   [2] *La Loca de la Casa.*
[3] *Fortunata y Jacinta.*
[4] As, for example, in the case of Carlos Golfín's wife, or in that of Doña Guillermina, "Vírgen y fundadora."

and it must not be expended without circumspection. Do good works by all means—but first of all make certain that your "good" actions will not defeat their own ends. The time for showy heroics is now past. How, then, can the individual and the nation best utilise their energies? The answer which Galdós offers to this question can, we think, easily be divined from his works. He has, however, left it on record in his Introduction to Salaverría's *Vieja España* (1907) where, after suggesting an epitaph for the Cid,[1] he remarks: "The Spanish people retains the pattern of those virtues which gave it predominance in the age of heroic and glorious deeds. But the heroic ages are gone and we have come to live a peaceful and industrious life, without swords and all the rest of the flummery of Mars; *fighting human ills with the weapons of the arts and sciences*."[2] Since these words were written by Galdós events have given the lie to certain of his affirmations; but the ideal held forth is, possibly, one which the modern world has a right to claim as especially its own.

Galdós may justly be regarded as the founder of the new school of writers, which grew to maturity after the disaster of

---

[1] This is, perhaps, worth quoting here: "Here we lie alseep—I, the good Cid and my Jimena—they do not keep me under lock and key—nor do they bind me with chains—for however loudly they call me—I shall not leave this sepulchre. It has finished its course—the sun of my famed powers—and the battles which to Spain—will give new prestige—are not won with Tizonas—nor Coladas nor Babiecas." ["Aquí yacemos dormidos—yo el buen Cid y mi Jimena—Non me guardan con cerrojos—ni me aferran con cadenas— que por mucho que me llamen—no he de salir de esta fuesa. Terminó su curso el sol —de mis sonadas proezas—y las batallas que a España—han de dar prestancia nueva—non se ganan con Tizonas—ni Coladas ni Babiecas."] —Prólogo, pp. x.-xi.

[2] "Conserva el pueblo castellano la matriz de las virtudes que le dieron predominio en la edad de las heroicas grandezas. Pero los tiempos heróicos pasaron y hemos venido a un vivir pacífico y laborioso, sin espadas ni demás chiriambolas de Marte, *combatiendo el mal humano con las armas de las artes y la ciencia*" (op. cit., Prólogo, p. xxxv.).

1898. There is, indeed, little in Angel Ganivet's *Idearium Español* [1] which we cannot find expressed either implicitly or explicitly in the *Novelas Contemporáneas*; and Ganivet's work was the Bible of the spiritual renascence which followed the disaster. In it he uses the term "abulia" to designate the spiritual malady from which his country is suffering, and he seeks a remedy for the disease in the right use of the native energy of Spain. Like Galdós, he has no sympathy with a cosmopolitanism which pours scorn upon "las cosas de España." It is within, he affirms, that Spain must look for salvation. The *Novelas Contemporáneas* also anticipate many of the views expressed by Ricardo Macías Picavea in his gloomy work, *El Problema Nacional.* [2] Picavea attributes the national malady to two innate defects of character—the predominance of passion over will (cf. Ganivet's *Idearium*) and the lack of any sense of abstract justice. The first is responsible for the alleged Spanish tendency to live in the present without making adequate provision for the future; the second for the administrative corruption which disgraces the public life of Spain. Friendliness and family affection are admirable qualities —but they should not provide a motive for the filling of a public appointment! This prevalence of nepotism in public affairs was, as we have seen, admirably satirised by Galdós in his portrayal of Manuel José Ramón del Pez, "indefatigable apostle of that venerable routine upon which rests the noble edifice of our glorious national apathy," [3] and his innumerable relations. Picavea suggest no remedy, for he conceives the

[1] This book was written in 1897, when Ganivet was Spanish consul at Antwerp.
[2] 1899.
[3] "Apóstol nunca fatigado de esas venerandas rutinas sobre que descansa el noble edificio de nuestra gloriosa apatía nacional" (vide *La Desheredada*, cap. xii., pp. 195–6).

malady to be incurable. A less pessimistic view was, however, taken by other members of the "generation of the disaster." Ramiro de Maeztu hopes for progress along the lines of industrial development [1]; Luís Morote thinks that salvation is only to be found by abandoning a vain policy of adventure abroad and by expelling as many priests as possible [2]; Rafael de Altamira looks for the cause of Sapin's disease in the economic realm. The stream of national energy has, he affirms, been swallowed up by the soil, from which it must now be diverted.[3] The germ of practically all the views expressed by the prophets of regeneration can, indeed, be found in the novels of Galdós. Ganivet's explanation of Spanish mysticism as a "sanctification" of the race's primitive sensuality was thought startling and revolutionary when it was advanced—but is it not merely a general application of Galdós' theory as to the real significance of mysticism in the individual? Is not Ganivet's interpretation of Spanish religious fanaticism as a species of "masochism"—a turning by the Spaniard against himself of the sadistic fury accumulated by the nation during eight centuries of battle with the Moors—quite in keeping with Galdós's excursions into morbid psychology? Are not the strictures which Miguel de Unamuno passes upon a sterile "casticismo" [4] anticipated by Gloria in her famous review of Spanish civilisation in the Golden Age? Are not his views as to the materialism which underlies the apparent idealism—even the religious idealism—of Spain's great age, very similar to those which scandalised the estimable Don Juan de Lantigua?

[1] Vide *Hacia otra España* (1899). Sr. de Maeztu has probably changed his opinions since he wrote this book! The outlook for industrialism is scarcely hopeful to-day.

[2] Vide *La Moral de la Derrota* (1900) and *Los Frailes en España* (1904).

[3] Vide *Psicología del Pueblo Español* (1902).

[4] Vide *En torno al Casticismo* (1902).

Unamuno is at one with Galdós in his view that only in the broader and more vital ideas of old Spain—expressed in literary form by Cervantes—can the key to the problem of modern Spain be found: in the idealism of Don Quixote tempered by the sturdy common-sense of Sancho Panza. Is not this conception of a *practical* idealism extolled throughout the novels of Galdós? Unamuno also comes forward with a defence of the ordinary business of life, which, he points out, is not devoid of imaginative, poetic spirit. Without the creative urge the most commonplace material things, or rather the things we mistakenly regard as commonplace, such as railways, factories, harbours, etc., could not have been brought into being. Passion, virility, moral energy must not be expended carelessly or, even with high motives, misapplied.

The diagnosis of Spain's malady was further developed by Martínez Ruiz ("Azorín"), in his novel *La Voluntad*, and by his friend Pío Baroja in a number of works, especially *Vidas Sombrías* and *Camino de Perfección*. These two writers continue the work, initiated by Galdós in the *Episodios* and *Novelas Contemporáneas*, of revealing Spain to Spaniards, and of making Spaniards intelligible to themselves. Both "Azorín" and Baroja agree with Galdós in tracing to "abulía" the source of their country's ills. Inspired, possibly, by the *Episodios* of Galdós, Baroja wrote his *Memorias de un hombre de Acción*, a series in which he studies the origins of contemporary Spain. The hero, Don Eugenio de Aviraneta, an historical figure, is essentially a man of action; a great promotor of sedition and revolt—the type of audacious adventurer which Baroja especially admires. Action is, indeed, the keynote of Baroja's work, but—and this is where he differs greatly from Galdós—the activity which Baroja extols is not necessarily either constructive or purposeful. He loves action for its own sake and demands from life, at any cost, "something dynamic." [1] His is a vagabond spirit, and his love of wandering is reflected in nearly all his books—especially in *Zalacain, el Aventurero* and *Las Inquietudes de Shanti-Andía*. He also differs from Galdós in his attitude towards the poor and unfortunate. In *La Busca* and *Mala Hierba* he gives us a masterly picture of low-life in Madrid—but that life is studied with a detachment and a lack of sympathy which is almost inhuman. Galdós was, as we have seen, essentially Christian in his attitude towards the problem of poverty. Baroja is pagan, Nietzschean; but, again unlike Galdós, he never indulges in deliberate propaganda. He shares Flaubert's horror of didactic art; and it is this dislike of moralising which distinguishes his work from that of Korolenko, with whom he has been compared.[2] Baroja is Galdós de-Christianised and purged of tendencious proclivities. Just as Galdós startled his countrymen of the post-revolution epoch by his attacks upon clericalism and conventional moral standards, so Baroja appears after the disaster of '98 with a more fundamental, if less resounding, challenge. While deploring the misinterpretation which he believes it to have suffered, Galdós holds fast to the Christian code of ethics. He does not doubt for one moment that life is worth while, nor does he question the general desirability of the existing social order. Baroja has a profound contempt for modern civilisation and for the moral teachings of Jesus Christ. He is the Spanish apostle of force, and the "relentless logic of facts." To the strong alone should come the "glittering prizes," and a society which exalts a Laodicean

[1] Cf. J. B. Trend, *A Picture of Modern Spain: Men and Music*, p. 74.
[2] Cf. Salvador de Madariaga, op. cit.

virtue as the ideal code of morality is both corrupt and foolish. "We must live the natural life, the savage, primitive life—we must bring up our children in the school of force. Let us despise empty ease. Life has no charm when we are not tormented by the spur of grief or wounded by the caress of love." [1] Thus does González-Blanco sum up the philosophy which Baroja substitutes for the humanitarian positivism of Galdós. Although the two creeds are diametrically opposed, Baroja would have been impossible, or at least unlikely, without Galdós, who, by his revolt against what was evil in the existing order, prepared the way for an attack upon that order itself. He cannot be relieved of a certain responsibility for much that was thought, said and written by the "generation of '98," and almost all the great figures in contemporary Spanish fiction must look to him as their master. He is, indeed, a unique figure in the history of the modern Spanish novel.

His position in the history of modern European literature is more difficult to determine. To Spaniards, and to students in the Spanish field, he must always appear as a giant, if only by comparison with the pigmies whom he immediately succeeded. Is he, however, entitled to rank as a European novelist of the first order?

Some would deny him greatness of any description [2]; while others, as we have seen, unite in according him the highest

---

[1] "Hay que vivir la vida natural, salvaje, primitiva—hay que educar a nuestros hijos en el instinto de la fuerza. Desdeñemos el reposo banal. La vida no tiene encantos si el aguijón del dolor no nos atormenta o la caricia del amor no nos hiere" (vide A. González-Blanco, op. cit. cap. x., p. 751).

[2] Orlando Lara y Pedraja says of him: "He has no outstanding qualities . . . and on that account he is, rather than a novelist, a writer of talent, of taste." ["No hay en el ninguna cualidad que sobresalga . . . y por eso, más que un novelista, es un escritor de talento y buen gusto"] (vide op. cit., p. 433 *et passim*).

praise. Let us deal in the first place with the vexed question of originality. Galdós has been compared with Balzac, with Dickens and with Dostoievsky. What, if anything, does he owe to these writers? If he has borrowed, how far has he succeeded in employing the alien material to create something new, something indisputably Spanish?

No writer, however individual, can altogether fail to be influenced by the literary atmosphere of his age; and it is scarcely surprising that Galdós should have fallen under the spell of the great novelists of France, England and Russia. He has himself admitted that his reading of Balzac impelled him to write the *Novelas Contemporáneas*—a Spanish "Comédie Humaine"—and with Balzac he has, naturally, frequently been compared.[1] From Balzac he undoubtedly borrowed the general scheme for a series of inter-related novels; and in productivity he almost rivals the great French realist. Like those of Balzac, his plots develop innumerable ramifications, and he revels in genealogical trees! His observation is as minute and exhaustive as that of Balzac. No detail escapes his eye, and all is faithfully recorded.[2] Like Balzac, he is especially interested in the bourgeoisie, and in money-making. The majority of his characters move, as do those of Balzac, in circles where financial soundness is one of the cardinal virtues and poverty one of the deadly sins. Hence the countless subterfuges and petty domestic meannesses to which many of his creations are obliged to resort for the sake of "keeping up appearances." And

---

[1] "Galdós is, first and foremost, the Spanish Balzac." ["Galdós es, ante todo, el Balzac español."]—A. González Blanco, op. cit., cap. v., p. 373.

[2] One must not overlook the influence of Zola in this connection. The mass of technical detail of a scientific and medical nature which Galdós introduces into many of his works is, as we have remarked elsewhere, in the authentic naturalistic vein.

hovering in the background there is always a Gobseck or a Torquemada!

There are other general resemblances between the two "human comedies"; but it would not, in our opinion, be justifiable to conclude from such similarities that Galdós is to be dismissed as a mere imitator. The social conditions which he was describing were in many respects similar to those treated by Balzac, and a likeness between the works of the two is, consequently, only to be expected. While, however, he is no slavish imitator, Galdós lacks the creative force of Balzac, the intensity of genius which characterises the supreme artist. Acute psychologist as he was, Galdós could never have given us a Eugénie Grandet or a Père Goriot. He rarely becomes one, as it were, with his characters; rarely exhibits to a high degree a passionate sympathy with his creations. There is nothing of the poet in Galdós; and talent is only too frequently obliged to do the work of inspiration.[1] He is also, as we have observed, too fond of the rostrum. It would, perhaps, be unkind rather than inapt to describe Galdós as Balzac turned schoolmaster.

The comparison with Dickens has, as Sr. de Madariaga remarks,[2] become a commonplace of Spanish criticism. It suggests itself naturally — for Galdós' affection for things English, and, especially, the novels of Dickens, is well known. There is a rich vein of humour in the work of Galdós which,

---

[1] Cf. M. de Revilla, *Revista Contemporánea*, año iii.–iv., tom xiii., March-April 1878, pp. 118–24: "Cold, reflective and reasoning by nature, in him talent does the work of inspiration, and contrives to imitate it with such skill that it easily succeeds in deceiving the reader." ["Frío, reflexivo y razonador por naturaleza, el talento sustituye en él la inspiración, y logra remedarla con tal arte que facilmente consigue engañar al lector."]

[2] Vide op. cit., p. 86.

in view of the fact that he admired that writer, has been dubbed somewhat too hastily, we think, "Dickensian." It is difficult on closer examination to discover any relationship between the sly irony of Galdós and the hearty jollity of Dickens. The latter, as is well known, was prone to a certain exaggeration, almost amounting to caricature, in his deline-ation of humorous types. He is quite deliberately funny. With Galdós the humour is more subdued, and his comical situations seem to arise more naturally out of the incidents of the story. He does on occasions, as we have seen, deliberately imitate the mock heroics of the English writer; [1] but there is, we venture to assert, no temperamental affinity between the two novelists. Dickens was the greater genius and Galdós, in many respects, the better artist.[2] The characters of Dickens are on the move the whole time. They do not as a rule stop to analyse or be analysed; for their creator has no use for psychology which clogs the action. He does not trouble, as does Galdós, to unravel mixed motives. There are, however, certain similarities of method between the two writers. Dickens, like Galdós, fre-quently introduces his characters by giving us their "dossier." Like Galdós, also, he attaches great importance to details of dress; and, like Galdós, he is interested in abnormal psychology. He was himself subject to bad dreams, and was, he tells us, for long haunted by the face of a corpse he saw at a morgue. Abnormal states of consciousness play a large part in his work [3]; and, as Sr. de Madariaga remarks, one of his best known heroes, Barnaby Rudge, .is a half-wit. Dickens, however,

[1] Notably in cap. xii. of *La Desheredada*.
[2] This is a bold saying, but we believe it to be justified. Madariaga (op. cit., p. 86) puts forward this view—but he is notoriously unorthodox.
[3] E.g. the visions of Mistress Affery in *Little Dorrit*; the "double consciousness" of John Harman in *Our Mutual Friend*; Doctor Manette's loss of memory, etc., cited by Sr. de Madariaga, op. cit.

unlike Galdós, is not concerned with these matters as a psychologist. He is attracted by abnormality because it is uncanny and supplies an atmosphere of dread. His "abnormals" are indeed, in the tradition of the "novel of terror," which enjoyed a great vogue at the time when he began to write and by which he was to some extent influenced. To these similarities of detail we must add the general resemblance which arises from the fact that both writers used the novel as a means of propaganda. In all essentials, however, they are utterly different. Dickens is a great lyrist. In his work emotion and sentiment predominate, while Galdós, as we have remarked, is rational, analytic—very rarely spontaneous in emotion.

Although his mildly benevolent and slightly academic muse fades into insignificance beside the sombre, terrible genius of Dostoievsky, Galdós is perhaps scarcely inferior to the Russian in his power of unravelling subconscious motives. Like those of Dostoievsky, his characters are usually neurotic or in some way mentally unstable. Like Dostoievsky, he is especially attracted by mystics and madmen, whom he regards as more closely in touch with the unseen world than are normal human beings. He did not, however, as did Dostoievsky in his cataleptic states, experience personally the curious ecstasies of the deranged. There is a detachment about his attitude which suggests at times the psychological laboratory; he is interested in his abnormals as "cases" rather than as human beings. His outlook on life is essentially sane and healthy-minded: free from morbidity himself, he cannot enter imaginatively into the psycho-pathological state which is unconscious of its own abnormality. Dostoievsky, like Spinoza, was a "God-tormented" man. Life to him was an insoluble problem, a problem which kept him continuously upon the rack of feverish introspection. He did not seek merely to portray human existence, but to justify that existence, which he found inexplicable. Galdós accepts life unquestioningly; and to all its problems he finds an answer in the exercise of charity. Charity, to him, is the central fact of human existence. He does not theorise about it or endeavour to explain its *raison d'être*. It is there: and that for him is enough.

In conclusion, it would, perhaps, be extravagant to claim for Galdós a place beside Balzac, Dickens, Tolstoy or Dostoievsky in the hierarchy of European letters. That he does, however, deserve an honoured place therein, and that he is, in the most significant sense of the word, the creator of the modern novel in Spain, we have here endeavoured to show.

FINIS

APPENDICES

(I)

THE NOVELS OF BENITO PÉREZ GALDÓS

A CHRONOLOGICAL SURVEY

Dates in brackets are those given by Galdós at the end of his novels and refer to the period at which the books were written.

In April 1868 he published a story—*La Conjuración de las palabras*—which was reprinted, together with *La pluma en el viento, El artículo de fondo, La mula y el buey, Un tribunal literario, La princesa y el granuja*, and *Junio*, in *Torquemada en la Hoguera*, 1889.

YEAR	NOVELAS CONTEMPORÁNEAS	EPISODIOS NACIONALES
1870.	*La Fontana de Oro* (Madrid, 1867-8). *La Sombra* (Madrid, Nov., 1870). First published in *La Revista de España*, 1871, tom. xviii. Reprinted in 1890 in 1 vol., together with three other small works—*Celín, Tropiquillos*, and *Theros* (1887).	
1871.	*El Audaz: historia de un radical de antaño* (Oct., 1871). The short stories *El artículo de fondo* and *La pluma en el viento o el viaje de la vida* (dated Madrid, April, 1872), and (Sept., 1872), *Un tribunal literario*, belong to 1871. The two last were first published in the *Revista de España*, vol. xix., 1871; vol. xxviii., 1872. *El Audaz* occupies many numbers of *La Revista* for the years 1871-2.	

YEAR	NOVELAS CONTEMPORÁNEAS	EPISODIOS NACIONALES
1873.		*Trafalgar* (1st series) (Madrid, Jan.–Feb., 1873).
		La Corte de Carlos IV. (Madrid, April – March, 1873).
		El 19 de Marzo y el 2 de Mayo (Madrid, July, 1873).
		Bailén (Oct.–Nov., 1873).
1874.		*Napoleón en Chamartín* (Jan., 1874).
		Zaragoza (March – April, 1874).
		Gerona (June, 1874).
		Cádiz (Sept.–Oct., 1874).
		Juan Martín, el Empecinado (Madrid, Dec., 1874).
1875.		*La batalla de los Arapiles* (Madrid, Feb. – March, 1875).
		El Equipaje del Rey José (2nd series) (Madrid, June–July, 1875).
		Memorias de un cortesano de 1815 (Madrid, Oct., 1875).
1876.	*Doña Perfecta* (Madrid, April, 1876). First published in *La Revista de España*, 1876, XLIX and L (March–May).	*La segunda casaca* (Madrid, Jan., 1876).
		El grande Oriente (Madrid, June, 1876).
		El 7 de julio (Madrid, Oct.–Nov., 1876).
		In Dec. *La mula y el buey, cuento de Navidad* (a short story).

Year	Novelas Contemporáneas	Episodios Nacionales
1877.	*Gloria* (2 vols.) (Madrid, Dec., 1876,— Madrid, May, 1877).	*Los cien mil hijos de San Luis* (Madrid, Feb., 1877). *El Terror de 1824* (Madrid, Oct., 1877).
1878.	*Marianela* (Madrid, Jan., 1878).	*Un voluntario realista* (Madrid, Feb. – March, 1878).
1879.	*La Familia de León Roch* (3 vols.) (Madrid, June, Oct., Dec., 1878).	*Los apostólicos* (Madrid, May–June, 1879). (In Jan. 1879 Galdós composed the novelette *La princesa y el granuja*.) *Un faccioso más y algunos frailes menos* (Santander, Nov.–Dec., 1879).
1881.	*La desheredada* (Madrid, Jan.–June, 1881).	
1882.	*El amigo Manso* (Madrid, Jan.– April, 1882).	
1883.	*El doctor Centeno* (2 vols.) (Madrid, May, 1883).	
1884.	*Tormento* (Madrid, Jan., 1884). *La de Bringas* (Madrid, April–May, 1884). *Lo Prohibido* (1st vol.) (Madrid, Nov., 1884).	
1885.	*Lo Prohibido* (2nd vol.) (Madrid, March, 1885).	
1886.	*Fortunata y Jacinta* (vols. i., ii., iii.) (Madrid, Jan.–May–Dec., 1886).	
1887.	*Fortunata y Jacinta* (vol. iv.) (Madrid, June, 1887). *Celín, Tropiquillos,* and *Theros* (Madrid, Nov., 1887).	

Year	Novelas Contemporáneas	Episodios Nacionales
1888.	*Miau* (Madrid, April, 1888).	
1889.	*La Incógnita* (Madrid, Nov., 1888—Feb., 1889).	
	Torquemada en la hoguera (Madrid, Feb., 1889).	
	Realidad, novela en cinco jornadas (Madrid, July, 1889).	
1890.	*Angel Guerra* (vol. i.) (Madrid, April, 1890); (vol. ii.) (Santander, Dec., 1890).	
1891.	*Angel Guerra* (vol. iii.) (Santander, May, 1891).	
1892.	*Tristana* (Madrid, Jan., 1892). *La Loca de la Casa* (Oct., 1892).	
1893.	*Torquemada en la cruz* (Santander, Oct., 1893).	
1894.	*Torquemada en el Purgatorio* (Santander, June, 1894).	
1895.	*Torquemada y San Pedro* (Madrid, Jan.–Feb., 1895). *Nazarín* (Santander, May, 1895). *Halma* (Santander, Oct., 1895).	
1897.	*Misericordia* (March-April, 1897). *El Abuelo, novela en 5 jornadas* (Santander, Aug.–Sept., 1897).	
1898.		*Zumalacarregui* (3rd series) (Madrid, April–May, 1898). *Mendizabal* (Santander, Aug.–Sept., 1898). *De Oñate a la Granja* (Santander, Oct.–Nov., 1898).

YEAR	NOVELAS CONTEMPORÁNEAS	EPISODIOS NACIONALES
1899.		*Luchana* (Santander, Jan.–Feb., 1899).
		La Campaña del Maestrazgo (Santander, April–May, 1899).
		La estafeta romántica (Santander, July–Aug., 1899).
		Vergara (Santander - Madrid, Oct.–Nov., 1899).
1900.		*Montes de Oca* (Madrid, March–April, 1900).
		Los Ayacuchos (Madrid, May–June, 1900).
		Bodas Reales (Santander, Sept.–Oct., 1900).
1902.		*Los Tormentos del 48* (4th series) (Madrid, March–April, 1902).
		Narváez (Santander, July–Aug., 1902).
1903.		*Los duendes de la camarilla* (Madrid, Feb. - March, 1903).
1904.		*La revolución de julio* (Santander, Sept., 1903; Madrid, March, 1904).
		O'Donnell (Madrid, April–May, 1904).
		Aita Tettauen (Madrid, Oct., 1904—Jan., 1905).
1905.	*Casandra, novela en 5 jornadas* (Santander, July–Sept., 1905).	*Carlos VI, en la Rápita.* (Madrid, April-May, 1905).
1906.		*La vuelta al mundo en la Numancia* (Madrid, Jan.–March, 1906).

YEAR	NOVELAS CONTEMPORÁNEAS	EPISODIOS NACIONALES
1906.		*Prim* (Santander, Madrid, July–Oct., 1906). (In 1906 Galdós published a volume, *Memoranda*, which contains 13 studies written at different periods.)
1907.		*La de los tristes destinos* (Madrid, Jan. – May, 1907).
1908.		*España sin Rey* (Madrid, Oct., 1907—Jan., 1908).
1909.	*El caballero encantado* (Santander-Madrid, July–Dec., 1909).	*España trágica* (Madrid, March, 1909).
1910.		*Amadeo I* (Santander-Madrid, Aug.–Oct., 1910).
1911.		*La primera República* (Madrid, Feb.–April, 1911). *De Cartago a Sagunto* (Santander - Madrid, Aug.–Nov., 1911). *Cánovas* (Madrid - Santander, March–Aug., 1912).
1912.		
1915.	*La razón de la sinrazón, fabula teatral absolutamente inverosimil en cuatro jornados* (Madrid, 1915).	

(II)

SHORT BIBLIOGRAPHY

of works dealing wholly, or in part, with the novels of Galdós

I. GENERAL (NINETEENTH-CENTURY SPANISH NOVEL)

EL P. FRANCISCO BLANCO GARCÍA, *La Literatura Española en el Siglo XIX.* (3rd ed. Madrid, 1909, parts i. and ii.).

ANDRÉS GONZALEZ-BLANCO, *Historia de la Novela en España desde el Romanticismo a Nuestros Días* (Madrid, 1909).

J. M. AICARDO, *De Literatura Contemporánea* (Madrid, 1905).

RAFAEL DE ALTAMIRA, *Psicología y Literatura* (Madrid, 1905): *De Historia y Arte (Estudios Críticos)* (Madrid, 1878).

JOSÉ MARÍA ASENSIO, *Fernán Caballero y la Novela Contemporánea.* Vide Fernán Caballero, *Obras Completas,* vol. i. (Madrid, 1893, etc.).

II. BIOGRAPHY AND CRITICISM (SPANISH)

M. MENÉNDEZ Y PELAYO, *Discurso leído ante la Real Academia Española en la recepción publica del 7 de feb. de 1897.*

EL P. BLANCO GARCÍA, op. cit. part ii. cap. xxvii. pp. 489–508.

ANDRÉS GONZÁLEZ-BLANCO, op. cit. cap. v. pp. 370–449.

LEOPOLDO ALAS ("Clarín"), *Galdós. (Obras completas de Clarin,* vol. i.) (Madrid, 1912).

L. ANTÓN DEL OLMET y A. GARCÍA CARRAFFA, *Galdós* (Madrid, 1912).

"ANDRENIO" (Gómez de Baquero), *Novelas y Novelistas,* pp. 11–112 (Madrid, 1918).

GUILLERMO DENDARIENA, *Galdós : su genio, su espiritualidad, su grandeza* (Madrid, 1922).

ANTONIO ALARCÓN CAPILLA, *Galdós y su obra* (Madrid, 1922).

SALVADOR DE MADARIAGA, *Semblanzas literarias contemporáneas* (Barcelona, 1924).

III. Articles, Reviews, etc. (Spanish)

Emilia Pardo Bazán, *El estudio de Galdós en Madrid*. (*Nuevo Teatro Crítico*, Aug. 1891, pp. 65–74.)

Orlando Lara y Pedraja, *Novelas españolas del año literario*, in *La Revista de España*, vols. xciv. and c. (Madrid, 1884).

"El Licenciado Pero Pérez," *La España Moderna*, in *La Revista de España*, No. lxii. pp. 66–67 (Feb. 1894).

J. León Pagano, *Al Través de la España Literaria*, pp. 77–112. (Barcelona, 1904).

Luís Morote, *Teatro y Novela*, pp. 59–75 and 259–270 (Madrid, 1906).

"El Bachiller Corchuelo" (González-Fiol), *Benito Pérez Galdós* (in *Por Esos Mundos*, vols. xx. and xxi., vol. xx. pp. 791–807; vol. xxi. pp. 27–56).

"Azorín" (Martínez Ruiz), *Lecturas Españolas*, pp. 171–76 (Madrid, 1912). Also, by the same author, an article in *Blanco y Negro*, No. 1260, entitled *Don Benito Pérez Galdós* (11 July, 1915).

"El Caballero Audaz" (Jose María Carretero), *Lo que sé por mí* (1st series), pp. i.–ii. (Madrid, 1915).

Luís Ruiz Contreras, *Memorias de un desmemoriado*, pp. 65–72 (Madrid, 1916).

Luís Bello, *Ensayos e imaginaciones sobre Madrid*, pp. 95–129 (Madrid, 1919).

E. Diez-Canedo, *La Vida del Maestro*, in *El Sol*, 4 Jan., 1920.

Antonio Maura, *Necrología de D. Benito Pérez Galdós* (Madrid, 1920).

IV. Foreign Criticism

A. Savine, *Le naturalisme en Espagne* (Paris, 1885).

Archer M. Huntington, *Pérez Galdós in the Spanish Academy*, in *The Bookman*, v. pp. 220–22 (1897).

W. H. Bishop in Warner's *Library of the World's Best Literature*, vol. xi.

Boris de Tannenberg, *Benito Pérez Galdós* in *Bulletin Hispanique II*. pp. 340–50 (1900).

Christian Brinton, *Galdós in English*, in *The Critic*, vol. xlv. pp. 449–50 (1904).

R. W. Waldeck, *Benito Pérez Galdós, Novelist, Dramatist and Reformer*, in *The Critic*, vol. xlv. pp. 449–50 (1904).

R. E. Bassett, *Modern Language Notes*, xix. pp. 15–17 (1904).

F. Vézinet, *Les maîtres du roman espagnol contemporain*, pp. 41–128 (Paris, 1907).

Articles dealing with Galdós will be found also in the following journals, etc: *Correspondant*, 10 avril, 1885 (de Tréverret); *Revue Bleue*, 9 mai, 1885 (L. Quesnel); *National Zeitung*, No. 56, 1885 (M. Landau).

V. Translations

(1) English

Doña Perfecta, a tale of modern Spain. Translated by D. P. W., London, 1886.

Doña Perfecta. Translated by Clara Bell. New York, 1883.

Doña Perfecta. Translated by D. P. W. New York, 1883.

Gloria. Translated by Clara Bell. New York, 1882.

Gloria. Translated by Nathan Wetherell, London, 1879.

La Familia de León Roch. Translated by Clara Bell. New York, 1888.

Marianela. Translated by Clara Bell. New York, 1883.

Marianela. Translated by Helen W. Lester. Chicago, 1892.

Trafalgar. Translated by Clara Bell. New York, 1884.

Zaragoza. Translated by Minna Caroline Smith. Boston, 1899.

La Batalla de los Arapiles. Translated by Rollo Ogden. Philadelphia, 1895.

(2) French

Doña Perfecta. Translated by L. Lugol. Paris, 1885.

Marianela. Translated by A. Germond de Lavigne. Paris, 1884.

El Amigo Manso. Translated by Julien Lugol. Paris, 1888.

Misericordia. Translated by Maurice Bixio. Paris, 1900.

(3) German

Doña Perfecta (2 vols.). Translated by J. Reichall. Dresden and Leipzig, 1886.

Gloria. Translated by Dr. Augustus Hartmann. Berlin, 1880.

El Amigo Manso (*French Manso*). Translated by E. von Buddenbrock. Berlin, 1894.

Trafalgar. Translated by Hans Parlow. Dresden and Leipzig, 1896.

Marianela. Translated by E. Plücher. Breslau, 1888.

(4) Italian

Nazarín (*Sicut-Christus*). Translated by Guido Rubetti and José León Pagano. Florence.

Gloria. Translated by Italo Argenti. Florence, 1901.

Marianela. Translated by G. Demichelis. Bologna, 1880.

La Fontana de Oro. Translated by G. Demichelis. Milan, 1890.

Doña Perfecta, Translated by Cunes. Milan, 1897.

(5) Dutch

Doña Perfecta. Translated by M. A. de Goeje. Leiden, 1883.

(6) Danish

Fra Perfecta. Translated by Gigas. Copenhagen, 1895.

(7) Swedish

Doña Perfecta. Translated by K. A. Hagberg. Stockholm.

León Roch. Translated by A. P. de la Cruz Frölich. Copenhagen, 1881.

Torquemada en la Hoguera (*Torquemada paa haalet*). Translated by Johanne Allen. Christiania and Copenhagen, 1898.

INDEX

A *Picture of Modern Spain*, 228
Abnormal psychological types, 116 *et
seq.*, 133, 136, 137, 163 *et seq.*, 176,
186 *et seq.*, 190; in Galdós and in
Dickens, 232; in Galdós and in
Dostoievsky, 233
"Abulia" and the social problem, 105,
150, 223; and the "generation of
'98," 225; attitude of Baroja, 227
Agents provocateurs, activity under
Fernando VII., 48
Alarcón Capilla, Antonio, 58 n.
Alarcón, Pedro Antonio de, 25 *et seq.*,
36; priority of Galdós to, 216
Alas, Leopoldo ("Clarín"), organises
banquet in honour of Galdós, 34
Alicante, Galdós in, 32
Altamira, Rafael de, and the social
problem, 226
Alvareda, founder of *La Revista de
España*, 33; editor-in-chief of *El
Debate*, 33
Angel Guerra, 129, 185 *et seq.*, 186 n.,
209, 221
Anti-clericalism of Galdós, 117 *et seq.*,
222 *et seq.*
Anti-traditionalism, 86
Antiquary, The, Spanish translation
of, 12
Aristocracy, attitude towards, 108 *et seq.*
Atala, vogue of, in Spain, 11
"Ateneo," the, Galdós and, 37
Ateneo Viejo, El, Galdós and, 35
Autobiographical element in *El Doctor
Centeno*, 157
Avellaneda, Gertrudis Gómez de, 15
Avellaneda," "la, 36, 221; importance
of, in development of Spanish novel
of manners, 16
Ayer, Hoy y Mañana, 9
"Azorín," and Galdós, 227

Balzac, 76, 217 n.; and Pedro Antonio
de Alarcón, 25; literary relationship
with Galdós, 31; admiration of
Galdós for, 34, 157; influence of,
on Galdós, 130; debt of Galdós to,
230 *et seq.*

Barbero de Madrid, El, 6
Barcelona, Galdós in, 32
Baroja, Pío, and Galdós, 227 *et seq.*;
debt of Galdós to, 229
Bigotry, treatment of, 73, 76, 81, 91,
95
Böhl de Faber, Cecilia ("Fernan
Caballero"), 19 *et seq.*
Bonaparte, Joseph, 4
Bride of Lammermoor, The and *El Señor
de Bembibre*, 14
Burell, Julio, a friend of Galdós, 35

Caballero, Fernán, 20 *et seq.*, 36, 221
Cabrerizo's *Colección de Novelas*, 11 n.,
12
"Caciquismo," attacks on, 146, 180
Café Universal, a haunt of Galdós', 30
Calderón, Serafín Estébanez de, *El
Solitario*, 4; and the novel of
manners, 220
Calle de Serrano, No. 8, residence of
Galdós at, 32
Camino de Perfección, 227
Camús, friendship with Galdós of
29
Cánovas del Castillo, Antonio de, 4;
and banquet to Galdós, 34
Carrera de San Jerónimo, the, in
1820–3, described in *La Fontana de
Oro*, 40
Cartas del Pobrecito Holgazán, 2
Casandra, 213 *et seq.*
Castelar, Galdós hears speeches of, 32;
and banquet to Galdós, 34
Castro, Fernando, 29
Catalina, Manuel, and Galdós' early
ambitions as a dramatist, 30
Catholic orthodoxy, revival of, 19
"Cerebralismo" of Galdós, 74, 129,
171
Cervantes, 216, 217, 227; influence of
in England, 1; and *género de costum-
bres*, 3; imitation of, in *Doña
Perfecta*, 131
Character, power of delineating, 76,
106, 118, 132, 150, 152, 154, 159,
170, 179, 180, 195, 205

R   245